POTTER STINKS

POTTER STINKS

Gender and Species in J. K. Rowling's *Harry Potter* Series

Keridiana Chez

University Press of Mississippi / Jackson

The University Press of Mississippi is the scholarly publishing agency of
the Mississippi Institutions of Higher Learning: Alcorn State University,
Delta State University, Jackson State University, Mississippi State University,
Mississippi University for Women, Mississippi Valley State University,
University of Mississippi, and University of Southern Mississippi.

www.upress.state.ms.us

The University Press of Mississippi is a member
of the Association of University Presses.

Publisher: University Press of Mississippi, Jackson, USA
Authorised GPSR Safety Representative: Easy Access System Europe -
Mustamäe tee 50, 10621 Tallinn, Estonia, *gpsr.requests@easproject.com*

Library of Congress Control Number: 2025934083

Hardback ISBN 9781496857316
Paperback ISBN 9781496857323
Epub single ISBN 9781496857330
Epub institutional ISBN 9781496857347
PDF single ISBN 9781496857354
PDF institutional ISBN 9781496857361

British Library Cataloging-in-Publication Data available

CONTENTS

POTTER STINKS

INTRODUCTION

More than two decades after the publication of the *Harry Potter* series, which boasts a staggering six hundred million in global sales ("Scholastic Marks"), a *Washington Post* op-ed declared that "there has never been a better time to read J. K. Rowling's books" (Rosenberg). What inspired this declaration was Rowling's use of Twitter and her site to make a series of problematic statements, sparking a controversy that fractured her previously devoted fanbase. A furious war of words has since raged as scholars, bloggers, tweeters, and redditors debate whether the creator of the beloved series is a transexclusionary radical feminist (TERF).

For a long time, the most vehement detractors of the series seemed to be either those who felt affronted by the popularity of children's stories among adults or those who fretted over whether *Harry Potter* promoted witchcraft.[1] While some scholarship rightly takes the *Harry Potter* texts to task, many readers—critics and casual alike—herald the texts as valuable tools for teaching feminism, supporting diversity and inclusion, and inculcating humane values. Most seem to agree that the "enemy" are snooty bluebloods, white supremacists, sexist misogynists, and those who would abuse, enslave, or seek to exterminate nonhumans.

Social scientists back up these interpretations. Anthony Gierzynski's *Harry Potter and the Millennials: Research Methods and the Politics of the Muggle Generation* (2013) surveys millennials, then in college,[2] on the political "lessons" of the series, finding that *Harry Potter* "did play an important role in the political development of those Millennials who became fans" by influencing them to become more liberal and politically engaged, more tolerant and accepting of difference, more skeptical of governing figures, and less accepting of violence as means to an end (75). A 2015 study published in the *Journal of Applied Social Psychology* trumpets *Harry Potter*'s "greatest magic" as the reduction of prejudice against minority groups, such as immigrants, homosexuals, and refugees (Vezzali et al.), and its findings made the rounds with headlines such as "Why Everyone Should Read Harry Potter" in *Scientific American* (Stetka) and "Reading Harry Potter Might Make You a Better Person" in *Smithsonian Magazine* (Lewis). In 2016, when movements against the recently elected president began to take shape, many found solidarity in the rallying cry "Dumbledore's Army!" as a symbol of resistance and unity.[3]

Since the series' feverish initial success—perhaps my first experience of what I would now call a viral phenomenon—Rowling has gained and retained control over a powerful platform, the likes of which few authors can boast, with the development of what is known as the Potterverse, a sequel (*Cursed Child*, 2016) and a cinematic trilogy prequel (*Fantastic Beasts*, 2016, 2018, 2022), and an online following fourteen million strong as of the time of this writing. As many scholars have identified, Rowling is an example of an "undead" author—one that "[haunts] their texts, acting as [a] particularly privileged fan . . . and providing extensions and 'authorized' interpretations" (Duggan 159). Wielding the courts as well, "she and Warner Brothers have long sought to maintain control over the fandom, fans' activities, and fans' interpretations of her texts" (160). And thanks to her spate of online activity in recent years, it has become impossible to write about *Harry Potter* without talking about, as Beth Sutton-Ramspeck puts it, "the hippogriff in the room" (viii): the question of Rowling's transexclusionary politics.

From depicting troubling trans villains in her recent novels to deriding a headline referring to "people who menstruate" for not using the word "women" to uncritically amplifying the voices of people known to be antitrans (J. Bird; Burns), Rowling roused suspicions about her politics in the years before 2020. The question of Rowling's trans-exclusionary politics became undeniable with the publication of her June essay "J. K. Rowling Writes about Her Reasons for Speaking Out on Sex and Gender Issues." Framing herself as a well-intentioned researcher who only accidentally aligned herself with trans-exclusionary tweeters, Rowling attempted to proclaim support for trans people while reaffirming ideas that hurt them. In the aftermath of this essay, many die-hard fans vowed to stop buying *Harry Potter* products. Many penned essays to express their heartbroken disbelief that the same person who authored works that promote empathy and tolerance could also promote views harmful to a painfully vulnerable population. Some compared Rowling to Lord Voldemort, the series' Hitlerian villain—and the clamor for her "cancellation" ironically inspired Vladimir Putin to publicly proclaim his solidarity with the author (Levin). (Rowling quickly disclaimed the connection [Siad et al.].)

As the world reeled from the discovery of a novel and lethal coronavirus, Rowling employed her presumably increased online time to fracture her fanbase by publishing an essay that I received as if not evidently antitrans, then an affirmation of her lack of concern for the difficult challenges faced by trans people. Rowling's trans-exclusionary politics have significantly impacted my perception of *Harry Potter*, casting a retrospective shadow over the series. By insisting on inserting herself both in the postpublication interpretation of her texts and trumpeting her views against expanding options for people who identify as trans, Rowling has made it very difficult to talk about her texts without considering her politics. For many, too, not only has our perception of Rowling changed—indelibly affecting how we interpret her intentions in writing the series—but *we* have also changed. My political beliefs, which have evolved beyond the ideologies of my younger years, have also influenced how I approach the act of rereading the books. Thanks to social media–fueled discourse, many have become more educated as well as empowered to speak up against abuses, erasures, and microaggressions. To those more on the left of the political spectrum, a more progressive and robust liberalism may include a focus on bringing about systemic and/or institutional justice, seeking inclusion and equality rather than tolerance, challenging the anthropocentrism on which human society is premised, and dismantling rather than merely revising the gender binary. This book is my attempt to articulate the interpretive dynamic among me as a reader, the text, and my sense of the author as shaped by what I now know of her politics and to offer a counternarrative to the trend in *Harry Potter* studies of downplaying the limits of the liberalism espoused by the series.

Potter Stinks: Gender and Species in J. K. Rowling's "Harry Potter" Series serves as an account of how much has changed since the launch of the series in terms of how we perceive gender, species, and other key cultural discourses through which we navigate our identities and social existence. In patriarchal societies, gender, class, and species are "linked oppressions" (Kemmerer 13), which, while not operating identically, are often "sustained by the very same tropes" (Deckha).[4] In *Harry Potter*, Rowling tells us she is a feminist and humane toward animals by promoting very salient messages across its pages: women and girls can be capable, smart, and heroic; mothers perform valuable work; and heroes liberate nonhumans from captivity and enslavement. These messages remain relevant and laudable. Yet she dangles these empowered female characters only to persistently sabotage them, just as she raises issues of humaneness only to quietly undercut them, producing a best-selling series that promotes feminism and humaneness in limited forms. In *Harry Potter*, women, girls, and nonhuman beings are presented as helpful, valuable even, yet in need of the leadership of human males. Nonhuman characters are deemed worthy in direct proportion to their willingness to help human characters. I remain grateful for a positive portrayal of a female character being smart and a male character that says no to abusing a nonhuman—but also unsatisfied. If there is indeed a long arc to justice, then these thresholds feel outdated and insufficient, and we must challenge how, by design, the novels declare these goals good enough.

Chapter 1, "Nicer Patriarchies: *Harry Potter's* Raised Glass Ceiling," argues that while offering an alternative world where gender ostensibly presents no barrier to opportunity or achievement, *Harry Potter* masks the ways in which female characters are largely reviled for their femininity. Despite overt feminist messaging, the general portrayal of female characters across the series promotes a dangerous contempt for the female bodied.[5] While some exceptional female characters—Fleur Delacour, Minerva McGonagall, Ginny Weasley, and Hermione Granger—are allowed entry into some domains that have been traditionally monopolized by men, the texts simultaneously reserve a narrow path of success exclusively for males. Effectively, female participation is increased and recognized as valuable to a higher degree, but females are still deemed to lack an elusive amalgam of traits that are tied exclusively to the male sex—the bodies that, according to the series, are best equipped to wield authority. Patriarchy is thus reasserted on the basis of a shrinking but sacrosanct area, preserving an essentializing gender binary that shortchanges women and girls of authority and recognition. The glass ceiling is raised—yet reinforced—as the female characters toil within a system designed to be male led and male favoring.

Chapter 2, "Bros before Chos: Masculinities and Male Homosociality in *Harry Potter*," explores Rowling's portrayal of male homosocial dynamics in the larger context of heteronormativity in the series. While less abrasive than they might be, the masculinities celebrated in *Harry Potter* remain steeped in a hierarchical structure that lionizes a select few. Male characters coded as superior (Albus Dumbledore, Harry) are shown to greatly benefit from the support of other males (Cornelius Fudge, Ron Weasley) but only to the extent that they can accept the duties and responsibilities of their unequal places. The inferiorly regarded male must manage his insecurities and resentments, while the superiorly regarded male attempts to accommodate those feelings by cultivating a façade of humility—a façade that requires the cooperation of many others who support and praise the "superior" male.

This model of more positive homosocial cooperation also maintains *Harry Potter*'s "nicer" patriarchy. As the crude wording suggests, the idea of "bros before hos" rests first and foremost on the categorization of females as sexual objects that threaten patriarchal power by attempting to supplant male homosocial bonds. Heterosexual relationships are the only ones possible, yet they are presented as potentially disruptive to the all-important work of men. *Harry Potter*'s message is clear: no matter how seductively any girl might entice, males need to prioritize their relationships with other males.

The next chapters articulate how gender and species discourses operate in wizarding society, intersecting with questions of ethics, technology, and labor as well as gender and species fluidity and trans identities. Harry is often held up as a model of integrity—in *Deathly Hallows*, Professor Dumbledore's posthumous apparition declares him "a remarkably selfless person" (716)—and our affection for the hero who frees Dobby has prevented a critical examination of the logic and boundaries of his empathy toward nonhuman beings. Chapter 3, "Moral Mediocrity: The Minimal Standards of *Harry Potter*'s Anthropocentric Humaneness," focuses on the wizarding world's reliance on the consumption and exploitation of nonhuman creatures and then untangles the textual strategies through which Harry's anthropocentrism is presented as legitimate and even especially humane. Nonhumans are not to be abused, and some deserve help—and that is something—but the lowness of this bar is concealed by the puffed-up presentation of Harry as a human(e) hero, overly praised for what we should consider the bare minimum. As small acts on behalf of nonhumans are praised as humane even though they primarily advance human ends, humaneness appears to be the collateral benefit of anthropocentric choices.

Meanwhile, Rubeus Hagrid and Hermione are ridiculed for wasting their efforts on undeserving beings and ill-fated attempts to address systematic enslavement, respectively, making it clear that Rowling's position is to promote, at best, an anthropocentric humaneness.

The next chapter continues the argument seeded in chapters 1 and 3—that apparent concessions to Othered groups become ways to further extract their labor in support of patriarchy. Despite the nearly unlimited potential of magic, some characters are perpetually in want, and there is much labor from which characters are not spared—especially nonhumans and women. Chapter 4, "Why Work? Magic, Technology, and the Value of Manual Labor in *Harry Potter*," posits two theories for why Rowling refuses to spare her characters from suffering that their magic should have rendered unnecessary. One is that the texts rely on inconsistent and problematic class stereotypes to quickly distinguish "good" from "bad," inspiring sympathy for some while summarily denigrating others. The second theory is that Rowling is profoundly invested in the idea of "working hard," echoing widely held social anxieties about the dangers of technology: the fear that overreliance on technology leads us to ruin of body, mind, and spirit. As a reply to these fears, *Harry Potter* conjures a pastoral ideal where magical technology is not overused. Yet the appearance of moderation is achieved on the backs of animals, women, and house-elves, and their willingness to happily labor without magic as a regular practice is what creates this society with a "healthy" relationship to technology. The inequalities of this system are effectively rendered appealing by a discourse that romanticizes the manual labor that is conveniently performed by the Othered. By bringing them to the fore, this chapter exposes not only *Harry Potter*'s pernicious overvaluing of labor for labor's sake but also the pitfalls of an escapism that relies on visions of a simpler past.

Chapter 5, "The Chosen One: The Limits of Self-Determination in *Harry Potter*," examines the role of autonomy in forming identity in the series, highlighting the tension among self-image, social acceptance, and the limitations imposed by the wizarding world's norms. One of *Harry Potter*'s more overt messages is that we can—indeed must—choose who we "truly" are and that self-determination defies biology and circumstances. However, while Rowling ostensibly promotes the idea of personal choice, the series also positively portrays a society that systematically restricts and confines individuals through practices such as name limitations, omniscient magical technologies, and societal suspicion toward those who challenge boundaries.

On one level, *Harry Potter* presents hybridity as fantastical fun—plants nip and develop acne, hippogriffs serve as loyal pets, and characters can change aspects of their body at will—but on another level, boundary-blurring and trans figures are suspect. Despite the vast magical potential, a wide range of choices are apparently beyond even the magical pale. The more transformation seems possible, the more *Harry Potter* insists that who one "truly" is remains fixed and unchangeable: one is what one was born to be. In Rowling's vision, identities (along with rights and privileges) rightly attach largely to natal morphological classifications.

In the epilogue, "Rowling Also Stinks: Fandom and the Problematic Living Author," I share my reaction to Rowling's trans-exclusionary views and how it has affected my approach to the texts. This wildly popular series indelibly influenced its first generation of readers and, if ongoing sales are any indication, continues to be voraciously read and reread by new and old readers, myself included. The characters may be flawed and wizarding society far from utopian, demanding that we critically examine the limitations of the liberal ideologies of its creator and its time, but it remains an imagined world that is creatively rendered and often hilarious. As a cultural touchstone, *Harry Potter* also functions as a litmus test for values, prompting the "*Harry Potter* generation" and new readers alike to examine where they stand in relation to these formative texts. In closing, I meditate on how we might still use—and perhaps enjoy—problematic texts, even when we learn that their authors espouse values that we deem harmful and use their wealth and power to spread those views.

A Note about Terms

As the Rowling TERF debate shows, the meanings of certain key terms used in this project are in flux. In this book, "feminine" and "masculine" refer to socially constructed gender traits and roles—discursively tied to aspects of our bodies—which are ever evolving and can differ across cultures and subcultures.

"Male" and "female" are terms that sort all people into two categories based on two biological checklists, irrespective of gender identifications. It is still useful to have terms to denote these biological checklists, even as the checklists are themselves flawed and unsettled areas of debate. For example, at the time of this writing, *Merriam-Webster's* online dictionary defines "female" as "of, relating to, or being the sex that typically has the capacity to bear young or produce eggs," which would mean, for example, that anyone infertile and/or past menopause is no longer female. That is clearly not how we use the terms colloquially. (Paradoxically, *Merriam-Webster* also says that "female" means "having a gender identity that is the opposite of male," conflating sex and gender entirely.) As for "women" and "girls," while I would wish for the terms to expand and be revised in their usage to refer to gender identity so as to also include trans people, *Merriam-Webster* still defines those terms as the equivalent of female.

Of course, *Harry Potter* does not describe any character's genitalia or chromosomal make-up, but I will use "male," "female," "women," and "girls" to refer to the characters according to how Rowling very evidently means to sort them. For example, we do not know what Harry's chromosomes or genitals are, but I will describe him as a male character or a boy because that is how Rowling intends him to be read.

Abbreviations

SS—*Harry Potter and the Sorcerer's Stone*
CS—*Harry Potter and the Chamber of Secrets*
PA—*Harry Potter and the Prisoner of Azkaban*
GF—*Harry Potter and the Goblet of Fire*
OP—*Harry Potter and the Order of the Phoenix*
HBP—*Harry Potter and the Half-Blood Prince*
DH—*Harry Potter and the Deathly Hallows*
CC—*Harry Potter and the Cursed Child*

CHAPTER 1

NICER PATRIARCHIES

Harry Potter's Raised Glass Ceiling

"One of my best friends is Muggle-born," said Harry, "and she's the best in our year."
—*HALF-BLOOD PRINCE*

"Hermione," said Harry, shaking his head, "you're good on feelings and stuff, but you just don't understand about Quidditch."
—*ORDER OF THE PHOENIX*

On the surface, Harry Potter's remarks seem refreshingly generous: he concedes that Hermione Granger is the "best" not only at school—granting her ascendancy in the realm of scholarly achievement, so long a male preserve, but also in the traditionally female area of emotion. In his allocation, Harry cedes significant ground while appearing to hold back very little. His apparent largesse feels like a satisfying feminist victory, yet what Rowling sets aside for her male characters is far more significant than it might appear.

Indeed, female characters gain access to a larger share of the pie only to find that some of these areas of achievement have become less desirable than when they were considered the exclusive purview of men. Hermione dominates in the realm of knowledge and book learning, yet her intellectual prowess is depicted as both essential and paradoxically less valuable than what Harry brings to the table. While she is also granted expertise in "feelings and stuff," his phrasing suggests that this traditionally female area of excellence remains beneath his notice. As if in compensation to the boys, the smaller slice that *Harry Potter* preserves for male excellence is, in turn, elevated in importance. Quidditch might sound insignificant compared to intelligence or emotional savvy, but it comes to represent the traits the series will decree the most valuable: physical agility, quick wits, and steady nerves in the face of danger. Every apparent feminist victory is thus both generous and limited—and this pattern is fundamental to why critics have been polarized over whether the *Harry Potter* series is feminist or sexist. It is both.

On one hand, the novels feature substantive elements that clearly promote female characters. Despite identifying Rowling's "ambivalence" toward feminism, Rivka Temima Kellner praises Rowling for creating "a world of impressively emancipated and empowered women" (367), a reading echoed by Atje Gercama, who describes Rowling's wizarding society as one "characterized by far-stretching gender equality" (38). Female characters are shown to be capably employed outside the home in the same professions as male characters (shopkeepers, lawmakers, office clerks, professors, Aurors), and maternal figures are presented as important influences in the hero's character development (Weiss 19). Across the series, female characters outperform male classmates at school, serve as Hogwarts Heads of Houses, lead the ministry's Magical Law Enforcement Department, play on mixed-sex sports teams, and vanquish evil in battle. All the essays in Christopher E. Bell's 2012 collection *Hermione Granger Saves the World: Essays on the Feminist Heroine of Hogwarts* argue for Hermione's recognition as a feminist role model: "an exemplar" of "what real-world, modern feminism means in contemporary Western society" (Bell 4) and the "true hero" of the films (Alexander 22). At the same time, female characters are not held to an impossibly idealized standard; evil female characters exist alongside male villains, "[doing] away with the oft-promoted stereotype that women are naturally peace-loving, nurturing, good souls" (Gercama 38). Rowling's presentation of masculinity was also refreshingly temperate for its time: the series' main villain embodies a toxic, power-hungry masculinity that is defeated by the male hero and his primary father figure, Albus Dumbledore, encouraging a less toxic version of masculinity that embraces an ethics of love and self-sacrifice (Bausman 51).[1] While finding that the series "[resonates] with gender stereotypes of the worst sort," Ximena Gallardo-C. and C. Jason Smith argue that Harry follows a "Cinderfella" trajectory, making "major choices in the first four books [that] belie a preference for the feminine" ("Cinderfella" 191, 199)—an arc that, for them, is sufficiently redemptive. In the same vein, Tara Foster reads Harry as an "emotional hero [that] undercuts the binary that privileges masculinity/mind/reason over femininity/body/emotion" (120).

On the other hand, there is the inescapable fact that in this saga, "Harry is the Sun and the women are planets at varying distances from him" (Cordova 22). While *Harry Potter* includes many female characters, they are the hero's supporting cast, "[implying that] the primary role of women in society is the care, socialization, and education of men *at any cost*" (Gallardo-C. and Smith, "Cinderfella" 193). To Elizabeth E. Heilman and Trevor Donaldson, Hermione appears "primarily an enabler . . . rather than an adventurer herself," consigned to a maternal role by her needy male peers (146–47). By and large, few female characters are differentiated as individuals, leading Heilman and Donaldson to conjecture that "Rowling was using her 'cut and paste' function" to populate Hogwarts (150). Overwhelmingly, the females are portrayed as "giggly, emotional, gossipy, and anti-intellectual" (150), as well as overly sensitive, chatterboxes, groupies, and sex objects (Gallardo-C. and Smith, "Cinderfella" 193–94). As for the male characters, they also largely conform to stereotypes, with the "strong, adventurous, independent type" revered, while the "weak, unsuccessful male is mocked and sometimes despised" (Heilman and Donaldson 155). Gender nonconformity is largely discouraged, and, as Tison Pugh and David L. Wallace argue, same-sex attraction is omitted as an impossible consideration ("Heteronormative Heroism" 263).[2]

This chapter first argues that *Harry Potter*'s girly-girl stereotypes are more harmful than hitherto recognized, particularly for how the series posits this flavor of femininity as not only contemptible but dangerous. Paradoxically, *Harry Potter* links girliness to the supposed threat posed by female sexuality—a perception that legitimizes sexual violence against women. The second section contends that scholarship that praises the maternal figures in the series tends to neglect the strong narrative thread that rebukes those same maternal figures for stifling male potential. Together, these sections establish that the vast majority of the female characters in *Harry Potter* are presented in ways that are harmful to the female bodied.

The third and fourth sections focus on the select female characters that have been held up as examples of feminist figures—Fleur Delacour, Professor

Minerva McGonagall, Ginny Weasley, and Hermione—whose representation suggests Rowling's desire to support patriarchy even as she challenges it. What has been called Rowling's ambivalence toward feminism belies a more problematic pattern: how patriarchy responds to evolving gender norms by giving to take, granting concessions only to then devalue those concessions and retrench the male claim to leadership roles. While first conceding certain bastions of traditionally masculine superiority to a select few female exceptions, the texts then carefully set aside a narrower avenue of achievement for a select few male bodies. This sacrosanct area may appear a modest reserve, but it grounds the male claim to the top of the hierarchy so that, despite the female characters' recognized superiority over expanded areas, the male characters appear more suited to wield power. These conditions essentially rachet up the glass ceiling: female participation is indeed increased and recognized as substantive and valuable—compared to their historically more stringent exclusion from most avenues of power and recognition—but females remain coded as fundamentally unsuited to the top positions. In *Harry Potter*, girls and women might be able to develop the "brains" but are deemed to lack the right "personality" to break past the now-raised glass ceiling. Together, this redrawing of the gendered spheres not only reasserts a problematically essentialized gendered binary but also reestablishes the rightness of patriarchy—in a way that shifts onto female bodies a lot more work and responsibility in exchange for a limited measure of power and credit.

Dangerous Girly Girls and Rape Culture

Many have persuasively called out the female stereotypes that *Harry Potter* revels in, particularly the plethora of indistinguishable girly girls that giggle, shriek, and obsess about their appearance to the exclusion of other interests. Gallardo-C. and Smith argue that Rowling's choice to repeat problematic gender stereotypes was, "by mirroring the child's real-world experiences in a slightly altered form," one of the "most [effective]" ways to "address issues of gender" ("Cinderfella" 192). But perhaps the question was never whether the texts reflect stereotypes per se but rather whether the texts promote such views as correct. As Eliza T. Dresang puts it, "From a feminist point of view, it is possible . . . for a stereotypic character to be . . . empowered only if she consciously subverts the stereotype" (221). If readers can identify a real-world discourse reflected in a text and be led by the text to recognize it as problematic, the text should rightly be considered as designed to promote productive challenges to the harmful gender discourses they reflect. In contrast, a text that only presents status quo gender discourses without calling them out as harmful and reductive ways of understanding our fellow humans will likely perpetuate these discourses by corroborating them. The burden would be entirely on readers to recognize, resist, and challenge the text.[3]

Not even the most protective reader has attempted to defend the series by enumerating examples where Rowling critiques as false the female stereotypes that she deploys—because there are virtually none. Instead, the texts direct readers to deride and dismiss girly girls. In *Goblet of Fire*, faced with the requirement of choosing an opposite-sex partner for the Yule Ball, Harry notices his female classmates as if for the first time and comes to unflattering, reductive conclusions: "They all seemed to Harry to be obsessed with the coming ball. . . . Girls giggling and whispering in the corridor, girls shrieking with laughter as boys passed them, girls excitedly comparing notes on what they were going to wear on Christmas night" (388). The text signals that this is from Harry's point of view, but his view is ratified by the "good" female characters. In *Half-Blood Prince*, the "violently pink" Wonder Witch section of the Weasley twins' joke shop features love potions and ten-second pimple vanishers, mobbed by a "cluster of excited girls giggling enthusiastically" (120) about the prospect of bettering their chances at securing male attention. Two notable exceptions, Hermione and Ginny, "both hung back, looking wary" (120), signaling to readers that the superior girl would behave differently than this unappealing "cluster." Similarly, in *Goblet of Fire*, a group of fangirls "squabbling over lipstick" swarm Viktor Krum, allowing Hermione the opportunity to "loftily" scoff at them (249). Hermione and Ginny are deployed to gesture that girliness is undesirable—and because a female character says it, it does not appear misogynist. In the cinematic *Half-Blood Prince*, Hermione calls the giggly, boy-crazy Lavender Brown a "daft dimbo" in front of Professors McGonagall, Severus Snape, Horace Slughorn, and Dumbledore—an incongruous declaration before authority figures in front of whom she is typically self-conscious and diffident.

"Male fantasy sex objects to seduce, beguile, and confuse males" (Heilman and Donaldson 152), the veela tell us more about the threat allegedly posed by females who wield this flavor of femininity to manipulate males. Among the discourses that either promote, condone, or forgive sexual violence against women, one of the most harmful and enduring is the idea that female sexual attractiveness is a weapon consciously wielded by unscrupulous females to control or debase helpless males. As Kate Harding discusses in *Asking for It: The Alarming Rise of Rape Culture and What We Can Do About It* (2015), being "perceived as pretty" and "being young" are two out of the eight factors that lead people to blame female victims for their rape (141). Female attractiveness is presumed to precipitate, and therefore excuse, sexual male aggression. According to the problematic logic of rape culture, females who unleash their sexual power are ultimately responsible for any sexual violence they may suffer. Like our own, wizarding society colludes in the belief that males are helplessly compelled to acquire the "advertised" sex—by deceit, duress, or force if necessary. Consider the unsympathetic Helena Ravenclaw's murder by the Bloody Baron: "Furious at my refusal, jealous of my freedom, he stabbed me" (*DH* 616). In short, an attractive female "asks for it."

In this light, the veela's drug-like effect on males is not as comical as first appears. In our introduction to the mascots of the Bulgarian Quidditch team, Harry registers them as "the most beautiful women [he] had ever seen" but quickly realizes that "they weren't—they couldn't be—human" (*GF* 103). With their shiny "moon-bright" skin and dazzling "white-gold" hair, these epitomes of Eurocentric beauty mesmerize males: "Harry stopped worrying about them not being human—in fact, he stopped worrying about anything at all. . . . Harry's mind had gone completely and blissfully blank" (103). The veela are depicted as intentionally using their sexual power on the (male) referee, players, and fans, effectively robbing them of free will. As they increase their dancing speed, Harry finds that his "dazed mind" is full of "wild, half-formed thoughts" of performing "very impressive" feats of masculinity, such as "jumping from the box into the stadium" (103); both Ron and he consider changing their team allegiances to Bulgaria.[4] The only way to resist the veelas' sexual power is for Harry to plug his ears and close his eyes (108). The veela then "[lose] control" and transform into monstrous harpies with "sharp, cruel-beaked bird heads, and long, scaly wings . . . bursting from their shoulders" (111). Upon this reveal, Arthur Weasley imparts some fatherly wisdom—"And *that*, boys, . . . is why you should never go for looks alone!" (112)[5]—implying that males will naturally, understandably, and inexorably be manipulated by women's looks and must learn to resist such a powerful force.[6]

Success or failure at resisting female sexuality becomes a measure of men within patriarchy.[7] Soon after, we see "three tall and beautiful veela standing in a clearing, surrounded by a gaggle of young wizards, all of whom were talking very loudly" (*GF* 125). A dishwasher claims to be a dragon killer that "[pulls] down about a hundred sacks of Galleons a year" (125), and the pimple-faced Knight Bus conductor falsely boasts that he is "about to become the youngest ever Minister of Magic" (126). They read as incels—unattractive men with low-status jobs who humiliate themselves by daring to expect the attention of extremely attractive females—but are treated as benign and comical because the veela's sexual attractiveness is ultimately to blame. Just as Harry almost flung himself out of the spectator box and the mesmerized referee ignored his duties,[8] these young men are depicted as if they are driven to lie—to present themselves dishonestly—to secure sexual access to the veela. How the veela feel about being "surrounded" by a "gaggle" of liars while hiding in the dark woods during a Death Eater attack on Muggles does not, apparently, merit description.

Fleur Delacour, the granddaughter of a veela, wields her beauty to similar effect, striking Ron speechless with a simple query about bouillabaisse. Turning "purple," Ron "opened his mouth to reply, but nothing came out except a faint gurgling noise" (*GF* 252). Nor is Ron the only "victim" of her brain-addling power: "As the girl crossed the Hall, many boys' heads turned, and some of them seemed to have become temporarily speechless, just like Ron" (252). Later, she is described as being "of such breathtaking beauty that the room seemed to have become strangely airless" (*HBP* 91); her beauty is suffocating. Like another incel, Ron humiliates himself by asking Fleur to the Yule Ball in full public hearing, then runs away. Despite not having witnessed the incident, Harry attempts to alleviate Ron's shame by blaming Fleur: "It wasn't your fault, I bet you just walked past when she was turning on the old charm for Diggory and got a blast of it" (*GF* 399). According to Harry's logic, the presumption is that it is Ron's "fault" that he asked out a girl he should have known is out of his league. Harry tries to shift that blame onto Fleur for having incited Ron—an innocent bystander to her "blast"—to humiliate himself, even as he conjectures that she was attempting to attract only one specific male—Cedric Diggory. The idea that female sexuality has a mind-impairing effect on males fuels the claim that males ought not to be held responsible for whatever their actions might be in the face of such a power. This is a rape-legitimating discourse that we should now be well familiar with—*she asked for it, she caused it, he could not help himself*, and *it was not his fault*.[9] In addition to these drooling teenage boys, the *Daily*

Prophet photographer, a "paunchy" adult man, ostensibly there to work, is also presented as distractedly "watching Fleur out of the corner of his eye" as she chats with Cedric (302). His pedophilic ogling is, by Harry's logic, also Fleur's fault. Echoing this misogynistic and pedophilia-justifying scene, *Deathly Hallows* also depicts Fleur's eleven-year-old sister, Gabrielle, "batting her eyelashes" and throwing the almost seventeen-year-old Harry a "glowing look" (108). Ginny gets jealous, as if the preteen should be considered a proper rival.

Love potions feature as a way for witches to acquire veela-like power over males, suggesting that this critique of female sexual power also applies to lesser mortals. It seems beyond hypocritical for the twins—who, despite their relentless bullying of Ron, present as generally likable and ultimately heroic characters—to refuse to sell their love potions to their sister as an exception to the female behavior from which they contrive to profit (*HBP* 120).[10] In the *Half-Blood Prince* movie, only the girls in Professor Slughorn's Potions class covet the cauldron of Amortentia, which the book calls "the most dangerous and powerful potion in this room" (186); in the book, a dozen girls conspire to dose Harry with such a roofie. Despite Hermione and Ginny's disinterest in the pink section of the store, they had earlier giggled with Molly Weasley about "a love potion she'd made as a young girl" (*PA* 70). We learn that Merope Gaunt, Voldemort's mother, used a love potion to entrap (and rape) the "out-of-her-league" Tom Riddle Sr. to disastrous results. (Had she not, Voldemort would not have been born, abandoned, and orphaned.)

The texts are curiously careful to preclude the possibility of males resorting to love potions—even though, in reality, rape is by and large a crime with male perpetrators, with or without roofies. In *Harry Potter*, female characters are vilified for resorting to potions, while male characters jokingly speak about girls as if they are prey animals to be attacked and ensnared, as when Harry complains that they "move in packs" so that he cannot "get one on their own" (*GF* 388). Ron suggests they "lasso one" (388) and describes their plan to find dates "in a tone that suggested they were planning the storming of an *impregnable* fortress" (396, emphasis added). Harry also considers if he should "ambush [Cho Chang] as she was going to the bathroom," but alas, "she even seemed to go there with an escort of four or five girls" (396). In these scenes, the reader's sympathy is directed toward the boys, who are required by gender norms to do the asking: from their perspective, the girls are walking targets with defenses to be overcome.[11] The language is disturbing but passes as humor because the reader is invited to sympathize with the boys' anxiety. Similarly, the text presents as a laughing matter that Harry sneaks up on Gregory Goyle while in his Invisibility Cloak, when the latter is polyjuiced in the form of a little girl, to threaten her with creepy sexual advances: he "waited until he was right behind her before bending very low and whispering, 'Hello . . . you're very pretty, aren't you?'" (*HBP* 464). Girl-Goyle runs off screaming, and we laugh.

When Harry finally becomes interested in Ginny, she is described as arousing Harry's inner "monster" (*HBP* 287), again depicting the male response to female attractiveness as an irrational and irrepressible force that drives monstrous behavior. When he finally gets to kiss her, "the creature in his chest [roars] in triumph" (534).[12] Harry's "monster" also "[roars] its approval" of Ron's attempt to slut shame his sister, though he convinces himself—and the text encourages us to read this ironically—that his desire to "rip Dean [Thomas] limb from limb for kissing her" is a "brotherly feeling" (287, 289–90). The fact that Ginny vehemently defends herself against slut shaming and is portrayed positively for doing so at least signals to the reader that Ron and Harry are in the wrong for this double standard—but it is the same double standard that the texts otherwise embrace by blaming female characters for being attractive. To wit, no one tells Ron he's "moving fast" when he starts dating Lavender and their time together is spent exclusively snogging. Ginny satisfyingly calls him a "filthy hypocrite" (300), but she undercuts this callout by joining every other part of the text in dismissing Lavender as a sexual object on which Ron can practice and then discard. "It looks like he's eating her face," Ginny mocks, "but I suppose he's got to refine his technique somehow" (300).

The most hated Defense Against the Dark Arts professor in the series, Dolores Umbridge, also wields girliness as a weapon, but because she is coded as old and ugly, it yields less successful results. Despite looking like a "large, pale toad" with "a broad, flabby face, as little neck as Uncle Vernon, and a very wide, slack mouth" and "bulging" eyes (*OP* 146), Umbridge insists on performing girly femininity through her wardrobe, décor, voice, and mannerisms. She wears little hair bows (146), "a horrible pink Alice band," a "fluffy pink cardigan" (203), or a "fussy little pie-frill" (661). Her Hogwarts and Ministry of Magic offices are decorated in "lacy covers and clothes," with florals, doilies, and "a collection of ornamental plates, each decorated with a large technicolor kitten wearing a different bow around its neck," which strikes Harry as so "foul" that he is "transfixed" (265). Umbridge wields femininity to disguise her malevolent actions at Harry's hearing, simpering, "I'm sure I must have misunderstood you, Professor Dumbledore.... So silly of me. But it sounded for a teensy moment as though you were suggesting that the Ministry of Magic had ordered an attack on the boy!" (147). As we later find out she did order the attack, it is clear that she uses this girly affectation to cast doubt on Dumbledore's implication. Significantly, Harry seems to instinctively know to distrust her *because* of her girly affect: her "silvery laugh" makes "the hairs on the back of Harry's neck stand up" (147). Her "high-pitched, breathy, and little-girlish" voice elicit a "powerful rush of dislike that he could not explain to himself; all he knew was that he loathed everything about her, from her stupid voice to her fluffy pink cardigan" (212).[13] To Harry, girliness conceals some sort of threat, and the events of *Order of the Phoenix* prove his visceral repulsion correct. Umbridge's failed attempt at girliness posits even more clearly that such femininity is, in this portrayal, a calculated weapon against males—even as the texts erase how such femininity is, in reality, much more dangerous to the females who become more likely to be blamed for their sexual victimization.

Rowling was unlikely to be aiming to legitimize sexual assault,[14] but the propagation of such discourses is highly problematic. We should also consider other instances where a female character is blamed as if they caused and therefore deserve their victimization and are offered no assistance or comfort. When Hermione spends the Slughorn Christmas party eluding a groping Cormac McLaggen, who is "the size of a troll" (*HBP* 416) and has "more tentacles than a Snarfalump plant" (*HBP* movie), Harry's response is to "severely" tell her, "Serves you right for coming with him" (*HBP* 317). Hermione, too, asked for it. In the movie, Harry does at least help Hermione get away by feeding Cormac a vomit-inducing chew, but in both text and movie, it is presented as a joke that she has to dodge Cormac's groping (318). Hermione herself describes his unwanted sexual contact as being only on the same level of annoying as the fact that he only wants to talk about Quidditch (318), minimizing McLaggen's sexual aggression. Harry's refusal to empathize or "act the hero" (*OP* 734) on this occasion is particularly troubling because, in this text, Hermione has been Harry's main ally through a series of life-threatening Triwizard tasks. Similarly, when Hermione is slut shamed and physically injured by hate mail she receives because Rita Skeeter implies that she is romantically involved with Harry and Viktor, Harry tells her to just ride it out. Ron again blames the victim: "I warned her not to annoy Rita Skeeter! . . . She'd better watch out for herself" (*GF* 542). Hermione chooses to find out how Rita has been getting her information without their help—a mission that Ron dismisses as a "vendetta" (548). Does anyone have more active vendettas than Harry? Dudley Dursley, Draco Malfoy, Severus Snape, and, of course, Voldemort—and he receives ample support for all of them. His problems always become her problems, but her problems never seem to become his. Casting female sexuality as a dangerous power while downplaying male sexual aggression and blaming females for "deserving" bad behavior is a harmful and still-prevalent combination.

Mollycoddling Mothers

A vast majority of the female characters, then, are portrayed with the same problematic and broad brush. We turn next to some that appear to offer some redemption: the maternal figures who have so much impact on Harry's development.

We navigate difficult terrain with texts that praise self-sacrificing mother figures because of the cultural context that necessarily informs our reading. On one hand, denying a mother character "credit for their actions" simply "because they evolve out of a maternal instinct" may perpetuate the sexism inherent in the separate-spheres logic that has historically devalued caregiving (Kniesler, "Unbreakable Vow" 278). Indeed, "if modern feminism is about empowering women to choose whatever lives they find satisfying, Molly's choice should not be denigrated as inferior" (Sutton-Ramspeck 110). Child-rearing is difficult and valuable, and it would be wrong if such work could not be positively recognized, especially when women continue to do the majority of it. On the other hand, given the centuries of socialization and propaganda that have funneled females into motherhood, we ought to remain suspect of texts that appear to praise representations of self-sacrificing motherhood—particularly if they describe caretaking behavior as exclusively or primarily female—and we should avoid perpetuating the idea that motherhood is every female's most natural and desirable life pursuit. Even in a society where women can work outside the home without raising eyebrows, the idea that women's most essential function is to bear and raise children remains deeply ingrained. Every ode to a "mother's sacrifice" necessarily propagates a powerful discourse that attempts to funnel half the population into unpaid work and financial dependency in order to free the other half to amass and control capital. Until women are no longer taught to believe that their fundamental worth depends on childbearing and rearing; not expected to prioritize husband, home, and children over all other pursuits; and not pushed to choose between financial dependency and bearing the second shift, we cannot praise motherhood without caveats lest that praise become additional propaganda. Anyone who does not mind that their praise of motherhood, without contextualizing caveats, may be co-opted as sexist propaganda that funnels females to prioritize motherhood above all else should perhaps wonder why they do not mind.

Rowling's maternal figures are favorably represented for faithfully executing their caretaking purpose—and, indeed, it is valuable that traditional women's work is highlighted and praised in the texts. However, the texts do not do the work of untying female bodies from domestic caregiving. No witch mother appears to work outside the home for a salary except the largely off-screen characters of Marietta Edgecombe's mother (whose career pressures Marietta to snitch on Dumbledore's Army) and Neville Longbottom's mother (whose career caused her to be tortured into madness by Death Eaters, orphaning her son).

Moreover, the maternal figures are also shown to grossly overdo it. Professor McGonagall, for example, is rightly praised as one of Harry's maternal figures, a special "mother [replacement]" who "brings discipline and rigidity" (Hidalgo 71). I agree with Kate Glassman that McGonagall plays an influential role in Harry's development (153)—as fair a measure of a character's value to this Harry-centric series as any.[15] But a focus on McGonagall's virtues, without attention to the ways that the texts undercut her in comparison to Dumbledore, is unfair. Glassman asserts that "to underplay her role in the series does this complex character a grave disservice" (153), and I agree: my complaint is that it is Rowling who performs this disservice. Often, as when McGonagall exhorts Dumbledore to use his power to stop Harry from participating in the Triwizard Tournament, her role is to anxiously voice concern for his welfare. Readers both appreciate her concern and dismiss it; of course, the hero *must* face, and overcome, his challenges. The mother figure in Neville's life, his grandmother, is depicted as a well-meaning but domineering woman whose excessive maternal power restricts his development into a brave, capable wizard. (In Divination class, Neville shares a castration nightmare "involving a pair of giant scissors wearing his grandmother's best hat" [*OP* 238].) Similarly, the nurse Madame Poppy Pomfrey—"a nice woman, but very strict" (*SS* 301)—performs essential ministrations, but her nursing is repeatedly experienced as an annoyance by Harry, who finds her "fussing about" (304) stifling, as when he emerges from the lake during the Triwizard Championship and she "wrapped him so tightly in a blanket that he felt as though he were in a straightjacket" (*GF* 504). (Her "fussing about" has also "held" him up on a previous occasion [*SS* 304].) In *Prisoner of Azkaban*, she is a mere pawn to Dumbledore's larger scheme, used by him to corroborate Harry and Hermione's false alibi (420). In *Order of the Phoenix*, Harry disrespectfully dismisses Pomfrey's work by comparing how helpful it was, at a critical moment, to find McGonagall, "a member of the Order of the Phoenix," rather than "someone fussing over him and prescribing useless potions" (464). (Alas, McGonagall's great usefulness in this instance is merely to bring him to Dumbledore.)

No one can deny that Molly Weasley also has a profoundly positive influence on Harry, taking on the role of adoptive mother by immediately tending to him like one of her own: feeding him, remarking on his growth, fussing over the state of his clothes, and being anxious for his safety. Meri Weiss praises the way that Molly exemplifies this epitome of female service (21). Similarly, although rightly noting that Molly embodies "many of the pre-feminism characteristics of motherhood," Alexandra Hidalgo devotes her essay to lauding Rowling's elevation of such: "Rowling is making an argument for women like Molly, who happily and skillfully perform the role of housewife and mother, to also be viable representations of feminism" (74, 73). Molly's entire life and personality rests on being a mother and wife; taking care of her husband and children is all she wants and virtually all that her character is. A clucking mother hen, her appearances inspire our gratitude both because we want to see our hero comforted and because her excesses often provide comic relief.

Yet the series also punishes her for mothering. Naturalizing the idea that a mother's work must be taken for granted,[16] her sons mock her anxiety, as when Charlie Weasley describes her as "having kittens" about Harry's upcoming participation in the Triwizard Tournament and "imitated his mother's anxious voice" in a series of hysterical, italicized sentences that signal that no character takes her concerns seriously: "*How could they let him enter that tournament, he's much too young! I thought they were all safe, I thought there was going to be an age limit!"* (*GF* 328–29). The twins also mock her overprotectiveness with a "high-pitched voice that sounded uncannily like [their] mother's: '*You're too young, you're not in the Order*'" (*OP* 88). Moreover, she appears foolish when she, "in floods," believes Rita's article about Harry (*GF* 329). In *Order of the Phoenix*, Molly's main role is to (s)mother as she anxiously tries to prevent her children's and Harry's participation—all while cooking and cleaning for Grimmauld Place. All the men try to convince Molly to loosen the apron strings. Her performances of maternal protectiveness are juxtaposed against her calm, lax husband, who, for most of the texts, almost appears as another one of her (s)mothered children, concealing the "fun" aspects of his personality to avoid her furious overreactions. In an earlier book, in contrast to her "shrilly" anxiety when she underestimates Harry's courage, Arthur correctly surmises that Harry is "made of stronger stuff" (*PA* 65, 73).

When Molly "[rounds] on her husband" asking him to "back [her] up" in her attempt to restrict the children's involvement in the Order, Arthur is the one who appears the more sympathetic as he delicately disagrees (*OP* 89). Weiss argues that the scene exists to highlight how wonderful a mother figure Molly is as she clashes with Sirius Black and declares Harry is "as good as" her son (23; *OP* 90). This is partly correct; however, Molly is also immediately put in her place by Remus Lupin, who reminds her that she is not the only one who cares for Harry, and by Harry himself, who chooses more information: "He did not look at Mrs. Weasley. He had been touched by what she had said about his being as good as a son, but he was also impatient at her mollycoddling. . . . Sirius was right, he was *not* a child" (*OP* 90). Readers may also feel "touched" by her protectiveness, but we know that she is, in some fundamental way, wrong: the action must go on, and the children must face their challenges. Dumbledore later affirms what Harry believes—that to be held back from participating in dangerous adventures is to be infantilized and discounted—when he declares Harry has "earned [the] right" to actively participate in the Horcrux hunt (*HBP* 507). Moreover, all of Molly's anxieties are eventually proven to be misplaced, as ignoring her always leads to glory and success—including the success of the twins' business, Weasleys' Wizard Wheezes. Even in *Deathly Hallows*, Molly attempts to manipulate the trio into remaining in hiding, in contrast to every other (male) character, who readily sees that they must continue with Dumbledore's instructions (87). If she had her way, Voldemort would not be defeated.

Molly's excessive mothering—and its rebuke—are part of the script that the texts consign mothers to follow. Like McGonagall, Molly is overly protective so that Harry can be stifled, playing out a familial drama that requires the mother figure to serve as antagonist to her coming-of-age son. Just as Molly's extra hug for Harry makes him feel "embarrassed, but really quite pleased" (*PA* 72), Molly *has* to mollycoddle Harry, and he *has* to both like and dislike it, thereby forging his independence. Her protective love is appreciated and resented; her narrow, too-personal view disables her from understanding what must be done.[17] The teenage boy understands what she cannot: that one must take risks for the "greater good" (*DH* 508). Ultimately, the same traits that apparently elevate motherly figures are the same traits that are used to justify the limits of their relevance.

Vice-Presidential Female Characters

Given the backdrop of vapid, dangerous, and downright repulsive girly females and the attendant ties to rape culture discourses, it is already difficult to pronounce the series a feminist success, and any interpretation that attempts to do so by focusing only on a few exceptional female characters is suspect. At this point, the question is whether, in a veritable morass of problematic representations, a few standout female characters can redeem the whole. Unfortunately, in *Harry Potter*, the texts institute a glass ceiling that effectively prevents some of her most capable, powerful, and valuable female characters from being thought of as equally or more capable, powerful, or valuable as her top male characters.

The "glass ceiling" is a term popularized in the 1980s in analyses of corporate structuring, defined by the Federal Glass Ceiling Commission of 1995 as an "unseen, yet unbreachable barrier that keeps minorities and women from rising to the upper rungs of the corporate ladder, *regardless of their qualifications or achievements*" (qtd. in Cotter et al. 656). Operating alongside tokenism, the glass ceiling represents the willingness of men in power to grant promotions to a select few female employees, and only up to a certain level, while the organization remains male led and male favoring. Thanks to the glass ceiling's invisibility, calling out sexism becomes more difficult with the promotion of token figures, as defenders of the status quo can point to the few female exceptions that have been promoted as proof that all females have equal access and opportunity and do not make it to the top due to their own deficiencies or choices.

Perhaps it is surprising to begin a section about capable female characters with Fleur Delacour. Rowling clearly does not present her as a feminist role model, but the way she undercuts Fleur is significant. The Goblet of Fire selects her as the best Beauxbatons representative for the Triwizard Tournament, and this is supposed to mean something; it certainly does when it comes to Harry, Cedric, and Victor Krum. Yet she appears to be included just so not all the champions would be male, then proceeds to come in last in every event. Readers are encouraged to enjoy every instance where the arrogant beauty queen is taken down a notch. In the second task, she is the only one to give up midway, wailing, "it was ze grindylows . . . zey attacked me" (*GF* 504), much in the tones of a caricature bemoaning that some petty hardship led her to break a nail. How did someone who bested a dragon (albeit the smallest of the four [327]) become unable to shake off a water pest from the Hogwarts year-three curriculum? Harry, whom she had dismissed as a "little boy" (275), not only ably manages the grindylows but saves her sister in her place. Harry later offers a weak defense on her behalf, saying "Fleur's not stupid, she was good enough to enter the Triwizard Tournament" (*HBP* 94), as if entry is where our expectations must be satisfied. Limping into the last task, she is nothing but a "scream [that] shattered the silence" (*GF* 624), after which her flirtation with the public sphere of achievement and glory quickly comes to a close. Postgraduation, she briefly "[works] part-time at Gringotts for [her] Eenglish [*sic*]" (*HBP* 92)—a transparent ploy to secure her future husband, Bill Weasley. At the moment of marriage, her dangerous beauty is finally rendered safe: the "radiance [that] usually dimmed everyone else by comparison, today . . . beautified everybody it fell upon," particularly Bill, who "looked as though he had never met Fenrir Greyback" (*DH* 144). She retires to homemaking, quickly becoming "rather like Mrs. Weasley" (511), aproned and in the kitchen fretting for her husband's safety well before the age of twenty. From haughty beauty to failed tournament champion to "slavish," adoring housewife (53), she appears to not "make it" because she cannot and does not want to. A character that, at least briefly, was accorded significant recognition for her competencies, Fleur ultimately is reduced to the poster child for misogynists of many kinds: an example of the haughty beauty that violent incels would rape and murder, the affirmative action candidate who cannot cut it, the "shrew" that needs to be tamed by the "right" man, and, finally, the everywoman that chooses to forego a career to become a dependent, happy housewife (and eventually mother).

In contrast to Fleur, who is included to come in last, Professor McGonagall is included to come in at second place. Gercama points to the fact that two out of four Heads of House are women and that, as deputy headmistress, McGonagall seems to perform capably when Dumbledore is temporarily removed: "This speaks to her capabilities as a talented wizard as well as to her capability to hold a position that comes with a lot of responsibilities and challenges" (37). Pugh and Wallace describe her as "Dumbledore's second-in-command" but find that her main achievements are to implement Dumbledore's will and "[defer] to his wisdom" ("Heteronormative Heroism" 271). "Prim where Dumbledore is broadminded, rigid where he is flexible, and unfair and hasty where Dumbledore is willing to listen and to be fair, at least where Harry is concerned" (Mendlesohn 175), McGonagall is purposefully contrasted to Dumbledore to her disadvantage in multiple scenes. No matter her capabilities and talents, it is nevertheless patent that the texts continually restrain her beneath the glass ceiling on which Dumbledore, the benign patriarch, stands. From the moment we meet her—when she, "a sensible person," cannot say "Voldemort" aloud and looks at Dumbledore in a "half admiring" way to compliment him as the "only one You-Know—oh, all right, *Voldemort*, was frightened of" (*SS* 11)—and every opportunity thereafter, she yields to Dumbledore as the clearly superior leader. McGonagall is an excellent executrix of his orders, as when he directs her to "alert the kitchens" (*CS* 330) or delay Umbridge (*OP* 474), but she does not take much decisive action of her own. She fails to even manage the impish Hogwarts poltergeist, Peeves, as he torments first years with water balloons; the best she can do is threaten to "call the Headmaster" (*GF* 172). Peeves ignores every other threat but finally responds to this equivalent of "I'm calling your father," suggesting that she ultimately has no authority without the patriarch who employs her. (Molly Weasley makes a similar appeal to patriarchal authority—"*You wait until your father gets home*"—when she chastises her sons in *Chamber of Secrets* [33].) The same applies with much higher stakes later: tasked to stand guard over Bartemius Crouch Jr., she fails to stop the Minister of Magic from bringing in lethal dementors. This time, threatening to call for father does not work: "I told him you would not agree, Dumbledore! . . . I told him you would never allow dementors to set foot inside the castle" (*GF* 702). Rowling puts McGonagall in charge at this critical juncture so she could, through her failure, propel the plot.

As with the analysis of Fleur, cataloging only how McGonagall is capable and strong without also analyzing how she remains limited by Rowling's glass ceiling would lead to a distorted view. McGonagall is, as Heilman and Donaldson fairly summarize, "a smart female of clearly secondary status" (148), and while such vice-presidential female figures could certainly be worse, Rowling does not allow them to be much better. The culminating effect of limiting capable females to this second-in-command position is to propagate a glass ceiling above which readers still cannot comfortably imagine female leadership. Moreover, Rowling tells us *why* females ought never to rise past that glass ceiling, and her position was already uncomfortably out of date in the late 1990s to early 2000s: no matter how capable of logic they might be, her female characters cannot control their emotions. "Sentimental and [lacking] in discernment," McGonagall is "book-smart, but not wise, powerful or brave" (Heilman and Donaldson 148). In contrast, "the intelligent man is multifaceted"; Dumbledore is a "distinguished-looking man who has many friends and confidants, a man who is not made fun of or intimidated by others, and a man whom everyone would like to know" (Mayes-Elma 92).

When she is temporarily taken out of commission in *Order of the Phoenix*, Harry thinks, "Dumbledore had gone, Hagrid had gone, but he had always expected Professor McGonagall to be there, irascible and inflexible, perhaps, but always dependably, solidly, present" (*OP* 730)—not as great as the other options, but simply there to be taken for granted. McGonagall cannot provide Harry with the freedom he needs, instead often appearing as a potential obstacle: "Professor McGonagall did not invite confidences; Dumbledore, though in many ways more intimidating, still seemed less likely to scorn a theory, however wild" (*HBP* 253). Their contrasting reactions to Harry slaying the basilisk are also telling: "Professor Dumbledore was standing by the mantelpiece, beaming, next to Professor McGonagall, who was taking great, steadying gasps, clutching her chest" (*CS* 327). The father figure makes Harry feel proud, while the mother figure's anxious reaction proves her inability to recognize that the danger is well past and success already attained. By book seven, even Harry displays greater emotional wherewithal than her when, in *Deathly Hallows*, he strikes a Death Eater in her defense, and his sudden appearance has her "clutching her heart" and "[struggling] to pull herself together" (*DH* 593). Not only has he surpassed her in emotional self-control, but "somehow her panic steadied him" (594); McGonagall is reduced to make the teenage boy look good. Even all her leadership during the Battle of Hogwarts is but an extended instance of her ably acting as Dumbledore's deputy since she rises to the occasion only after Harry tells her he needs support to "[act] on Dumbledore's orders" (595).

Harry's final love interest, Ginny Weasley, is fierce, capable, independent, and brave—and certainly deserving of being described as a feminist figure. But as a feminist figure, she, too, is viciously undercut.[18] What Harry seems to find especially attractive about her is that she "was not tearful; that was one of the many wonderful things about Ginny, she was rarely weepy" (*DH* 116). She is an exception to her sex—obsessed with Quidditch, likes derisive humor, and is emotionally hardy—because of an unusual amount of salutary male influence: "Having six brothers must have toughened her up" (116). The twins compliment her for her spellcasting "power" despite her smaller size (*OP* 100), betraying their troubling assumption that smaller bodies would possess less *magical* ability. She is invited to join the Slug Club on her own merits, but while Harry is presented as the master of all Defense Against the Dark Arts, Ginny's signature spell is the comical Bat-Bogey Hex, which causes bat-like bogeys to fly out of the recipient's nose.

Ginny appears quite good at Quidditch—that masculine proving ground where Draco Malfoy and Harry face off again and again[19]—but the texts are also careful to not make her as good as Harry. She helps the team rack up points ten at a time—the team points that never seem to matter in comparison to Harry's game-ending, one-hundred-and-fifty-point Snitch capture. George "fairly" declares her as "not bad" (*OP* 573), and while it is heartening to know that she became "so good" despite their "never [letting] her play with us" because she had been surreptitiously borrowing their brooms since the age of six (574), her Quidditch abilities are always praised with reservation to ensure that Harry remains superior at the sport. Consider his reaction when he learns that she is his replacement on the team after Umbridge bans him from playing:

> "Ginny Weasley," said Katie [Bell].
>
> Harry gaped at her.
>
> "Yeah, I know," said Angelina [Johnson], pulling out her wand and flexing her arm. "But she's pretty good, actually. Nothing on you, of course." (453)

The text carefully describes Harry's negative reaction as a nonverbal "gape" so that the hero would not be in the position of saying something unflattering about his future wife, but he is effectively struck speechless by the possibility that Katie could have thought Ginny his equal. The text then uses Angelina to voice what he cannot: that it is obvious to all that Ginny could not possibly replace him as Seeker, even if she is "pretty good." Their skepticism is borne out in the next game, when, by a "miracle," Gryffindor "only lost by ten points; Ginny managed to catch the Snitch from right under Hufflepuff Seeker Summerby's nose" (575). This appears as an achievement, but when Harry graciously compliments her catch, she attributes her success to chance: she was merely "lucky," the Snitch "wasn't . . . very fast," and her opponent had a cold, causing him to "[sneeze] and [close] his eyes at exactly the wrong moment" (575). Privately, Harry reasserts his superior ability: "He was quite impressed by Ginny's performance but he felt that if he had been playing he could have caught the Snitch sooner . . . if she hadn't hesitated, she might have been able to scrape a win for Gryffindor" (576). Ultimately, he not only blames her for the frustrating loss but also attributes her shortcomings to a lack of nerve and quick judgment. Ginny may have worked very hard at Quidditch since age six, but Harry is "a natural" (SS 167); Ginny capably contributes to the team, but Harry is "the youngest House player in about . . . a century (152).[20]

Cataloging the agency or capacities of exceptional female characters has its limits and must be paired with a bigger-picture analysis of how far a text lets them be recognized and rewarded with respect, power, and influence. If a gendered glass ceiling is represented in a text, the interpretive question is whether that text approves or challenges the glass ceiling that keeps them from the top positions. *Harry Potter* fails to challenge: these capable female characters are depicted as unable to rise to the top positions because they are not good enough. Fleur, McGonagall, and Ginny are three supporting female characters that Rowling sets up as capable enough to contribute—to matter—but not to lead. Is a text that promotes female characters as capable vice presidents to male presidents feminist? Compared to some, certainly, and, to that extent, the series must be credited. Even at present, too many still question whether females could outperform males at school, participate in physical sports and military defense, and be deputies of major institutions, and for that reason, Rowling's feminism still has relevance. Nevertheless, given the repeated textual reminders of their relative incapacity compared to male characters, *Harry Potter* feels much less feminist than it might first appear—particularly when, as Jeanne Hoeker LaHaie remarks, these "flashes of fully empowered female figures, girls and women" effectively "[distract] readers from the more consistently traditional depictions of females" that comprise the bulk of the series' female characters (125).

Preserving a (Shrinking) Male Sphere

Hermione's arc over the series offers the most detailed exposition of Rowling's glass ceiling. Like McGonagall, she is praised for her logic and intellect—an area that has historically been the domain of males. Despite this expansion into a realm of achievement that historically excluded females, however, Hermione is ultimately restrained by texts that specifically carve out select areas of achievement for the series' hero. In a give-to-take dynamic, *Harry Potter* appears to generously concede ability and give credit to the main female character only to devalue her functions and elevate those reserved for the main male character.

We are not short on textual evidence of Hermione's prowess at school given that her devotion to her studies is the butt of repeated jokes: "Every one of them had called Hermione a know-it-all at least once, and Ron . . . told Hermione she was a know-it-all at least twice a week" (*PA* 172).[21] Her studiousness is directly tied to what Harry thinks of as her "mania for upholding rules" (*HBP* 306), which is another recurring motif. "Little Miss Perfect" can be a downright nag (*OP* 566). While her superior knowledge and spellwork contribute greatly to the quests, Hermione's studious perseverance also makes her seem dull, arrogant, and uptight to her peers. When they first meet, Hermione sounds "bossy" and makes the boys feel insecure because they "hadn't learned all the course books by heart" (*SS* 105, 106). Harry is particularly "dazed" because, through her "background reading," she "[knows] all about" him, and she wonders aloud at how he has not bothered to gather more knowledge about himself (106). Harry does not respond to her implied critique positively; as per Farah Mendlesohn, "Harry's friendship with Hermione is grudging and his willingness to humiliate her in public no better than Malfoy's treatment of his acolytes" (174). Moments in the text suggest that he quietly compares himself to her and does not enjoy "losing," such as when she talks about grades or rightly surmises that Draco's challenge to a duel had been a trick: "Harry thought she was probably right, but he wasn't going to tell her that" (*SS* 159). Before the troll encounter that forges their friendship, Harry finds Hermione "interfering," and she is unflatteringly described as "hissing at them like an angry goose" when she tries to stop them from going to meet Draco for the illicit midnight duel (155). Ron loudly proclaims "no one can stand her" after she publicly bests him at Wingardium Leviosa (172). In short, she is initially rejected because her in-your-face knowledge, cleverness, and conscientiousness make the boys feel inadequate.

Sorcerer's Stone explicitly claims that surviving the troll in the bathroom is a critical bonding experience leading to the formation of the trio. It is the aftermath of the incident, however, that defines the *terms* of their new bond. After the pivotal experience, Hermione takes the blame in a way that allows the boys to escape punishment and reap rewards, causing House points to be deducted in her name and added in the boys' names. Katrin Berndt commends Hermione for her "generosity of character" (165). According to Rachel Armstrong, Hermione is subverting her initial positioning as "damsel in distress" by "taking action": "This assertion is *brave*" (241). Gercama cites this moment as an example of her "moral development"; Hermione has learned to be attentive to people's needs (41). Yet what Hermione does that so endears her to Harry and Ron is to tell two lies; one is highly unflattering to herself, which assuages the boys' resentment ("I went looking for the troll because I—I thought I could deal with it on my own—you know, because I've read all about them" [*SS* 177]), and the other excuses the boys' rule breaking ("They didn't have time to come and fetch anyone" [*SS* 178]). Through the first lie, she admits to the boys that she *is* an arrogant know-it-all—and invites McGonagall to punish her for it. Hermione could have simply omitted this first lie and absolved them all, which would still credit the boys as her saviors and still be "brave," "taking action," etc. But instead, the boys' acceptance of Hermione—and perhaps the readers', to whom Hermione has been introduced as a bossy know-it-all—hinges on her first agreeing that having greater book knowledge and earning better grades does not make her superior or deserving of more authority in relationship to them.[22] Precisely through that unnecessary first lie, Hermione opts to have McGonagall take her down a notch so that the boys—uncomfortable with her knowledge and cleverness—will accept her. Depressingly, it works.[23]

The text takes care to frame our perception of what Hermione says as being impressive because she told "a downright lie to a teacher" (*SS* 177), casting the boys' acceptance of Hermione as being due to her learning to be looser about rules. As Heilman and Donaldson note early on (156), and as

Beth Sutton-Ramspeck's *Harry Potter and Resistance* (2022) argues in toto, rule following and respect for institutional authority are not lauded traits in the series, and if we are to like her, Hermione has to be weaned off the habit. Critics such as Gercama argue that Hermione must "grow up" over the series by learning to be more like the rule-defying boys (41).[24] Yet even as far into the series as *Half-Blood Prince*, she is represented as clinging to ministry-approved textbooks and spells. To the extent that she learns that many of its leaders are ill-deserving of blind allegiance, I would agree that Hermione is improved, though it is unclear whether the texts credit the boys for this growth.[25] After all, her main challenges to the ministry's authority are the Society for the Promotion of Elfish Welfare (S.P.E.W.) and Dumbledore's Army, and in neither case do the texts attempt to attribute her flouting of authority to the boys' influence (certainly the opposite is true when it comes to S.P.E.W., which she pursues despite their attempts to dissuade her).

What Hermione does appear to learn from the boys is to enable, or at least not snitch on, the boys' self-interested rule breaking.[26] Both boys consider her as being "nicer" for learning to "become a bit more relaxed about breaking rules" (*SS* 181), as if calling them out for rule breaking is a form of personal unkindness. In *Prisoner of Azkaban*, when he uses the Marauder's Map to sneak into Hogsmeade for an afternoon of fun, despite the danger, a smugly "grinning" Harry asks her whether she is going to report him. She passes the implicit test when she says, "Oh—of course not—" (199). She fails, however, when the broom-crazy Harry refuses to let teachers know about his mysterious receipt of the Firebolt and Hermione tells McGonagall. She immediately reverts, in Harry's mind, to someone who causes undue "interference" (233), and the boys shun her for weeks until the Firebolt is returned. This shunning teaches her a lasting lesson; she does not snitch again. The boys even taunt her with the knowledge that their friendship is conditioned on her silence, as when she believes Harry has illegally dosed Ron with Felix Felicis to win a Quidditch game and Ron demands, "What are you going to do, turn us in?" (*HBP* 298). Ruthann Mayes-Elma makes a powerful point: the pattern of female characters who enforce the rules (and are resented for it) and male characters who break the rules is particularly problematic when the rules are (given who is in power) set by men: "So if women are supposed to follow the rules, but men are not held to that same standard, who are the rules set up for? The answer to that would have to be 'women.'... [M]en are shown to be 'above' the system/rules" (87).

Despite my analysis so far, perhaps it still feels like I am not giving enough credit to Hermione's representation as their intellectual superior. Yet it is significant that she could have been rendered more brilliant but was not. For example, the texts describe the teen Dumbledore as a genius, winning "every prize of note that the school offered" and "soon in regular correspondence with the most notable magical names of the day," even publishing in "learned publications such as *Transfiguration Today, Challenges in Charming*, and *The Practical Potioneer*" (*DH* 17); the teen Snape revised Potions textbooks and invented spells; and the teen James Potter and Sirius Black aced exams without study and became secret Animagi.[27] Compared to these male characters, Hermione is merely a girl who is logical, works very hard, has developed great memory, and follows instructions well. Bill and Percy Weasley (*CS* 46), and possibly Barty Crouch Jr. (*GF* 556), achieved a complete set of twelve O.W.L.s (Ordinary Wizarding Levels), whereas Hermione only manages eleven (*HBP* 103), with no prizes, publications, or innovations.[28] Perhaps Remus's pronouncement that Hermione is "the cleverest witch of [her] age" is accurate only because he specified cleverest *witch* (*PA* 346).

In fact, Hermione appears to possess gifts that no one even wants: Harry becomes increasingly anti-intellectual as the series progresses, making room for Hermione's expansion into that area while conveniently sparing him from having to lose to her in head-to-head competition. As a young boy, Harry's interest in reading sets him apart from Dudley, "who never read anything" (*SS* 80). In *Sorcerer's Stone*, he finds his schoolbooks "very interesting" and eagerly names his owl Hedwig because he found the name in *A History of Magic* (88). Yet he goes from being described by the narrator in book three as a "highly unusual boy" for reading this book by flashlight under blankets and "really [wanting] to do his homework" over the summer holidays to claiming in book seven that he "might've opened [*A History of Magic*], you know, when I bought it . . . just the once" as a badge of pride (*PA* 1; *DH* 318). Obtusely, during *Order of the Phoenix*'s summer holiday, he is desperate enough for information about the magical world to lay by flowerbeds to listen to the news and "[scavenge Muggle] newspapers from bins" on the street but not enough to do more than skim the front page of the *Daily Prophet* (3, 73). Despite the ways that his knowledge about magic and the magical world is repeatedly shown to be deficient, he never picks up a book out of choice other than for Quidditch. The only exception is in *Half-Blood Prince*, wherein he enjoys reading the teenaged Snape's annotations, and that exception is carefully carved out: "He did not usually lie in bed reading his textbooks; that sort of behavior, as Ron rightly said, was indecent in anybody except Hermione, who was simply weird that way" (237–38).

Moreover, Hermione's intellectual prowess is also undercut by her tendency to hysterics, which many critics have noted. In *Sorcerer's Stone*, she identifies Devil's Snare and knows how to beat it but falls prey to her nerves: "wringing her hands" (278), she ludicrously forgets that she can light a fire by magic.[29] Once in safety, Harry pays her a meager compliment for "[paying] attention in Herbology," and Ron immediately reminds us that Harry was the one to not "lose his head in a crisis" (278). To some degree, the text does redeem Hermione right after when she solves Snape's potions puzzle, this time exhibiting, as Dumbledore later describes, the "cool use of logic in the face of fire" (305). However, her "cool" logic here highlights how forced the previous scene is. She also lacks the nerve for flying—"this was something you couldn't learn by heart out of a book—not that she hadn't tried" (144)— and "[lacks] confidence on a broomstick" all the way to the last book (*DH* 53). In *Deathly Hallows*, after they are attacked in the Muggle coffee shop, the boys calmly identify the unconscious Death Eaters, but Hermione interrupts "a little hysterically": "Never mind what they're called! . . . How did they find us? What are we going to do?" (166). Hermione's hands shake so much that she accidentally cuts Ron trying to free him from his ropes. "Somehow her panic seemed to clear Harry's head" (166)—like the McGonagall scene cited earlier, female panic "somehow" has a fortifying effect on Harry.

These hysterics certainly make the male characters *appear* more capable. Even as she saves Harry from Nagini-Bathilda in *Deathly Hallows*, something about her performance—perhaps her choice of spell or her aim—is deficient: her ricocheting spell breaks Harry's wand. Dresang argues that Hermione's hysterics are "out of line with her core role in the book" (223) and Meredith Cherland finds that they mar her portrayal to the point that Hermione is "one of the least credible characters in this series" (278), but her repeated hysterics at critical junctures serve what for Rowling is a vital purpose: they create a handicap that allows Harry to outshine Hermione even if she is more logical, intelligent, knowledgeable, hardworking, and generally better at spellwork. After all, how great is her superior spellwork if she cannot reliably perform under pressure?[30]

Rowling's take on what makes Harry superior despite his anti-intellectual stance can perhaps be summarized by how she describes his approach to the troll in the dungeon: he "did something that was both very brave and very stupid" (*SS* 176).[31] This is the shrinking male sphere: Hermione gets the smarts, but it takes his stupid bravery to save them from the troll. In one of the most troubling conversations of the series, Hermione explicitly divvies up their realms and assigns greater value to his:

> "Harry—you're a great wizard, you know."
> "I'm not as good as you," said Harry, very embarrassed, as she let go of him.
> "Me!" said Hermione. "Books! And cleverness! There are more important things—friendship and bravery and—oh Harry—be *careful!*" (287)

She gets the "books" and "cleverness," but they are not as "important" as his "friendship and bravery" (287). Hidalgo acknowledges that Hermione "may be selling herself short" but considers the contrivance as a laudable instance of Hermione sacrificing herself to mother Harry, despite their being the same age: "By downplaying the value of academic achievement in order to make Harry feel better about himself, she may be selling herself short, something that mothers at times do in order to make their children feel accomplished when they doubt themselves" (83–84). To some readers, so long as Hermione has "grown through her mothering," having her repeatedly sell herself short for Harry to "feel accomplished" can be a feminist victory (84).[32] This kind of reading might encourage females to continue to hinge their value on a very traditionally feminine form of self-sacrifice (self-erasure) while the same series exhorts males to hinge *their* value on traditionally masculine forms of self-sacrifice (glorious battle). In this view, males might risk their lives at key moments, but females risk their selves as a way of being. One form of sacrifice is not definitively worse than the other, but it is a troubling binary, particularly when the masculine is privileged in relation to the feminine. More critically, Mayes-Elma describes Hermione as, "without even thinking, [putting] him back up on the pedestal from where he had climbed down, where society has told girls that boys should be" (91). Rowling, with careful forethought, frequently has Harry climb off his pedestal so Hermione can thrust him back on it.

This gendered apportionment is also quite starkly shown by their O.W.L. results: Harry secures a smattering of grades ranging from "Poor" to "Exceeds Expectations," with a single "Outstanding" in Defense Against the Dark Arts (D.A.D.A.), while Hermione earns ten "Outstandings" and one "Exceeds

Expectations" in D.A.D.A. (*HBP* 103). The range of female achievement has expanded to every subject area *except* one—the one that the series ultimately argues is the most important and that is reserved for Harry. The text insists, without convincing explanation, that the Patronus Charm—a D.A.D.A. spell that Harry masters after copious private lessons with Remus and which the mastery of so greatly impresses the head of Magical Law Enforcement, the O.W.L. examiners, and his Dumbledore's Army (D.A.) peers—is "the only spell [Hermione] ever has trouble with" (*DH* 263). The hysterics that Dresang and Cherland find so inconsistent with Hermione's character are made central to her character precisely so that readers might buy the premise that she (whose childhood was likely filled with happy memories) simply cannot get it together and think happy thoughts in the face of danger.[33]

Despite and in part because of her flaws, however, Hermione *is* a worthy feminist role model. I will readily agree that the texts portray Hermione as essential, and I do not think that Hermione's hysterics undercut her completely—she just hits Rowling's narrative glass ceiling.[34] Perhaps because she *is* elevated in so many ways, Rowling felt she had to be viciously undercut so as to not overshadow her designated hero. Across the series, Hermione remains, sadly, the loudest voice to declare, again and again, that her intellectual achievements are secondary to Harry's brave-and-stupid ones. Hermione exclaims that forming the D.A. under Harry's leadership is "much more important than homework!" because "we've gone past the stage where we can just learn things out of books" (*OP* 325). In saying this, she consigns all her achievements to a beginner or preparatory "stage," as compared to the advanced level at which Harry operates. (This is a particularly odd claim when Harry learned most of his D.A.D.A. spells *from books* during *Goblet of Fire*, with her coaching.) In one of the more unbelievable articulations of Harry's D.A.D.A. superiority, he argues that he is not suited to lead the D.A. because Hermione has historically bested him at D.A.D.A. examinations. This puts her in the position to declare that, indeed, almost all her scores have been superior but none of that counts relative to the singular time he scored higher: "You beat me in our third year—the only year we both sat the test and had a teacher who actually knew the subject" (*OP* 326). Yet in the third-year examination, an obstacle course that tested for practical ability, Hermione "did everything perfectly" except when the boggart appears as Professor McGonagall telling her she has failed her exams (*PA* 319). The text does not remind us that Harry had many extra hours of tutelage from

Professor Lupin with a boggart nor of the fact that when the class had its one session on dealing with the creature, Hermione did not even get a turn (140). Yet she insists that this exam result should stand as proof positive that Harry is better at D.A.D.A. Hermione is also the one who organizes the D.A. and calls for an official vote to make his leadership "formal" and to give him "authority," allowing Harry to have the position and power while still performing humility (*OP* 391). Immediately after, the text describes Hermione as speaking "bossily" (392), an unflattering word choice that emphasizes her lack of the authority that she just conferred on Harry.

In his exaggerated modesty, Harry attributes his field achievements to "luck," "fluke," or "help" but then invokes the same binary of stupid bravery versus book-smarts that positions him as superior to Hermione: "You think it's just memorizing a bunch of spells and throwing them at him, like you're in class or something?" (*OP* 327, 328). In fact, no one suggested that he should be the one to lead the D.A. because he has successfully "[memorized] a bunch of spells"—if that were the measure, it would be Hermione—but after setting up this straw man, Harry manages to come off as humble as he articulates precisely why he is better suited to lead the D.A.: he is the one who the texts have established to have the reliable ability to "think straight" in the face of life-threatening danger. Harry appears to pay lip service to the idea that book-smarts are the correct measure of value only to confirm that stupid bravery is the superior measure. While Hermione is unquestionably better at almost every type of magic—Harry can only surpass her in Potions under Professor Slughorn by following the "alternative instructions" written in by the Half-Blood Prince (*HBP* 189), ultimately not understanding any of the concepts—the series carves out D.A.D.A. for his exclusive supremacy based on the specious premise that D.A.D.A. cannot be learned out of a book. Even his brief Potions success is aggrandized in these terms; Ron describes it not as simply following an alternative text but as another instance of instinct and nerve: "He took a risk and it paid off" (192).

It is unfortunate, and harmful, that when Rowling apportions her separate spheres, she ascribes the hard work to the heroine and "instinct" to the hero.[35] Ultimately, Hermione's intellectual and magical capabilities—which are significant and, in many ways, superior to Harry's and Ron's but never *brilliant*—position Hermione to do a lot more work for much less of the glory. Some have written about men avoiding domestic work through "strategic incompetence"—essentially, by feigning an inability to competently perform those duties and tasks traditionally foisted on females while denying the possibility that those shortcomings should translate to incompetency in other areas. (The same man who cannot organize a children's birthday party or track a family's calendar should, logically, also lack the skills to organize a company's finances or track a multilevel project.)[36] As per Bell, Harry is "often flatly incapable of success—sometimes to the point of utter ineptitude" (6), but as he has been so carefully protected by the texts, no one feels pressed to question his entitlement to authority and leadership.

Rowling sells readers the idea that boys are less capable of cooking, mending wounds, paying attention, taking notes, organizing study schedules, doing research, and packing a bag, yet these shortcomings conveniently do not negatively impact their lives nor render them unable to succeed in the areas in which they choose to invest, particularly because Hermione picks up the slack. After the bonding troll incident in *Sorcerer's Stone*, the text notes how "lucky" Harry is to now have her friendship because now she can help him with his homework and he can play more Quidditch (181). Both boys seem to survive by copying from her, "[managing] to scrape passes" in History of Magic only with her notes (*OP* 229) and relying on Hermione finishing or correcting their work—at times, emotionally manipulating her. In another example of many, Harry relies on Hermione to "look over (in other words, finish writing)" his Herbology essay, freeing him to meet Dumbledore for more important business (*HBP* 426). As Ron later quips, they simply never have to read *Hogwarts: A History*, a text with knowledge that repeatedly proves important: "What's the point? . . . You know it by heart, we can just ask you" (*GF* 548). When Hermione appears to be resentful of always giving them her class notes, Ron says, "We just haven't got your brains or your memory or your concentration—you're just cleverer than we are—is it nice to rub it in?" to "mollify" her into continuing to help them (*OP* 229). She is so pleased to be considered more capable that she allows them to continue to mooch off of her labor and falsely elevate their grades.

In essence, years of academic underachieving have resulted in the two boys simply being less able at most magic, which in turn excuses them from menial responsibilities. Charms, a "soft" subject (*HBP* 174) taught by the diminutive Professor Filius Flitwick, is a catch-all for essential, but generalized, spellwork (conjuring, levitating, summoning, banishing, cheering, color changing, lighting, unlocking, severing, producing water, cleaning). Hermione's prowess is particularly in such Charms, which thrusts her in the position of doing most of the prosaic support work of life, whether it be using a "N.E.W.T. [Nastily Exhausting Wizarding Tests] standard" Protean Charm to create a communication device for the D.A. or melting them an "easier path through the untouched snow" (*OP* 398, 451). In contrast, Harry's capabilities only come into play on special occasions—and to special acclaim.

Throughout *Deathly Hallows* especially, as they lose access to institutional and familial support, Hermione takes on the bulk of the work to make up for their loss. All summer, Harry does nothing to prepare for their Horcrux hunt except to nostalgically empty his school trunk. When he cuts his finger on a broken mirror fragment, he thinks to himself that he should perhaps learn a wound-mending spell from Hermione (*DH* 14)—but, of course, he never does ask, for what would be the point? She will be there to do it. In contrast, Hermione spends the summer mastering difficult spells, such as the Invisible Extension Charm, Obliviate, and a slew of protective enchantments; researches Horcruxes; makes complicated arrangements for her parents' safety; and carefully packs survival essentials for all. Even though Harry is the only one who has ever been shown to have experience in cooking (helping his aunt fry bacon and eggs on Dudley's birthday [*SS* 19]), Ron makes the specious claim that the job of preparing their food has fallen primarily to Hermione only because she is "supposed to be the best at magic" and not "because [she's] a *girl*" (*DH* 293). But Rowling has actually arranged for Hermione to be the best at this kind of magic *because she is a girl*.

Further guaranteeing that Harry will be the one to accomplish the most glorious, credit-bearing achievements across the series is the formulaic contrivance of Hermione (and Ron, as well as all adults) conveniently exiting stage left to enable his one-on-one face-offs—a pattern adhered to in every book. Mendlesohn identifies this as following the courtier tradition, where the hero's companions "provide their skills to enable the hero to achieve specific things for which the *hero* and not they take the credit and the prize" (164). In *Sorcerer's Stone*, there is only enough potion for one person to go through to the last stage of the obstacle course, and Hermione makes her infamous books-and-cleverness speech (287).[37] In *Chamber of Secrets*, Hermione is first benched because she is polyjuiced into a human-cat hybrid. Then, she is literally petrified, and Harry pries the key knowledge (the piece of paper with the answer to what the monster is and how it travels) from her cold, stiff hand.[38] In *Prisoner of Azkaban*, Hermione gets in on the rescue while Ron is laid up, but Harry takes credit as the one who "saved all our lives" by successfully driving off a circle of dementors with the one spell Hermione mysteriously cannot master (412). In *Goblet of Fire*, Harry is the only of the three selected to be a Triwizard Champion, and while Hermione is in the background researching and teaching him essential spells, he is given the opportunity to essentially redo the challenges from *Sorcerer's Stone* alone and with higher stakes. His posse in *Order of the Phoenix* grows, but all are again incapacitated and cede the dueling stage to him. In *Half-Blood Prince*, Harry is the only one to receive special lessons and join Dumbledore in the dangerous Horcrux-locket hunt and the only one in the Astronomy Tower when Dumbledore is killed. In *Deathly Hallows*, every character takes a more active part, but as Melanie J. Cordova notes, all the Horcrux destructions receive some articulation—and quite lengthy scenes when done by Harry or Ron—but Hermione's is pithily described off scene and as an occasion where Ron let her have a turn (31). The focus is on how it "was Ron, all Ron's idea! . . . He was *amazing*! . . . Amazing!" (*DH* 622–23). The final Battle of Hogwarts sees many rise to heroism, but when it comes to Voldemort, Harry states the obvious: "It's got to be me" (737).

Many critics have granted Rowling leeway for this sidelining, citing genre conventions to excuse her authorial choices. If the sidelining were the only evidence of Hermione being undercut, this reasoning would be more satisfying. William V. Thompson, for example, blames the fact that the fantasy tradition is "heteronormative and largely patriarchal" and seems to grant Rowling leeway for that reason: "How can such a girl character be anything but subject to the hero of such a story?" (184). After lowering the bar thus, Thompson concludes that Rowling successfully "creates a character in Hermione that operates in such a way to both resist and undercut the overarching limitations of heroic fantasy" (184). Sarah Margaret Kniesler also notes the practicality of giving the titular hero the heroism: "As the title character, it is necessitated that he [Harry], in most cases, be the character who completes the heroic task" ("Alohomora!" 93). As such, "this is a plot device, not a comment on gender politics, especially because Rowling has repeatedly stated in interviews that she did not consciously make Harry a male, but that was how he came to her" (93). With this passive language, Kniesler blames genre ("it is necessitated" by "plot" that his female companion be suppressed, as if gender analysis should be suspended if an author chooses to follow a sexist genre) and the muses (the male hero "came to" Rowling as if in a vision; no conscious sexism equals no sexism at all). Compare Kniesler's and Thompson's approach to Pugh and Wallace's, who take as their starting premise that the male-hero narrative necessitates not just the sidelining but the obliteration of all other male characters and thereby critique both the text *and* the problematic conventions ("Heteronormative Heroism" 261).[39] Moreover, this appeal to genre depends on ignoring the many authors who have written in the fantasy genre and inventively subverted or defied its problematic conventions. The recurring pattern of sidelining Hermione from the crucial action is not mere loyalty to convention but rather in line with Rowling's purposeful preservation of a glass ceiling.

Conclusion

As virtually all of *Harry Potter*'s female characters are presented as essentially stereotypical and flawed in the same trite ways, and not as products of their society, readers are left to assume gender differences are biological, propagating discriminatory stereotypes. Moreover, the prominent maternal figures present mothers as valuable influences that, in their excess, must be eventually resisted, ignored, and outgrown. Girls are presented with the false choice of either becoming mollycoddlers or working spinsters who, even at their best, cannot surpass or replace males in capability or value.

The few promising exceptions are methodically ranked second to their male counterparts at every turn—whether by directly undercutting female achievements, by lowering the bar for the males, and/or by raising the value of the males' achievements. Hermione, Fleur, McGonagall, Ginny, and Molly are limited feminist figures who are created by the author to accept second place in a shamelessly male-favoring world. Second place is certainly better than no place and, at the time of the series' publication, not something to be scoffed at, but surely that is and has always been an unnecessarily low bar.

Rowling's motivations for this elaborate glass ceiling are unclear. Perhaps she really could not create past the patriarchal conventions of the genres she chose, determined to follow through on the vision of a male hero that came to her. Perhaps she attempted to expand what females could do while reassuring conservative readers that this is not the end of gender difference or male authority. It could well be that none of this was strategic—that Rowling truly preferred a male-privileging gender binary if it would just allow some females to rise to second place. In any case, the messaging is problematic.

Rowling buttresses the zero-sum logic of the gender binary, where there are only two recognized genders, tied to two sexes, with distinct areas of excellence. On one hand, she shrinks the male areas to grant females intellectual prowess. On the other hand, she decimates the value of intellectual prowess as she hands it over to females. The binary is preserved, albeit with some adjustments, stubbornly still privileging the male over the female to produce, at best, a *nicer* patriarchy.

CHAPTER 2

BROS BEFORE CHOS

Masculinities and Male Homosociality in *Harry Potter*

We've taken what you'll sorely miss.
—*GOBLET OF FIRE*

The battle still raged inside his head: *Ginny or Ron?*
—*HALF-BLOOD PRINCE*

Inseparable since their first train ride to Hogwarts, Harry Potter and Ron Weasley have a best-friend relationship that is indelibly shaped by tension. Their complicated dynamic is contingent on Ron's ability to repress his jealousy over Harry's wealth, fame, athletic prowess, and greater magical talent, an emotional burden at which Ron—after a lifetime overshadowed by five older brothers—is well practiced. Long-fomenting cracks and fissures in their relationship erupt in *Goblet of Fire*, however, as Harry rises to unprecedented popularity as Triwizard Champion. When Ron—the person he would most "sorely miss" (*GF* 465)—refuses him his company, Harry pines for him intensely: his need is unspeakable and desperate.

There is a relative lack of scholarship on masculinities and male relationships in *Harry Potter*. Much of what exists compliments the series for making "toxic" masculinity the literal enemy, embodied by Voldemort, that is successfully vanquished by "a skinny, black-haired, bespectacled boy" (*OP* 1) who embraces humility, mercy, and love. Cassandra Bausman, for example, argues that "love is almost figured (if to Harry's dismay) as his super-power . . . set against that of Voldemort's traditional, terrifying brand" (49), while Karen Sugrue identifies that Albus Dumbledore's masculinity should be considered "toxic" and corrected by Harry's more emotionally open, friendship-building approach (149). Terri Doughty acknowledges that the books "do not problematize masculinity" per se but nevertheless finds it "reassuring" and productive that the texts offer boys a less violent "path of maturity to follow" (253, 257).[1] Similarly, Casey A. Cothran argues that the series deserves praise for proffering Harry Potter's masculinity as a salutary model: "Rather than sexist, [Rowling's] work struggles to articulate and define the nature of a positive masculinity" (131). To many, a text that assigns certain attributes or behaviors based on a binary concept of natal genitalia is not a problem so long as those revised scripts are seen as more desirable or beneficial. Thus, an essentializing masculinity that encourages males to "lose themselves in a violent struggle for authority, blinded by a preoccupation with power" would be obviously problematic, but an essentializing masculinity that "places an important focus on self-awareness and self-control" would be welcome (131).

Indeed, *Harry Potter*'s overt message is the importance of love and friendship. Happy teamwork gets things done—yet the friendships that Harry cultivates are not without their conflicts. In *Harry Potter*'s patriarchy, male characters are always in competition with each other, and only a minority are considered worthy of power. Their relationships are governed by a set of rules that attempt to regulate potential conflict between males, bringing relative peace to a pecking order that keeps a select few men on top. In the previous chapter, I discuss how Hermione becomes part of a Harry-centered trio by proving to the boys that she understands that her superior book learning and spellwork do not make her more suited to power; she does most of the accommodating. In contrast, Rowling's male characters navigate their inequalities differently, with accommodations made on both sides.

First, the chapter compares the series' presentation of two pairs of male characters: Albus Dumbledore and Cornelius Fudge, a pair that fails to maintain positive homosocial bonds, and Harry and Ron, a pair that largely succeeds. According to Rowling, for a homosocial bond to be successful, the inferiorly regarded male must learn to live with his insecurities and resentments, while the superiorly regarded male must continually make accommodations for those insecurities and resentments by cultivating a façade of humility—a carefully calibrated dynamic requiring the cooperation of many others. It is a significant amount of work, but if successful, *Harry Potter* says, the homosocial bond can empower both. But at whose expense? The males lower on the hierarchy certainly bear the brunt of the emotional labor. As the next section shows, Rowling's portrayal of homosociality also promotes certain troubling rules of male-male loyalty, including the rule that males must aid and, if necessary, abet each other such that questionable choices cannot be questioned.

The rules of male homosocial loyalty also include, as the last section discusses, carefully protecting against the possibility that a heterosexual relationship might supplant the all-important male-male bond. Popularly called "bros before hos," this discourse encourages males to view their homosocial bonds as easier and more satisfying compared to onerous relationships with enigmatic females. As the wizarding world operates largely according to a gender binary that is strictly heterosexist, this creates an apparent dilemma for the hero: Who will be his mate? Harry's inexpressible feelings toward Ron across the series are then juxtaposed against Harry's first crush on a girl, Cho Chang—a character that was always meant to be a mere pause in the short journey to marrying Ron's little sister, Ginny. No matter how seductively Cho (or eventually, Ginny) might entice, Rowling's position is that the hero needs to prioritize male relationships above all others, promoting patriarchal interests. Analyzing how homosociality regulates his choice of wife, the last section of this chapter charts how *Harry Potter* normalizes the subtle and relentless ways in which a patriarchy can marginalize most females from mattering except to the limited extent that they may be useful to men.

Revising and Reassessing Masculinities

"More than just male-male friendships and bonding," male homosociality "is a fixture of social life that promotes oppressive versions of masculinity because of its structural characteristics" (Vogels 226). Researchers have identified homosociality as operating according to three primary tenets:

(1) *emotional detachment*, a meaning constructed through relationships within families whereby young men detach themselves from mothers and

develop gender identities in relation to that which they are not; (2) *competitiveness*, a meaning constructed and maintained through relationships with other men whereby simple individuality becomes competitive individuality; and (3) *sexual objectification of women*, a meaning constructed and maintained through relationships with other men whereby male individuality is conceptualized not only as *different from* female but as *better than* female. (S. Bird 121)

Largely through claims of essentialism—that is, that biology creates two opposite genders that only find complementarity through heterosexual union—people identified as male by their natal biology have been encouraged to cultivate a gender identity that is not feminine. Under patriarchy, although most men could be considered superior to women by virtue of the sex designation that marks them as not female and not feminine, all men are not deemed equal: one iteration of masculinity is considered the standard against which all others are (de)valued. The ability to claim superiority based on masculinity has typically depended on competing with other males, "using such 'markers of manhood' as occupational achievement, wealth, power and status, physical prowess, and sexual achievement" (Flood 341). In the last several decades, the male figures at the top of the masculinity pyramid—the masked superhero, the Rambo-type musclehead, the cutthroat Wall Street titan, and the playboy billionaire—have been represented as lone and fundamentally lonely men. Their relationships with other men have been primarily defined by the need to dominate or best them, whether that be at physical size and prowess, the amassing of resources, and/or the sexual conquest of women.

None of these valuations are set in stone, of course: "When historical conditions and social patterns in society change, the hegemonic position can also be confronted and questioned, meaning that hegemony is never absolute or fixed" (Hammarén and Johansson 3). At any given point in any given patriarchal culture, male bodies are always vying for ascendancy—to assert a better presentation of that hegemonic masculinity perhaps or to scuffle for primacy against other lower-ranked masculinities or even to alter or displace that hegemonic masculinity. Given ever-shifting discourses, Nils Hammarén and Thomas Johansson rightly critique the tendency to regard homosociality as only productive of male-male competition (3). Urging for a more "dynamic" view that accounts for certain kinds of positive bonding ("horizontal homosociality"), they argue that groups of men can and do strive for "group cohesion, togetherness, and intimacy, rather than interpersonal competition and the creation of male hierarchies" (3).

A positive representation of a male body behaving in a historically disallowed way—emotively, vulnerably, cooperatively—appears a victory, and, to some significant degree, it is. Compared to testosterone-heavy masters-of-the-universe stereotypes, a skinny young wizard who values his friends appears a refreshing alternative indeed. Certainly, if a body is enabled by that novel positive representation to feel licensed to behave in a new way—particularly, in the polar opposite of its usual grain—it can feel profoundly liberatory. We are so used to analyzing how hegemonic forms try to stamp out the nonhegemonic that we cannot help but cheer when the latter appears to receive any positive validation—forgetting, perhaps, that cultural narratives can tolerate a surprising amount of contradiction to preserve male power and that nonhegemonic narratives are not necessarily better.

In his essay on masculinity, Steven L. Arxer encourages an additional layer of analysis. Arxer explores how hegemonic masculinity can become "hybrid," appropriating nonhegemonic practices "as a way to protect and reproduce gendered power and privilege" (390). It is not enough to identify nonstereotypical gender representations and declare victory when there is a distinct possibility that such "new" practices can be quietly co-opted into the service of patriarchy. "In appearing 'softer,'" hegemonic masculinity can adapt to changing norms, thereby "[presenting] itself as less opposed to femininities and as an unlikely candidate for the maintenance and perpetuation of patriarchy" (394), effectively flying under radars that are attuned only to more flagrant or established sexism.

Patriarchy is adaptive and sneaky: the vast array of aggressive male role models might, for example, make us welcome representations of cooperative male bonding with relief, but we are perhaps too quick to assume that the proffered alternative is wholly positive. Nonhegemonic homosocial bonds that appear more inclusive of different masculinities may in practice be easier on men and boys and therefore antisexist, but this greater latitude for males may still be *at the expense of females.* Subverting stereotypes is therefore not enough: we must continue to inquire and assess how proposed alternative models may remain limited. In *Harry Potter*, male homosocial bonds are governed by a revised set of discourses that attempt to regulate homosocial competition—not to squash it, because *Harry Potter*'s patriarchy depends on its continuation, but to maintain it in such a way so that those who better embody hegemonic masculinity (as it adapts and evolves) can benefit from the support and service of other males. While cooperative homosociality is in some ways encouraged, it remains pervasively hierarchical, and competition remains rife.

Male Homosocial Cooperation and the Humble Hero

According to Rowling, males must engage in ongoing accommodations wherein the "inferior" male manages his jealousy and the "superior" male performs a reassuring humility that quells the worst pangs of that jealousy. Albus Dumbledore and Cornelius Fudge exemplify a negative homosocial bond wherein Dumbledore is regarded as superior, but Fudge cannot accept being the loser in the relationship. Harry and Ron, on the other hand, show how males who are unequal in talent, ability, and status can, through mutual work, maintain a positive homosocial bond. While Rowling presents this as a positive model, as I will show, this more cooperative model is also fraught with issues.

First, the problem pair: Dumbledore and Fudge. Famous even in youth as "the most brilliant student ever seen at the school," Dumbledore proceeded to publish and invent and to vanquish their generation's greatest threat, Gellert Grindelwald (*DH* 17). Perhaps projecting, the eulogizing Elphias Doge hypothesizes that Dumbledore must also have made his brother jealous: "Being continually outshone was an occupational hazard of being his friend and cannot have been any more pleasurable as a brother" (18). To be close to someone so greatly regarded is to live continually obscured in their shadow, always seen as lesser than or rendered invisible. If "inferior" males fail to placidly take their inferior place, *Harry Potter* says, they can create societal conflict as they lash out in futile attempts to supplant the "superior" male. Various exchanges between Dumbledore and Fudge illustrate what happens when a malcontent attempts to buck against his lower place in the hierarchy: he inevitably loses, and his envy then fuels vindictive reprisals that can harm others in their purview.

Throughout the series, Fudge is presented as an inferior man who favors the outward signs of power, obtaining the post of Minister of Magic that was thrice offered to, and rejected by, the humbler Dumbledore (*HBP* 443). In the first few books, the two men appear to get along professionally because Fudge recognizes and accepts his inferiority. *Goblet of Fire* ends with an explicit break, however, with Fudge misinterpreting Dumbledore's advice, which "sounded like a mere statement," by reacting instead "as though Dumbledore were advancing upon him with a wand" (709). By *Order of the Phoenix*, they have become enemies. The time of having "[pelted] Dumbledore with owls every morning, askin' fer advice" has given way to a blustering Fudge that wants to stamp Dumbledore out (*SS* 65). "Deep down, Fudge knows Dumbledore's much cleverer than he is, a much more powerful wizard," Remus Lupin explains, "but it seems that he's become fond of power now, and much more confident. He loves being Minister of Magic, and he's managed to convince himself that he's the clever one" (*OP* 94).

Much of the conflict in *Order of the Phoenix* stems from Fudge's refusal to accept that he is inferior in talent, intelligence, ability, presentation, and popularity. Subjecting Harry to the full Wizengamot for a hearing on underage magical use is one such attempt—Dumbledore and Fudge appear to be on trial rather than Harry. During their very public confrontation, Dumbledore showcases his cool, collected, always-in-control masculinity, while Fudge quickly unravels, unable to control his emotional response to stress and conflict. Dumbledore speaks with a "quiet voice," even "cheerfully," and "[strides] serenely across the room" with a "perfectly calm expression" to face off with the "obviously flustered," "thoroughly disconcerted" Fudge (*OP* 139). Successfully engaging the Wizengamot's attention, Dumbledore emerges victorious by projecting a certain model of masculine authority—he is the elder statesman wielding civility to put Fudge in his place. The scene is an exercise in synonyms: Dumbledore speaks "pleasantly" with "an expression of polite interest" (139); "calmly" and "quietly but clearly" (146); "politely" and "mildly" (147); and "courteously" (148). The most hostility that he allows himself to show is when he contradicts one of Fudge's assertions "politely as ever, but now with a suggestion of coolness behind his words" (148). In contrast, the cartoonish Fudge is described with emotive words, some of which animalize him: "icily," "barked," "forcefully" (146); "snapped" as he "turned brick red" and "a shade of magenta" (147); "snarled," "blustered," "at the top of his voice," "roared" (148); "shouted, banging his fist on the judge's bench and upsetting a bottle of ink" (149); and "savagely," turning "a deeper shade of puce" (149). The more he feels power slipping away, the more aggressive Fudge becomes, attempting to attain by force the respect that he cannot legitimately earn. Refusing to admit his obvious deficiencies, Fudges goes on to abuse the power of the ministry to attempt to bring Dumbledore's domain, Hogwarts, to heel.

In contrast, the homosocial bond between Harry and Ron illustrates how, in patriarchy, cooperation for mutual benefit can be achieved between unequal males. Unequivocally and relentlessly, the texts "lionize Harry's masculinity as dominant" by keeping Ron down (Pugh and Wallace, "Postscript" 189): "Ron is Tonto to Harry's Lone Ranger, Robin to his Batman, and thus Ron can never match Harry in terms of his accomplishments, whether they be sexual, intellectual, athletic, or heroic" (Pugh and Wallace, "Heteronormative Heroism" 272). It is not merely that Harry is rich and famous; he is better in every way.[2] As Lauren Byler aptly puts it, Ron suffers "repeated subjection to experiencing his own averageness" (121), and it is an inferiority constantly produced by direct contrast to Harry. Both boys embrace anti-intellectualism, but the texts always denote Ron as being just a little bit worse at school. For example, Hermione looks over both their work but hands Ron a whole sheet of corrections and a conclusion to copy, while to Harry she says, "Yours is okay except for this bit at the end" (*OP* 300). Both boys fail to turn vinegar into wine, but Harry's vinegar merely turns to ice, while Ron's flask dramatically explodes (*HBP* 515). During their O.W.L.s, Harry is embarrassed that he changed his rat's size instead of its color but comforted by the fact that Ron "had caused a dinner plate to mutate into a large mushroom and had no idea how it had happened" (*OP* 713). Harry "hobbled" out of Crouch-Moody's (Barty Crouch Jr. polyjuiced as Professor Alastor "Mad-Eye" Moody) D.A.D.A. class with the unique achievement of being able to "throw off the [Imperius] curse entirely," and the next sentences quickly tell us that Ron "had had much more difficulty with the curse than Harry" (*GF* 232). Harry's array of O.W.L. grades are decidedly average, but he has one "Outstanding" in the most valuable subject (Defense Against the Dark Arts). When he glances at Ron's O.W.L. results, he notes only that "there were no 'Outstandings' there" (*HBP* 103). "Despite the fact that he is physically larger and more developed (as evidenced by his moustache)" (Pugh and Wallace, "Heteronormative Heroism" 272), Ron is also described as less talented and lacking the necessary nerve for the violent sport of Quidditch. Ron has much to be jealous of: when he finally gets on the team, Harry bemoans that he is "not performing to" the "standard" of the Keeper he replaces (*OP* 400). In his very first game, Harry must "[save] Weasley's neck" (412) by, predictably, quickly catching the Snitch.

These comparisons frequently make Ron appear woefully pathetic, such as when Crouch-Moody says Harry and Hermione would make good Aurors, and Ron desperately offers a thought while "looking hopefully at Moody as if he too wanted to be told he had the makings of an Auror" (*GF* 570). Although, in their first encounter with the veela at the Quidditch World Cup, both boys appear to be equally susceptible to the femmes fatales' powers (103), Harry is shown to become quickly impervious to the worst of their effects, while Ron spontaneously joins the "gaggle" of underwhelming young wizards who lie to the group of veela during the Quidditch World Cup riot: "Did I tell you I've invented a broomstick that'll reach Jupiter?" (126). Even years later, when the quarter veela Fleur Delacour is engaged to his brother, he remains embarrassingly vulnerable to her presence (*HBP* 93).

Not only does Harry best Ron at every level but he is also presented as a fundamentally superior character. Farah Mendlesohn describes Harry as an "almost incomprehensibly . . . nice child" (162), while Ron often derives pleasure from bullying and unkindness.[3] There are several examples of his propensity for petty bullying, as when he "casually [turfs] a first year out of one of the good armchairs by the fire so that he could sit down" and displaces his anger about failing his Apparition test by "goading" Moaning Myrtle, which "put fresh heart" into him (*HBP* 257, 462). While Harry is declared "a remarkably selfless person" (*DH* 716)—a hero who has "never sought" power but is thrust into it and therefore "best suited" to possess it (718)—Ron is a bit too much like Fudge: he relishes power and hungers for attention. Hermione rightly conjectures that, having "all those brothers to compete against at home," Ron is particularly sensitive to being overshadowed by the Chosen One at school (*GF* 290). When attacked in the middle of the night, Ron finds, "for the first time in his life, people were paying more attention to him than to Harry, [and] it was clear that Ron was rather enjoying the experience" (*PA* 270), in contrast to our humble hero, who vocally complains about receiving so much attention. In *Goblet of Fire*, having been used as a tournament target for Harry to rescue, he actively attempts to foment more attention: "Harry noticed that Ron's version of events changed subtly with every retelling," featuring himself as an active participant rather than the damsel in distress (509). Having received the coveted Prefect's badge in their fifth year over Harry, Ron "kept moving his . . . badge around, first placing it on his bedside table, then putting it into his jeans pocket, then taking it out and laying it on his folded robes, as though to see their effect on the black," finally "[wrapping] it tenderly in his maroon socks and [locking] it in his trunk" (*OP* 168). In *Half-Blood Prince*, he is perfectly happy to play in a Quidditch match even when he thinks Harry dosed him with lucky potion (293). In the final moments of *Deathly Hallows*, when Harry must consider what to do with the all-powerful Elder Wand, Ron's impulse is to keep it, and his greed contrasts unfavorably with Harry's heroic choice to forego that kind of power (749). There are ample reasons why being friends with Harry would incite in Ron a relentless sense of always competing—and always losing. As the Chosen One's friend, Ron's condition is to "always [be] shunted to one side whenever people see [Harry]" (*GF* 290). Ron's lot is to accept his status, and, for the most part, he does; as Hermione says, "He puts up with it, and he never mentions it" (290).

For his part, Harry has a lot of work to do as well. In *Half-Blood Prince*, for example, Ron's resentment reaches dangerous levels as Professor Slughorn pointedly singles out Harry and Hermione for attention—treating Ron as if he "was not present" or as if he were a "display of Cockroach Clusters" (233, 244).[4] Attentive to Ron's increasing "bad mood" (234), Harry intentionally schedules Quidditch practices to coincide with Professor Slughorn's dinner party invitations: "This strategy meant that Ron was not left out, and they usually had a laugh with Ginny, imagining Hermione shut up with McLaggen and [Blaise] Zabini" (244), the Gryffindor who is aggressively pursuing Hermione and a Muggle-born-hating Slytherin, respectively. This strategy is doubly protective of the male homosocial relationship—both in keeping Ron included and in excluding Hermione in a way that exposes the female of the trio to gender (and, if we consider the witch-Muggle divide as allegorical, racial or species) harassment.

More subtly, Harry must never actively seek attention nor behave as if he enjoys it when he receives it, assuaging Ron's insecurities through an elaborate construct of humility to the point that Harry appears to possess unreasonably low self-esteem. Some of these iterations of humility are discussed in my previous chapter—and there are yet more, each contrived to cultivate his humble, modest persona. What is important to Rowling is that Harry is "famous . . . without tryin'" (*CS* 117)—that he be famous without ever appearing to have sought fame.

In *Goblet of Fire*, Ron's festering insecurities and resentments erupt when Harry is selected as a Triwizard Champion: this is "just one time too many" for the beleaguered Ron (290), who withdraws from their friendship for the first time. Harry cannot seem to fathom why: "'*Jealous?*' Harry said incredulously. 'Jealous of what? He wants to make a prat of himself in front of the whole school, does he?'" (289). Harry's response makes him appear humble, even though not much earlier he had indulged in a daydream of himself as the victorious champion, very much *not* making a prat of himself in front of the whole school: "a series of dazzling new pictures," "arms raised in triumph in front of the whole school, all of whom were applauding and screaming" (192). While the reality of the risks can be expected to dampen his enthusiasm, the same person who so clearly saw the potential for glory in the opportunity ought not now be "incredulous" that Ron might be jealous to not have that same opportunity land on his lap. Harry's inability to conceive of Ron's feelings reveals the solipsism that blinds him from empathizing with the best friend who lives in his shadow, hungering for a fraction of the attention that he blithely takes for granted.

Significantly, Harry knows that he must conceal any desire to be recognized as the best, to garner even more acclaim and praise, or be the center of attention—he has to be someone who "[doesn't] ask for it" (*GF* 290). His "dazzling" daydream is illicit (192); his desire for more attention is taboo. For Harry to appear as a likable, humble hero, he must not only conceal any desire for more glory but also continually disclaim credit for, sometimes even awareness of, his achievements. At the same time, the texts shower him with the attention he always claims to dislike by planting other characters to herald his achievements in his stead. In the previous chapter, I discuss how some of these instances of Harry's exaggerated humility put Hermione in the position of raising Harry's self-esteem at her expense. But Hermione is not the only one to perform this work: the persona of the modest hero is maintained through a community of admirers tasked to sing the praises he cannot. Mendlesohn rightly notes that "the flattery of Harry by the wizard world is easily as unpleasant as that of Dudley by his parents" (171)—partisan, idolatrous, and shallow—and his companions serve to "[create] moral authority around the person of Harry Potter" (165). There are many more examples, such as when Molly Weasley thanks him for saving the poisoned Ron with a timely bezoar in *Half-Blood Prince*: "You saved Ginny . . . saved Arthur . . . now you've saved Ron" (403). In response, Harry "muttered awkwardly," "Don't be . . . I didn't . . ." (403). His sentences are unfinished because to finish them would be to contradict fact; he *did* save them all. Attractively, he seems to want to disclaim credit for what he has done, inciting Arthur Weasley to also gush, "Half our family does seem to owe you their lives" (403).

In the rare event that he is *not* being praised or given special attention by his entourage, however, Harry is abruptly cured of his apparent humility. Consider *Order of the Phoenix*: at the novel's opening, we encounter an unusually immodest-sounding Harry. Ron and Hermione appear to be included in important business while he is stuck in Privet Drive, leading him to feel as if his capabilities are not being recognized as they ought to be: "Why wasn't he, Harry, busy? Hadn't he proved himself capable of handling more than they? Had they forgotten what he had done?" (*OP* 8). Receiving only pithy responses about his encounter with the dementors, he resents the lack of praise: "Wasn't *anybody* going to say 'well done' for fighting off two dementors single-handedly?" (35). Finally confronting his friends, the humility façade is fully, if briefly, lifted: "I've handled more than you two'd ever managed and Dumbledore knows it—who saved the Sorcerer's Stone? Who got rid of Riddle? Who saved both your skins from the dementors? . . . Who had to get past dragons and sphinxes and every other foul thing last year? Who saw him come back? Who had to escape from him? Me!" (66–67).

Soon after, he implodes again when Ron receives the honor of being named Prefect but, this time, has the self-control to keep his resentments to himself. Draco's later taunt accurately captures his state of mind: "How does it feel being second-best to Weasley . . . ?" (*OP* 194)—a novel concern for famous Harry Potter. "Anxiously probing his own feelings," he wonders whether his belief that he deserves the badge over Ron makes him "as arrogant as Draco Malfoy": "Did he think himself superior to everyone else? Did he really believe he was *better* than Ron?" (166). Given how the texts insistently denote Ron as inferior in every way, Harry's "small voice" seems to be insisting on the lie that he must continually tell himself so as to not feel "arrogant." Continuing the argument, he carefully parses out that, when it comes to heroic "adventures," he did the most. While *"Ron and Hermione were with me most of the time,"* he notes, *"they didn't fight Quirrell with me. They didn't take on Riddle and the basilisk. They didn't get rid of all those dementors the night Sirius escaped. They weren't in that graveyard with me, the night Voldemort returned"* (166–67). Again, Harry proves how aware he is of his many achievements and how much he esteems himself—and fairly enough, but it starkly contrasts with his propensity to play dumb about why he is popular or worthy of praise.

The Prefect-badge debacle is Harry's first time getting a small taste of what it always feels like to be Ron, and it is enough to send him into a

tailspin, exposing how very much he does, despite the texts' protestations
to the contrary, believe himself to be entitled to the attention and admiration he receives. As it turns out, his "bitterly" insisting that he would "swap"
places with Ron "any time he wants" is just the luxurious thought of someone
who usually enjoys the privilege of attention (*GF* 290). Despite his middling
grades—as well as regular detentions, demerits, and unchecked curfew-
and boundary-breaking—somehow Harry still feels entitled to a position
that entails helping the administration enforce school rules. In truth, what
deranges him is that, in this one instance, Ron has been ranked above him.
The façade of humility dissolves as soon as he is put in the position of feeling
that "*Ron must have something*" he does not (*OP* 167). It is only during this
jealous tailspin that he is able to have a somewhat more honest conversation with himself about the fact that he does, secretly, consider himself to
merit more esteem than Ron—that, perhaps, Ron does have ample reason
to be jealous of him.

To his credit, Harry manages to rein in his jealousy about the Prefect
badge—he would not, as "Ron's best friend in the world, . . . ruin this for
Ron when, for the first time, he had beaten Harry at something" (*OP* 167)—
exemplifying, in this rare moment, just a fraction of the self-soothing that
Ron must continually engage in. However, Harry rises above his jealousy in
part by mentally putting Ron back in his lower place. Concluding that he was
denied the badge because he has been too adventurous, too daring, "caused
too much trouble" (167), he reassures himself that Ron's elevation to Prefect
is actually a form of insult. The text also helps by suggesting that Molly's
encounter with the boggart (foregrounding the very real danger they now
face after Voldemort's return) puts into perspective how childish it was to care
about being Prefect at all: "It seemed extraordinary to him that barely an hour
ago he had been worried about . . . who had gotten a prefect's badge" (178).
Thus, the text quickly reasserts Harry's superiority over Ron by decreeing
the latter's achievement to be mere child's play, and every moment thereafter
that Ron polishes his badge or enjoys his power further infantilizes him.[5]

As if in anxious compensation for these unflattering opening scenes, the
humility dance then repeats in *Order of the Phoenix* multiple times. Several
chapters later, Harry appears unbelievably dense when he disclaims his fitness to lead a D.A.D.A. student group, requiring his friends to twice iterate
the same achievements that Harry was so capable of bellowing at the novel's
opening. The text again allows him to play dumb—*Who, moi?*—to which

Hermione replies, "Isn't it obvious? . . . I'm talking about *you*, Harry" (*OP* 326). Effectively inviting the elaboration of compliments, he replies, "About me what?" (326). The text describes Harry as being "sure the pair of them were pulling his leg," eager to contest Hermione's claim that he is "the best in the year" in D.A.D.A., crediting "luck" or "fluke" for his successes (326–27), which again requires Ron and Hermione to list his achievements. (I analyze this scene in the previous chapter.) A few pages later, Hermione must again repeat that "there's no point pretending that you're not good at Defense Against the Dark Arts," with another iteration of his amazing abilities: "You were the only person last year who could throw off the Imperius Curse completely, you can produce a Patronus, you can do all sorts of stuff that full-grown wizards can't" (331). Hermione could be said to be calling him out for "pretending" to be humble, but everything about the novels is calculated to make readers believe that his humility is sincere.[6]

Harry's humility construct is an elaborate façade that conceals how much public adulation he requires to sustain it. A humble hero is certainly more appealing than an arrogant one, but, interestingly, he cannot even be *self-assured*. It is a fascinating dynamic: surrounded by companions who are ever ready to rebut his self-effacements, the hero maintains both his authority *and* his reputation for humility. Thanks to these frequently staged reminders, readers find it hard to agree with Snape that he is as arrogant as his father was (*OP* 650).[7]

At the Hog's Head, a surly skeptic inspires the novel's *fifth* reiteration of Harry's feats by his peers: corporeal Patronuses, which inspire his peers to be "deeply impressed"; killing the basilisk, which elicits whistles, "awestruck looks," and a soft "wow"; saving the Sorcerer's Stone, which leaves a classmate's "eyes . . . as round as Galleons"; and the Triwizard Tournament tasks, which evokes "a murmur of impressed agreement around the table" (*OP* 342).[8] As before, Harry's apparent humility ("He was trying to arrange his face so that he did not look too pleased with himself" [343]) becomes an opportunity for more praise to be heaped. Demurring, he explains that he "had a lot of help with all that stuff," even though Harry earlier had, when "anxiously probing" his resentment about the Prefect badge, thought he deserved credit for the key achievements. But because he pulls off his performance of humility, his peers immediately dismiss the value of the help he received as readily as he had. Michael Corner points out he handled the dragon alone; Susan Bones notes that "nobody helped you get rid of those dementors this summer" (343).[9]

Had his peers instead questioned whether he had really done all this himself, perhaps he might have once again bellowed his curriculum vitae in all caps.

To be clear, I believe Rowling intended to present Harry as a moody teen-ager maturing into his role as a natural-born leader, but the texts contain sufficient evidence to allow us to read Harry's humility as a semiconscious performance. Is the ideal man supposed to be great but pretend to never know it or develop low self-esteem and depend on an entourage to periodi-cally remind him of his greatness? In effect, the superior male must learn to cultivate a social dynamic whereby he typically never needs to ask for atten-tion—and has the luxury to claim that he has never done so—because it is automatically and regularly given. In turn, his burden is to protest and demur and be ever anxious about appearing "as arrogant as Draco Malfoy" (*OP* 166). My point is not that Harry does not deserve attention and admiration—no one saves more lives than he—but rather to highlight how much Harry's heroic characterization relies on an elaborate psychodrama of performed humility, bordering on a delusion of low self-esteem.[10] This dynamic not only requires others to periodically buttress his self-esteem, even at their own expense, but also forces him to disclaim or contradict reality. The reality is that Harry is, as we have been told and as he well knows, superior to Ron in ways that the texts deem important—he *is* less selfish, petty, and rude; more likely to feel protective toward the downtrodden; and better at D.A.D.A. and Quidditch. And the reality is that he knows he is superior to Ron and feels entitled to more attention and power. But it is Harry's awkward job to perpetually act as if he does not recognize this reality—to maintain an elaborate façade of humility that nevertheless cracks the moment he feels he is not being appropriately recognized.

In a society that lionizes a select few over all others, resentments abound. While Ron grapples with his undercurrent of jealous resentment, Harry is always grappling with his own undercurrent of *entitled* resentment. To some degree, he resents having to make so many accommodations to con-tinually disclaim credit and disavow fame. In turn, this feeds the solipsism that reduces his capacity to recognize and empathize with the best friend who lives in his shadow, hungering for a fraction of the attention that Harry receives. Ron appears in an unflattering light—as desperate for attention— when he exaggerates his achievements, tousles his hair for an audience, or polishes his Prefect's badge. The ill-concealed hunger of the "inferior" male becomes further justification for his inferior position.[11]

Loyal Bromances

Despite all these required mutual accommodations, the series presents the male homosocial bond as the most valuable possible relationship. Harry copies Ron's scheduling choices wholesale, syncing their timetable completely, and continues that pattern every year (*CS* 252). All their leisure time is enjoyed together, and they bunk in adjacent beds. Were it not for summer holidays, Quidditch in years one to four, Prefect duties in years five and six, various detentions, and their two rifts, the two boys would have, by choice, spent every minute of their days and nights together.[12]

Part of the reason that male homosocial relations are superior, as per *Harry Potter*, is because boys just want to have fun: the anxious females in the series embrace rules that hamper what is posited as a male's natural preference for risk-taking, action, and adventure. After Harry shares his anxieties over Sirius's safety in *Goblet of Fire*, for example, Ron suggests a game of Quidditch in the orchard. Hermione believes herself to be speaking for Harry when she says, in an "I-don't-think-you're-being-very-sensitive sort of voice," that Harry would abstain because "he's worried, and he's tired" (*GF* 150). But Harry responds immediately that yes, he does want to play. Hermione leaves the room muttering, "*Boys*," suggesting this kind of response—seeking (distr)action, living in the moment, yielding to impulses—is exclusive to males (150).

In the series, blind loyalty exists only among male friends, which is of a kind where each boy easily puts aside his own opinions, even his own principles, to enable the other's schemes and whims and absolve the other of feelings of guilt or shame. Both boys are presented as extremely loyal to each other to the point that each backs the other's play even when they disagree. In the books, Harry—supposedly the heroic protector of the oppressed—never expresses disapproval of Ron's unkind remarks; his reaction is often omitted.[13] He admits to himself that Luna speaks an "uncomfortable [truth]" in describing Ron as "a bit unkind" but only mutters an uncommitted "I s'pose" in response (*HBP* 310, 311).[14] There is one other moment where the text acknowledges that Harry disagrees with Ron's immature behavior toward Hermione but chooses to keep this to himself for the sake of the homosocial bond: "He liked being back on speaking terms with Ron too much to speak his mind right now" (*GF* 432). These two examples suggest that Harry's other curious refusals to critique Ron's shortcomings are willful choices to preserve the homosocial bond.

In turn, Ron also withholds and shields Harry from critique. Contrast the reactions of his two best friends to one of Harry's more selfish instances of rule flouting. Having spied on Snape's memories of being cruelly bullied by his father and godfather, Harry becomes "desperate . . . to know of any mitigating factors there might have been, any excuse at all for his father's behavior" (*OP* 659). It is understandable, of course, that he would be deeply discomfited, but rather than wait or send an owl,[15] he impetuously latches on to an ill-advised plan to break into Umbridge's office to talk to his godfather. Careful Hermione begs him to abort. All her points are sensible and accurate, particularly when she notes the selfishness of his taking on such an unnecessary risk right after Professor Dumbledore has sacrificed his position as headmaster to protect Harry from being expelled for other rule breaking (667). Yet her counsel is described as "nagging" (661). Echoing the many representations of overly anxious female characters in the text, Hermione's wise counsel appears annoying and unsupportive. In contrast, "Ron seemed determined to give neither his opinion nor his advice" (667). "He would not look at Harry," suggesting that he does not support this plan, but he tells Hermione to "give it a rest, okay? He can make up his own mind" (667). The twins decree that Ron's laissez-Harry-faire attitude makes him "a true friend" (658).

Ironically, Ron's modeling of male loyalty reminds us of Remus's behavior in the very memory that inspires Harry's fireplace foray: the two more popular males, James Potter and Sirius Black, pounce on Severus Snape while Remus pretends to continue reading, "though his eyes were not moving and a faint frown line had appeared between his eyebrows" (*OP* 645). The loyal male friend feigns blindness, keeps his mouth shut, and tacitly supports his bros, even when they behave abusively. While Rowling seems to intend readers to read James and Sirius as bullies and Remus as their enabler, she does not seem to recognize that she promotes the same blind loyalty with Harry and Ron. When Hermione criticizes Harry's use of the Levicorpus spell, reminding him that Death Eaters had used it to torment Muggles, Ron jumps to his "aid" by insisting that they were "just having a laugh" while pointing a phallic sausage at her (*HBP* 241). It is little surprise that Ron also abuses his Prefect power to silence one of Harry's detractors, Seamus Finnigan (*OP* 219).

In Rowling's depiction, both the "inferior" and "superior" males benefit from mutual aiding as well as abetting, easily suppressing individual conscience for the sake of the homosocial relationship.[16] When Ron dares to "betray" Harry—as when Ron shares with Hermione that Harry has been "muttering in [his] sleep" (*OP* 681), lending support to Hermione's "nagging" Harry for not practicing his Occlumency—Harry is quick to retaliate, bringing up Ron's pathetic performance on the Quidditch field with "vindictive pleasure" and thus shoving the lower-tier male back in line (682). The attack reminds Ron, ears red, how much he stands to lose if he were to lose Harry's favor. Considering how Ron's self-esteem is crippled by his "abysmal goal-keeping record" (683), this is a vicious attack and would seem well out of proportion to Ron's transgression—except that Ron has "betrayed" him to a *female*—a crime against male homosociality.[17]

Given the undercurrent of resentments in the male hierarchy, the homosocial bond can explosively rupture at any time that the "inferior" male imagines himself more deserving or the "superior" one fails to perform humility, but the series also depicts it as easily reparable. Harry and Ron appear able to get over their anger, while female characters hold grudges. In *Goblet of Fire*, Harry cuts Ron off from apologizing so they can resume their friendship without further ado (358). But Hermione—a bystander to their rupture—is overtaken with excessive emotion. She "shouted, stamping her foot on the ground, tears splashing down her front" (358–59), embraces them in unwanted hugs, and "dashed away, now positively howling" (359). Ron declares her "barking mad" and directs Harry to look at his Triwizard task scores (359), cementing their gender's common ground: boys, unlike girls, move on.[18] In the aftermath of Ron's *Deathly Hallows* return, Harry's and Hermione's reactions are similarly juxtaposed. Harry is eager to resume the relationship on its previous terms with as little verbiage as possible. After a few lines on Ron's resentments, "simultaneously they walked forwards and hugged," his abandonment forgotten (379). In contrast, Hermione cannot immediately forgive; she becomes, in Harry's opinion, "quite demented" (380). Ron spends the next several days patiently bearing with her icy treatment, and we can easily see—from the many scenes of Molly's emotional volatility—how Arthur successfully modeled this kind of conciliatory behavior for his sons.

While Rachel Armstrong is right in saying that Hermione's relationship is "essential" to the boys (250)—in that they, perhaps literally, could not "last two days without her" (*Deathly Hallows: Part I* film)—the texts are fairly insistent in their goal of marking the male homosocial bond as more important than male-female ones. They operate as a trio, but the male homosocial bond is, to Harry, the one that feels more valuable. When Ron unfriends him in *Goblet of Fire*, Harry is absolutely bereft, though he will not admit it.

Hermione "impatiently" gives voice to their unspeakable feelings ("You miss him! . . . And I *know* he misses you—"), but Harry vehemently denies his attachment ("*Miss him?* . . . I don't *miss him*"), admitting privately that "this was a downright lie. Harry liked Hermione very much, but she just wasn't the same as Ron" (*GF* 316). After their reconciliation, "he couldn't believe how happy he felt; he had Ron back on his side" (365). He even believes that "Ron's indignation on his behalf" about Igor Karkaroff's unfair scoring "was worth about a hundred points to him" (360)—worth more than his position in the competition in which he risks his life and, implicitly, worth more than all the support that Hermione unconditionally provides.[19] At the beginning of the Triwizard Championship, though he has Hermione's and Hagrid's support, it has not sufficed: he "thought he would have coped with the rest of the school's behavior if he could just have had Ron back as a friend" (296). In contrast, when Hermione ceases speaking with the boys in *Sorcerer's Stone*, she is the only one to suffer, and when the two boys shun Hermione for telling Professor McGonagall about the Firebolt's mysterious arrival in *Prisoner of Azkaban*, they feel only relief. In *Order of the Phoenix*, Harry describes feeling "an odd sense of loss" only about Ron's being called away for Prefect duties on the *Hogwarts Express*, and even though he has also shared virtually all the train rides with Hermione, her absence does not register as a loss (184). Hermione may be essential in practical terms but not emotional ones. Both from his misery when Ron is absent and his happiness when Ron returns, it is clear how much the "superior" boy relies on his homosocial bond with an "inferior" friend.

Flirting with Homoeroticism

Given the intensity of their bond, the text is surprisingly silent about how this intensity renders the Harry-Ron bond homoerotic. For the second Triwizard task, Ron is correctly identified (perhaps by Dumbledore or by the Goblet of Fire) as the one Harry will most "sorely miss" (*GF* 465). Harry is the only one to have a same-sex friend serve as a hostage; the other two male competitors have female romantic-love objects taken from them.[20] This is not because Rowling's wizarding society is particularly tolerant of same-sex relationships: in addition to a complete lack of any character who is identifiable as not heterosexual (Pugh and Wallace, "Heteronormative Heroism" 263), the series makes it clear that it would be inappropriate if Harry's need for Ron transgressed that boundary.[21] Homosocial bonds have to guard against the possibility of *excessive* bonding—that is, the threat that intimacies of one allowed sort might lead to those of another sort.

The potential for homoeroticism appears as an ever-present threat, most clearly in the figure of the dementor. The choice of name for their attack, the "Dementor's Kiss" (e.g., *PA* 247), renders erotically sinister the idea that a male character (except for Mary Cattermole, only male characters are named as potential victims of their kiss) can be rendered apparently helpless against the sexualized assault. When he first learns what a dementor is, Uncle Vernon's reaction shows that the idea of a man being kissed against his will is horrible enough without the soul eating: "'Kiss you?' said Uncle Vernon, his eyes popping slightly. '*Kiss* you?'" (*OP* 34). Indeed, the attack on Dudley is described as an eroticized sexual assault: the dementor "was crouching low over him, gripping his wrists in its slimy hands, prizing them slowly, almost lovingly apart, lowering its hooded head toward Dudley's face as though about to kiss him" (19). Later, this threat of homosexual rape is projected unto Harry when Aunt Petunia wildly conjectures that Dudley has been demented—has lost his mind—because of Harry's "*thing*": "What did he do to you, Diddy? . . . Was it—was it you-know-what, darling? Did he use—his *thing*?" (26).

In two other instances, Harry also seems anxious about distancing himself from the charge of homosexual attraction. When Dudley taunts him about not being "brave in bed," he ridicules Harry for "*moaning*" in his sleep: "Who's Cedric—your boyfriend?" (*OP* 14, 15). Harry, of course, highly resents the implication. He is also "slightly alarmed" when asked by Molly to opine on whether the "good-looking" Bill Weasley ought to cut his hair (171) as if shrinking from assessing Bill's attractiveness more closely. Notably, Ron is repeatedly described as behaving similarly to a fangirl toward Viktor Krum—ogling, lusting after his autograph—behavior that the texts describe as shameful for a male (*GF* 249). In one case, Ron offers to give him his bed, and while he adds he would "kip on a camp bed" instead, his desire to have Krum share his bed is curious (249). Beth Sutton-Ramspeck astutely notes that Peter Pettigrew's fixation on James Potter, to the point that he might "[wet] himself from excitement" (*OP* 645), is "implicitly sexual" (Sutton-Ramspeck 69).

A threat can be code for a temptation: that which tempts us but is taboo feels like a threat to our abstinence. All the representations of the male desire for phallic broomsticks are, in this context, remarkable. Ron, "now walking around and around the Firebolt, taking in every glorious inch" (*PA* 223), admires Harry's broomstick with patently homoerotic overtones, mounting it with "an expression of ecstasy on his face" (256). When the aroma of Amortentia brings to mind what he finds most attractive, Harry thinks of "treacle tart, the woody smell of a broomstick handle, and something flowery he thought he might have smelled at the Burrow" (*HBP* 183). While the "something flowery" is meant to refer to Ginny, who had earlier been described with that smell, there is room for ambiguity. As the potion's fumes intoxicate him, "filling him up like drink[, a] great contentment stole over him; he grinned across at Ron, who grinned back lazily" (183). In this hazy moment, the phallic broomstick melds with the scent that reminds him of Ron's home and sister—and the two males exchange drunken grins *with each other*. Adding to the messy slippages, *Half-Blood Prince* is the same book in which Harry pretends to have roofied Ron with Felix Felicis, and Ron is then actually roofied by a love potion intended for Harry. Rowling's portrayal of a positive male-male friendship flirts on the edge of homoeroticism because of the intensity with which she insists that it is their primary bond above all others, yet same-sex desire remains taboo. Hermione's inclusion in the trio—a female attached to a pair of bonded males—serves the vital function of reducing the possibility that their intense bond might be read as homosexual. Hermione's constant presence reassures readers of the boys' heterosexuality, even as they appear unusually disinterested in heterosexual relationships until a later-than-average age.

The Burden of Heterosexual Coupling

Offering a reprieve from Horcrux hunting, Fleur (now Bill's domestic angel) suggests that the trio hide out in Shell Cottage, safe and comfortable. Her overprotectiveness reminds Harry of Mrs. Weasley—and "he was glad that the back door opened at that moment" (*DH* 511). Here, homoerotic temptation is unwittingly posited as the direct result of Harry's aversion to the heterosexual domestic arrangement that Fleur and Molly represent. But what is so repulsive about the traditional heterosexual marriage that would have Harry seeking "the back door"?

Whereas, in *Harry Potter*, male homosocial friendships appear easily reparable and much more satisfying—a narrative that conceals the accommodations that unequal males must make to manage their undercurrent of mutual resent-ments—romantic relationships with females are portrayed as far too much work. The trials and tribulations of heterosexual courtship come to the fore in *Goblet of Fire*, which, as Roberta Seelinger Trites notes, positions the fourth book as a significant milestone, where the characters "[experience] sexuality[,] almost a *de rigueur* rite of passage for adolescents" (477).

The *Goblet of Fire*'s Yule Ball is a major event that effectively requires het-erosexual coupling for attendance, as Professor McGonagall makes clear to a reluctant Harry whose "insides seemed to curl up and shrivel" at the very thought (*GF* 387). The boys, who have so far avoided entering the fraught world of dating, face pressure to quickly catch up. Given Rowling's plethora of girly girls—giggling, shrieking, and bland—Harry is ambivalent about pursuing romance, but *un*feminine girls are also unattractive to him.[22] Still, the boys understand the unspoken rule that the Yule Ball requires boys to ask out and be accepted by "the best-looking girl who'll have you, even if she's completely horrible" (395)—anything but a "troll" (394), Ron's slur for an unattractive female. (Most of the girls, in turn, appear to compete to attract desirable boys in equally shallow ways.) Awkward and inexperienced, the boys casually use predator-prey language to refer to the task of courtship; Ron jests they might need to "lasso" a girl to get her "on her own" (388).[23] No one other than Harry and Ron struggles quite so much: Neville finds the courage to ask Hermione, then, despite rejection, Ginny; Fred Weasley asks out Angelina Johnson by shouting his offer across the common room (394).

After both boys procrastinate, they are rejected by their respective choices (Harry by Cho, who has already accepted Cedric; Ron by Fleur) and are in dire straits. Ron suggests that Hermione could count as a "girl" for the pur-poses of the ball and tries to essentially assign his sister to Harry like a piece of chattel (*GF* 401), but it has become too late for even these drastic options. Seized by eleventh-hour desperation, Harry settles for one of Hogwarts's most giggly gigglers, Parvati Patil—who, despite being one of the "best-looking girls in the year" and eager for the ball (411), inexplicably remains partnerless—and then secures her twin sister, also pretty and eligible, for Ron. As they step onto the dance floor, the music is "mournful," reflecting Harry's attitude (419). Parvati has to "[steer] Harry so forcefully that he felt as though he were a show dog she was putting through its paces" (415). Nevertheless, he reaps the social rewards of having an attractive girl on his arm, receiving compliments from male peers. Ironically, Harry is also "pleased" that neither of his foes, Vincent Crabbe and Gregory Goyle, "had managed to find a partner" and have, effectively, come as a same-sex pair (413)—precisely what Harry and Ron would have preferred to have been allowed to do in the first place and how they actually spend the majority of the ball.

Asking out a girl successfully requires impressing her in the predictable ways that are linked to the discourse of males as protectors and providers—be of means, handsome, and athletic. In each encounter with Cho Chang, his first crush, Harry feels immediately interpellated into the traditional heterosexual courtship mode. When, in *Order of the Phoenix*, Cho calls him "brave" for standing up to Professor Umbridge, a gender-appropriate compliment, Harry considers "accidentally-on-purpose showing her his cut hand" (283). Chicks dig the scars that bear evidence of masculine risk-taking, so the discourse goes. This masculine urge to impress (and the feminine propensity to be impressed) appears in the texts as a "natural" male response, further normalizing these gendered discourses. Having just defeated the Hungarian Horntail and being reasonably good-looking, with piles of inherited gold in the bank, Harry *should* be able to win at this particular game. Indeed, for someone with such a propensity to "act the hero" (734), a gendered burden to risk life and limb and rescue frail damsels should not present much of an imposition. Although titillated by the possibility of successfully inhabiting his assigned gender role, Harry fears what he sees as his gender's burden.

Boys are, according to the heterosexual script, also required to attend to girls' copious feelings: to charm, assuage, reassure, and patiently survive displays of the emotionality that, according to *Harry Potter*, they do not experience or understand. Thus, in *Order of the Phoenix*, Cho begins to appear more as a trap: in Hermione's words, Cho "[corners Harry] after the [D.A.] meeting" to initiate their first kiss (457). He recounts the experience in a way that posits himself as a passive victim: "She was the one who started it. . . . I wouldn't've—she just sort of came at me—and next thing she's crying all over me—I didn't know what to do" (459). Hermione points out what would have been obvious to someone able to regard Cho as a grieving person—"You just had to be nice to her" (460)—but Harry had been too caught up thinking about how she still looked "very pretty" despite her "red and puffy" eyes (456). He appears unable to feel basic empathy and to cope with Cho going off the expected script. "Whenever he had imagined a scene involving the two of them it had always featured a Cho who was enjoying herself" (460), but alas, real-life Cho does not conform to his fantasies. He has done the things that are supposed to impress girls—he has even grown taller—and does not understand why that is not enough to please her. Though he issues a "reluctant grin" when Ron helps him interpret the weepy kiss as a victory with his "triumphant gestures" (458), Harry becomes ambivalent about whether to pursue a relationship with Cho and all her emotions.

Despite Hermione's attempt to remind Harry that Cho is grieving, Harry tries to reductively interpret the situation according to what he assumes are her gendered expectations: "He ought to have asked her out; she had probably been expecting it and was now really angry with him" (*OP* 461–62). Although he had been able to perceive that three-hundred-odd pages earlier, as "Cedric had been Cho's boyfriend[,] the memory of his death must have affected her holiday almost as badly as it had affected Harry's" (230), he cannot read her properly now. All he can think to do when she begins crying is to awkwardly pat her on the back. Completely preoccupied with whether he is acting as he believes a male should in a heterosexual courtship, Harry is unable to engage with or comprehend Cho as a person. That night, he suffers a nightmare:

> Cho was accusing him of luring her there under false pretenses; she said that he had promised her a hundred and fifty Chocolate Frog cards if she showed up. Harry protested. . . . Cho shouted, "*Cedric gave me loads of Chocolate Frog cards, look!*" And she pulled out fistfuls of cards from inside her robes and threw them into the air, and then turned into Hermione, who said, "*You did promise her, you know, Harry. . . . I think you'd better give her something else instead. . . . How about your Firebolt?*" And Harry was protesting that he would not give Cho his Firebolt because Umbridge had it, and anyway the whole thing was ridiculous. (462)

Nightmare-Cho is here to collect: as a girl, she expects a courting male to hand over "loads of Chocolate Frog cards" as proof of his willingness to be a provider. Harry is anxious that he will not measure up—Has he "[lured] her there under false pretenses"? But, at the same time, he "protests" against fulfilling the "promise" of gifting her such a trove. In traditional heterosexual courtship terms, the nightmare suggests that he does not want to fulfill his appointed role of providing her with his hard-earned resources: Cho's demands are "ridiculous." Nightmare-Hermione takes Cho's side, suggesting that he give her his powerful broomstick, which is a threatened castration,[24] both for the phallic nature of the broomstick and the fact that it is an essential part of his success on the Quidditch field. To Harry, the prospect of giving either his accrued earnings or his source of power to a female romantic interest is literally the stuff of nightmares. While he enjoys the idea of "impressing" girls with his heroic achievements, he fears and resents the burden of "taking care" of them.

Perhaps there is something to Harry's apparently offhand comment in *Order of the Phoenix*, rebutting Cho's exclamation of how "pretty" Patronuses are: "They're not supposed to be pretty, they're supposed to protect you" (606). As Cho is repeatedly described as pretty across the series, this remark suggests that, at some level, Harry does not want girls to be the protégés but rather the protectors. Indeed, as the blessed recipient of his mother's powerful protection, which has proven essential for his survival, Harry may well prefer being in the position of protégé. All this heroism business just does not seem worth it if the point is to protect girls: in *Goblet of Fire*, even as he is being thanked by Fleur for having rescued her sister in the second Triwizard task—along with helping save Cho and Hermione—he finds himself "heartily wishing he'd left all three girls tied to the statue" (506).

Nevertheless, Harry remains attracted to Cho, and as she makes it incredibly easy for him to ask her out—having all but done the asking herself—they end up on a date to Hogsmeade. From the start, Harry seems to regret it. Their awkward conversation flows only when they talk about Quidditch, but this ease is broken when Pansy Parkinson makes fun of him for not being as good-looking as Cedric, making him feel like he is competing with a superiorly regarded male and failing to measure up. Cho leads him to Madam Puddifoot's, "a cramped, steamy little place where everything seemed to have been decorated with frills or bows" (*OP* 559). All the girliness that Cho finds "cute," Harry finds repulsive. The shop "was full of nothing but couples, all of them holding hands," filling Harry with dread that "perhaps Cho would expect him to hold *her* hand" (559). Why that prospect is so dreadful is not clear except that he is aware that he should be the one to make the move and he experiences that gendered expectation very negatively. When he espies another student, Roger Davies, kissing his date, "Harry wished they wouldn't; he felt that Davies was setting a standard with which Cho would soon expect him to compete" (559–60), again projecting onto Cho his own understanding of the heterosexual courtship script.

Their date completely unravels when, during another awkward silence, Harry asks her to come with him to meet Hermione. Despite noticing that

Cho's tone has become "cold" and that she looked "all of a sudden . . . rather forbidding," Harry focuses only on the self-imposed duty of behaving as he thinks a boy on a date ought to behave: by attempting to gain intimate access to the girl's body (*OP* 560). All the couples in the tea shop are holding hands; ergo, he must hold her hand. The oppressive sense of expectation seems to erase the question of whether Harry even desires it: he only feels "a mounting pressure to take hold of it" (560). The sense of intramale competition becomes yet worse when Cho shares that Roger had asked her out recently and that she had been at this same tea shop with Cedric last year. Through Hermione, the text normalizes his obtuse response, coding his behavior as average teen-boy awkwardness in the face of the confusing feminine sex. In *Harry Potter*, most of the female characters contrast against Rowling's presentation of males as emotionally "simpler" creatures—a binary that Hermione reaffirms. As Harry is completely "bemused," Hermione breaks down for him what Cho might be feeling "with the patient air of one explaining that one plus one equals two to an overemotional toddler" (572). While suggesting that Harry, too, can also be overly emotional, she also confirms his belief that he needs a translator because girls are irrational. Harry's mention of meeting up with Hermione is treated as an unintentional gaffe, casting Cho's angry reaction as excessive, while according to Hermione, Cho's similar mention of Roger and Cedric was instead a calculated attempt to gauge Harry's interest by inciting jealousy. Harry complains that Cho should have just asked him directly if he likes Hermione, and, without calling out Harry's own failure to be direct, Hermione blames Cho for not being "sensible" enough to be direct and castigates her entire sex for such manipulations (573).

The text is lighthearted and teasing about the boys' emotional incompetency, while girls are presented as playing manipulative games. Harry "fervently" agrees with Ron's remark that Hermione should write a book "translating mad things girls do so boys can understand them" (*OP* 573), effectively classifying all girls as frustrating enigmas that can only be managed by adhering to one-size-fits-all instructions. The text indulges in the notion that boys are congenitally incapable of comprehending Cho's effusive emotions by virtue of their sex, excusing Harry's failure to be empathetic or to understand and regulate his own emotions. Thus handicapped, Harry's only option appears to be to learn how to "charm" witches. In *Deathly Hallows*, Ron—once described by Hermione as having "the emotional range of a teaspoon" (*OP* 459)—has received an invaluable gift, *Twelve Fail-Safe Ways to*

Charm Witches, a useful book of scripts that appears to work even on the oh-so-clever Hermione (*DH* 113). This suggests that males can succeed in managing emotional females not by developing greater emotional depth but by learning how to protect themselves from the worst of their partners' excesses.

There are many small and infuriating moments where male characters speak to each other (at times literally) over the shoulders of emotional women. In *Deathly Hallows*, Molly, who does not participate in the dangerous trip to move Harry, waits at home to presumably fret by the clock with all hands pointing to "mortal peril." When her eldest arrives, she runs to him to embrace him, "but the hug Bill bestowed upon her was perfunctory. Looking directly at his father, he said, 'Mad-Eye's dead'" (*DH* 78). Similarly, some chapters later, the Auror Nymphadora Tonks apologizes to Harry for rushing off from his birthday party, but instead of responding to her, Harry directs his reassurances "more to Lupin than Tonks" (139). When Fleur "[makes] an impatient noise" over Harry's insistence that their Horcrux mission must remain secret, the text adds that "Bill did not look at her; he was staring at Harry" (484). In *Deathly Hallows*, Fleur walks into the kitchen where Bill is attempting to have a "private word" with Harry about dealing with goblins (516). Bill asks her to "wait. . . . [j]ust a moment," so she "[backs] out," a three-sentence interruption that adds nothing to the plot, pacing, or humor (516). Rather, it seems included because the exclusion of a female character underscores the seriousness of the conversation the men are about to have. What appears important is what the men communicate to each other while circumnavigating their emotional, inconvenient women.

In *Order of the Phoenix*, the Weasley twins suggest that, through extensive experience, they have learned how to manage their mother: the secret is to "head her off early, otherwise she builds up a head of steam and goes on for hours" (107). In this instance, Molly's screaming also sets off the "shrieks and screams" of Sirius's mother's portrait, linking all mothers—good or evil—by their emotional explosiveness (107). Arthur's strategy, behaving "meekly" and "imploringly" and tiptoeing around his wife (522, 507), is what Ron learns so well. Arthur's other main strategies are avoidance and dishonesty, proving, in *Deathly Hallows*, that he has learned nothing from the *Chamber of Secrets* flying-car debacle except to better hide his next illicit project, Sirius's flying motorcycle. The wife appears like an emotional handful, while the husband appears sympathetic in his efforts to not trigger her explosions: "Er, I'm hiding—that's to say, keeping—it in here. . . . I'm going to try and put it all back together again when Molly's not—I mean when I've got time" (*DH* 93). Similarly, although it is the rest of her family that has lived through the chaotic peril of the Quidditch World Cup, they are the ones who must comfort anxious Molly. She sobs and embraces the twins, who recognize that she is, at that moment, demanding rather than giving comfort. Her husband has to speak to her "soothingly" and "[prise] her off the twins" (*GF* 146); Hermione has to make her some tea, to which Arthur adds a shot of whiskey (147). Only after his wife's nerves are soothed like the chore that it is can he and his sons return to the pressing work of responding to the World Cup attack.

Most female characters also actively try to dissuade men from taking on risks and doing what needs to be done. Soon after, Lupin announces that "there's work to do" (*DH* 81), which Bill instantly recognizes as well: the need to go search for Mad-Eye's body. Neither of their female partners, Tonks and Fleur, recognize this "work" that needs doing without having it explained to them; instead, they ask as one unit where they are going, thinking only of keeping their men home safe. Considering that Tonks is described as Mad-Eye's special protégé, it is unflattering that she neither thought of the duty to protect his corpse herself nor volunteers to go. Molly also pipes in with a pleading "Can't it [wait]?" (81).

If this is Harry's future, he does not seem to want it. Seeing Cho after a lapse, he quickly cautions her, "Don't start crying again" (*OP* 637): he will neither charm, soothe, nor be held back. Because the majority of female characters are so unflatteringly rendered by the series, readers are encouraged to not only sympathize with the hero's rejection of heterosexual relationships but also blame girls and women as the primary enforcers of this unpleasant dynamic.[25]

Protecting and Preserving the Male Homosocial Bond

In *Harry Potter*, both homosocial and heterosexual relationships require work, but only the former is worth the hero's while; the latter is portrayed not only as a minefield but also as potentially disruptive to male homosocial bonds and the "important work" they enable.

Trites is partly right in arguing that "the tournament is a mechanism for Cedric and Harry to work out their male aggressiveness as they compete for the attention of the same girl" (478), yet it is important to distinguish how the boys manage to build positive homosocial bonds while in competition for the Triwizard Cup but not while in competition over Cho. According to Rowling, competing on the field can build positive male homosocial bonds, but competing for a female romantic interest can destroy them. Harry begins in the uncomfortable position of "inferior" male in relation to the older, more handsome, more confident Cedric, but because Cedric does not behave arrogantly and Harry can accept his second place, the boys are able to collaborate in the tournament: Harry tells him what the first task involves, and, in return, Cedric gives him a crucial tip for the second task. However, as soon as he learns that Cedric has successfully asked Cho to the Yule Ball before him, his view of Cedric is tainted: "He had been starting to quite like Cedric. . . . Now he suddenly realized that Cedric was in fact a useless pretty boy who didn't have enough brains to fill an eggcup" (*GF* 398). Suddenly, Harry cannot accept his inferiority relative to Cedric; he can no longer "overlook the fact that he had once beaten him at Quidditch, and was handsome, and popular, and nearly everyone's favorite champion" (398). As a result of his resentment, Harry puts off using Cedric's tip on the second task: "His less-than-friendly feelings toward Cedric just now meant that he was keen not to take his help if he could avoid it" (434). This delay places Harry in a precarious position when he ends up with only about a week to figure out how to survive underwater. Before Harry gallantly offers Cedric the opportunity to claim the Triwizard Cup together, he resists the temptation to take it for himself, even though he "saw Cho's face shining in admiration, more clearly than he had ever seen it before" (634). The text casts his decision as a conscious decision to choose positive male homosociality over heterosexual temptation—Cedric over Cho.

Viktor Krum and Harry are also Triwizard competitors without issue until Viktor mistakes Harry as a rival for Hermione's attentions. When Viktor pulls Harry aside to confront him, Harry is flattered that the older and taller professional Quidditch player had "thought he, Harry, was an equal—a real rival" (*GF* 553). Thankfully, no problematic love triangle exists: Harry can assure him that he and Hermione are only friends, and as a result, the two males can forge a positive homosocial bond. Viktor compliments Harry's flying, which makes Harry "[grin] broadly" and "suddenly [feel] much taller himself" (553); Harry duly returns a Quidditch compliment. Again, male homosocial bonds are shown to be capable of thriving even in intense and direct competition, enabling males to collaborate even as they compete, but that becomes apparently impossible when the competition involves a female.

The same happens with Ron, who initially gushes over Viktor but finds his feelings soured when his idol takes Hermione to the Yule Ball.

As per Rowling's portrayal, men and boys must carefully moderate their investments in their romantic interests so as to protect male homosocial bonds. As per Christina Vogels, "One way that homosociality encourages young men to denigrate women is through the rule that 'male-male relations' must be privileged over male-female ones. This rule specifically encourages young men to deprioritize women they are involved with romantically" (227). Ron offers multiple examples of transgressions of this rule. When he unwittingly overdoses on the love potion intended for Harry, Ron physically attacks him, boxing his ear because he "insulted" Romilda Vane (*HBP* 393), thus putting a girl above his homosocial bond. Similarly, when Ron begins dating Lavender Brown, he becomes far too invested at first. Not emotionally—it does not appear that he particularly even likes Lavender—but he certainly enjoys the snogging and cedes a lot of what was formerly Harry's time to her. The relationship leads to an "improved" Ron, as he is more confident, but "at a heavy price" as "Harry had to put up with the frequent presence of Lavender Brown, who seemed to regard any moment that she was not kissing Ron as a moment wasted" (304). Lavender is an annoyance, an obstruction, literally and emotionally "squeezing herself in between Harry and Ron" (312). Harry thinks to himself that if Ron also begins to call her by a cutesy pet name, like "Lav-Lav," he would have "to put his foot down" (392), suggesting that he believes he has the right to set limits on Ron's relationship. He also breaks out in a "shout of laughter" when Ron receives the "My Sweetheart" necklace from Lavender, making it clear that being claimed by a girl could not be allowed: "Nice. . . . Classy. You should definitely wear it in front of Fred and George" (338). Indeed, under the bro code, males are encouraged to "persecute those who break [the] rule by appearing *too* invested in their girlfriends" (Vogels 227). When, in *Goblet of Fire*, Fleur's inquiry for bouillabaisse leaves Ron "goggling," Harry's laugh is what "seemed to jog Ron back to his senses" (252); similarly, it is now his duty to police how much Ron behaves as if he is invested in Lavender. Thankfully for their homosocial bond, Ron manages through poor treatment to drive her away.

The greatest threat to their homosocial bond, from Harry's perspective, comes from the possibility of Ron and Hermione becoming a couple. Though their eventual coupling feels forced—endless bickering is perhaps not the potent aphrodisiac that Rowling pretends it is—by *Half-Blood Prince*, their mutual romantic interest is brought to the fore. This forces Harry to consider how he would be affected: What if they "started going out together, then split up," or, even worse, "what if they became like Bill and Fleur, and it became excruciatingly embarrassing to be in their presence, so that he was shut out for good?" (*HBP* 283). The former possibility would fracture their trio in ways with which Harry is more familiar, given the number of rows that they have already had. The latter, however, would be unprecedented: Harry might tumble from the trio's lynchpin to its third wheel. Harry gets a small taste of this at the beginning of *Order of the Phoenix* when Ron and Hermione are at Grimmauld Place without him, and he reacts very poorly: "He could hardly bear to think of the pair of them having fun at the Burrow when he was stuck in Privet Drive" (8). In *Deathly Hallows*, he describes feeling "strangely lonely" when he wakes up to find that Ron and Hermione fell asleep with their hands touching (176). Ron, too, is affected. In a bid to save itself, the Horcrux locket attempts to incite Ron to use Gryffindor's sword on Harry instead by taunting him with visions of Hermione preferring Harry, and it seems to almost work (378). Perhaps that is why Rowling does not have the two get together until the middle of the Battle of Hogwarts, on the precipice of ending the series.

Who is our heterosexual hero supposed to partner with? The series' answer to this conundrum is Ginny, whose virtues and limitations I discuss in chapter 1: ungirly but still definitely a girl and comfortably unthreatening. Ginny is, in short, the Weasley he can kiss. It is troubling that what Harry also values about Ginny is that she proves willing to protect her bond with Harry above her same-sex bonds—precisely what males in the series would *not* do for their heterosexual partners. In *Half-Blood Prince*, Harry gets off lightly for leaving Draco a bloodied mess. Everyone tries to protect Harry from his guilt except Hermione, so Ginny tells her to "give it a rest" (*HBP* 530), echoing Ron's exact words in defending Harry against Hermione's "nagging" in the previous book. The text does not acknowledge that Ginny's logic is poor in claiming that Harry needed to use a vicious spell because Draco sounded like he was about to use an Unforgivable Curse; after all, Harry is famous for using only Expelliarmus against even the Dark Lord himself.[26] Ginny proves she is ready to defend him at the cost of her relationship with Hermione: "Hermione and Ginny, who had always got on together very well, were now sitting with their arms folded, glaring in opposite directions" (530).

Yet while the female-female relationship is readily cast aside, the male-male relationship needs to be protected: "The battle still raged inside his head: *Ginny or Ron?*" (*HBP* 519). Having synced their lives together to the utmost possible, the two boys would have to effectively uncouple in order to make room for any substantive romantic relationship. "He would not risk his friendship with Ron for anything," which makes her "*out-of-bounds*" (290). The text refers to her as a "diversion" (*CS* 35) and a "distraction" (*HBP* 242) well before Harry becomes interested in her, and there is a moment, before they get together, when Harry delays using Felix Felicis to secure the crucial Horcrux memory from Professor Slughorn because he wants to use it to get with Ginny (472). On the surface, Harry interprets his dilemma—Ginny or Ron—as being due to Ron's "natural" desire to protect his little sister. Under the bro code, males are not supposed to prey on each other's sisters; he envisions Ron "shouting things like 'betrayal of trust' . . . 'supposed to be my friend'" (289). Wanting to protect one's sibling is lovely, but it is problematic to "protect" by aggressively policing one's sister from engaging in the behavior one unquestioningly accepts of one's own gender. (Witness Ron's use of Lavender for snogging practice, a treatment validated by Ginny; see previous chapter.) Perhaps Ron's concerns are actually the same as those that fuel Harry's anxieties when Ron becomes increasingly intimate with Hermione: the very real fear that a girl would take his place in Harry's affections. When Harry earlier attempts to pursue Cho, Ron also runs interference, harassing her about her Tornados badge with an "unnecessarily accusatory tone of voice" to drive her away (*OP* 230). With Ginny, he may be running similar interference under the guise of brotherly concern: "Ron seemed to be there at Harry's shoulder every time he saw Ginny," apparently refusing "to leave them alone together for longer than a few seconds" (*HBP* 519–20).

But the homosocial bond, for now, is safe. With Ginny waiting in the wings since age ten, it appears romantic when she is finally noticed by Harry in book six. Depending on the reader to fill in the blanks, the texts barely waste any lines on rendering their relationship.[27] A public kiss suffices to establish their long-foreshadowed union; not even Ginny's reaction is relevant. Instead, he emerges from the kiss to look past her and mark his victory over both Ginny's ex-boyfriend and the unworthy girl who had tried to ensnare him: "Harry looked over the top of Ginny's head to see Dean Thomas holding a shattered glass in his hand, and Romilda Vane looking as though she might throw something" (*HBP* 534). He notices that Hermione was "beaming, but Harry's eyes sought Ron" (534)—the person whose reaction matters the most. Securing Ron's blessing, Harry rejoices: "The creature in his chest [roared] in triumph" (534).[28]

The text then endeavors to make it appear as if Ginny is seamlessly integrated into his life, never threatening to steal him away from Ron. The next chapter opens with the four of them—one couple established, the other to be—in the common room, with Ginny "leaning against Harry's legs" (*HBP* 535), an appendage to his appendage. They exchange some words about Ron's continuing discomfort with seeing them "snogging each other in public," and Ginny shares a story about how she has affirmed Harry's masculinity to Romilda—another jab at the girly girls against whom Ginny appears superior (536). Ginny then becomes conveniently busy studying for her O.W.L.s, which frees the text from having to deal with the awkwardness of depicting how they operate as a couple while she is excluded from all the important Voldemort business. We know that they do continue to spend some "limited time" together but are not told what that amounts to in minutes or hours spent without Ron (539)—nor how Ron fills up his Harry-less time.

The rest of the novel hardly dares to fill in these blanks, rushing immediately into the action-packed locket retrieval and Dumbledore's dramatic death. In the lull before the funeral, as the emotions settle from their feverish pitch, the narrator describes the end of term as follows: "Harry, Ron, Hermione, and Ginny were spending all of their time together" (*HBP* 634). The ordering of the names significantly distances Harry and Ginny; she is the optional, occasional fourth wheel. The trio simply waits for her to go to bed (she conveniently retires early) before they talk about the Horcruxes (635). Indeed, it is difficult to understand how Harry and Ginny's relationship really functions, even just for these brief few weeks. What is the nature of their connection if a vast area of his life—the upcoming hunt for Horcruxes—is kept from her? And why must they be kept from her to begin with? Ironically, Harry now readily embraces the heterosexual male-as-protector script: she is excluded, ostensibly, to protect her because she is "his best source of comfort" (634). At the same time, she will never cramp his style; Ginny is the "superior" girl because she understands that to keep Harry, she must take what she can get and manage her anxieties. She "would not say, 'Be careful,' or 'Don't do it,' but [rather] accept his decision" (646). She accepts that she cannot make him stay with her ("I knew you wouldn't be happy unless you were hunting Voldemort. Maybe that's why I like you so much" [647]) and that he will not let her go (because Voldemort would "try and get to me through you" [646]). The novel that brings the couple together ends with their (temporary) breakup as she patiently waits for him to finish his "important work." We do not see them again as a couple until the epilogue, where "heteronormative relationships . . . triumph" (Pugh and Wallace, "Postscript" 190).

Conclusion

Harry Potter offers a tantalizing vision of positive male homosocial bonds between unequal males, so long as both parties engage in ongoing work that ultimately reinforces their inequality. Most of the burden is on the "inferior" male to manage his jealous resentments, but the "superior" male also has much work to do in pretending to a humility that is belied by his barely suppressed sense of entitlement. Yet Rowling idealizes this vision of friendship, elevating male homosociality above other bonds. Close relationships with females present a threat to this primary bond, promising few rewards other than sexual access and a begrudgingly necessary domesticity. The series' lesson to boys is to choose carefully: to learn to resist female sexual power and focus on selecting, among a sea of needy and weepy girls, the least demanding and most devoted prospect.

Thus, while positive representations of masculinities and male-male cooperation can appear beguilingly antisexist, even such can become propatriarchy when it remains the imperative, through the propagation of negative female stereotypes, that male bonds should always trump heterosexual bonds. Perhaps Rowling attempts to make palatable her proffered alternative to more toxic masculinities by reassuring readers that it is still, ultimately, in the interests of patriarchy.

CHAPTER 3

MORAL MEDIOCRITY

The Minimal Standards of *Harry Potter*'s Anthropocentric Humaneness

I'm a wizard, not a baboon brandishing a stick.
—PUNITIVE LINES SET BY PROFESSOR FLITWICK, *Half-Blood Prince*

Dobby is a free house-elf and he can obey anyone he likes and Dobby will do whatever Harry Potter wants him to do!
—HALF-BLOOD PRINCE

In *Chamber of Secrets*, Harry Potter reaps a vital lesson on interspecies relationships in the magical world.[1] Harry's first exposure to a commonplace wizarding chore—removing gnomes from the garden—initially "shocked" him: their job is to pluck up the little gnomes, spin them in the air, and hurl them out of the garden (*CS* 37). Although Ron Weasley insists that this "doesn't *hurt* them" (37), Harry is reluctant to engage in the prescribed violence. His instinctual compassion contrasts favorably against the Weasley boys who toss gnomes with casual relish but proves foolish when the first gnome, "sensing weakness, sank its razor-sharp teeth into [his] finger" (37). "Harry learned quickly not to feel too sorry" for the gnomes, chucking the offender nearly fifty feet and joining the Weasley brothers in rendering "the air . . . thick with flying gnomes" (37). Portraying human violence as defensive and righteous yet also playful and prosaic, the incident teaches Harry that a species can become categorically undeserving of his instinctual mercy simply because a single representative dared to resist violent human control. The reader, in turn, learns that the appropriate attitude is for the human(e) subject to feel the right feelings for the suffering of nonhuman creatures but to also keep such merciful feelings in check. Both lessons are vital components of the humaneness that *Harry Potter* espouses: be human(e) enough to feel the "weakness" of compassion for the nonhuman Other yet "strong" enough to fulfill the necessary work of anthropocentrism—in this case, safeguarding the human-designated space from nonhuman incursion. This ability to feel but limit his empathy is coded as desirably masculine.

Adoring fans of *Harry Potter* may object to this interpretation; many readers would maintain that the series fosters empathy toward Others, including nonhumans. Indeed, the "good" characters wage battle against wizard supremacists who seek to control, oppress, and/or exterminate Mudbloods, "half-breeds," and all other species; Harry eschews wizarding society's prejudices against giants and werewolves and frees an abused house-elf, along with a zoo snake, a condemned hippogriff, and an imprisoned dragon; Rubeus Hagrid challenges the demonization of "dangerous" creatures; and Hermione Granger attempts to establish the Society for the Promotion of Elfish Welfare (S.P.E.W.). To date, little scholarship has taken up the question of how *Harry Potter* reflects and informs attitudes toward nonhuman animals, but some of it reads the series positively. Jen Harrison argues that, through its rampant examples of hybridity and blurred boundaries, *Harry Potter* exposes how "their control over the human/nonhuman divide is illusory, and it cannot be maintained . . . the hierarchy is shown to be not merely unethical but unviable as well" (334). This echoes a position taken by Margaret J. Oakes in a brief portion of an article devoted to discussing the intersection of magic and technology in the series: that the fact that anything could prove sentient teaches us that "respect must be shown to every single thing" (126).

While I agree that such representations can serve as a call for "empathy toward others whose hierarchical differences are shown to be imaginary" (Harrison 329), looking at the totality of nonhuman representation in the series, it is difficult to conclude that the author who developed these representations was particularly moved to dismantle species hierarchies—or even to nurture readers' compassion for nonhuman animals. Peter Dendle offers a more compelling analysis, documenting how *Harry Potter* presents nonhuman exploitation dismissively or "for comic effect" and how the titular hero is overly praised as a "perennial liberator of all manner of creatures" (170, 166, 168). This chapter argues that *Harry Potter* promotes an anthropocentric humaneness, granting special cultural value to a low standard of concern for nonhuman beings. By analyzing this, we can recognize how low the bar is set and, more importantly, how literature can retrench no-longer-progressive beliefs. Upholding the conceit that the bar remains high and worthy of admiration—that the liberal subject is a human(e) hero—*Harry Potter* inhibits the kind of self-critique that might inspire self-reflection and change.

The first section of this chapter surveys how nonhumans are consumed and exploited in the wizarding world—for food, potions, class experiments, and as beasts of burden—in ways that the series never presents as ethical concerns. In the context of this widespread exploitation, the series' pretense that only "bad" characters mistreat nonhumans has the effect of lowering the bar, as some "good" characters espouse similar values with the texts' approval. The third section focuses on the nonhuman characters that Harry liberates from captivity (the zoo boa, the Gringotts dragon, Dobby, and Buckbeak) to show how Rowling carefully ensures that every act of service that Harry performs that benefits a nonhuman is actually an act to achieve anthropocentric ends. According to the series, the humane human is one that feels but ultimately *resists* the urge to sympathy and mercy to nonhuman creatures so that it is never their primary goal to prioritize nonhuman concerns. Moreover, not all captivity appears to matter. As discussed in the fourth section, two characters who take the humane urge too far—Hagrid and Hermione—emphasize the limits of Rowling's anthropocentric humaneness. These two characters are, as per the texts, excessive in their empathy for nonhuman Others—an excess coded as feminine. In closing, the chapter reveals the totalizing nature of the series' anthropocentrism by delineating how even nonhuman resistance is co-opted.

The Systematic Use of Nonhuman Beings

Part of the appeal of Rowling's world-making is that the world she creates is a magical replica of our own, mirroring many of the contradictions in our contemporary categorizations of the nonhuman species that we use, consume, hate, and/or love. For Rowling, the premise of human superiority is not fundamentally in question. As in our world, all nonhumans in the wizarding world are assumed to exist to serve human uses and are regulated and/or exploited accordingly.

One of the series' greatest compliments that can be paid to a nonhuman species is to be described as, in the words of Hagrid, "dead useful" (SS 81)—or, perhaps, usefully dead. Animal flesh is the highlight of the typical Hogwarts meal even as "the wizarding world's source of food . . . remains entirely mysterious" (Dendle 166–67). The menu of Harry's first Hogwarts feast features "roast beef, roast chicken, pork chops and lamb chops, sausages, bacon and steak" (SS 123)—a list meant to impress readers with the wide range of animal meats available in a single meal. Their potions are hardly vegan; ingredients include various animal parts, like unicorn horns, beetle's and eel's eyes, and bat spleens (81, 72). Violence and death are likely part of the process of procuring these consumables, but as the texts keep this process invisible, the mass consumption of animal products escapes ethical inquiry. Someone's failure to feel compassionate feelings when the violence is presently before them *would* be more troubling, but distance from violence does not fully explain why the characters of *Harry Potter*, like us, do not consider the failure to have compassion for out-of-sight cruelty to be at all problematic.

Every magical person's essential accessory, the wand, also depends on its animal core to work. Presumably, dragons must be dead for their heartstrings to be harvested, but we do not hear details of this procurement process. Instead, we hear two contradictory stories about gathering phoenix tail feathers and unicorn hairs. In one, the prolific Ollivander describes how Fawkes, Dumbledore's pet phoenix, "gave" the feather for the core of Harry's and Voldemort's wands (SS 85), as if Ollivander approached the bird and politely requested contributions. This language is contradicted by Ollivander sharing, like a war story, how he acquired the core for Cedric Diggory's wand from a unicorn that "nearly gored me with his horn after I plucked its tail" (GF 309). Either way, Ollivander presents himself to advantage, casting himself as both the gentle harvester and valiant procurer of the precious resources on which their practice of magic largely depends.

At Hogwarts, complementary subjects of study sort nonhumans into two broad categories. Care of Magical Creatures teaches each generation how to manage—"care" for—select nonhumans, but this is motivated by a desire to use them. *Fantastic Beasts and Where to Find Them* suggests that this stewardship model is at least a vast improvement over, for example, the Magical Congress of the United States of America's previous policy of "curse-to-kill" (xv), but the text is suspiciously vague about British policies of that time, likely to portray the English as the more humane. All the "care" is transactional if not exploitative: bowtruckles are studied so that wand trees might be safely approached (*OP* 259), nifflers are "useful little treasure detectors" (*GF* 543), and unicorns are pretty and have valuable hair (*HBP* 486). The more "interestin'" nonhumans that Hagrid features in his classes may be dangerous (*OP* 439), but he justifies their inclusion by how useful they are to humans (hippogriffs and thestrals provide transportation if trained or conciliated).

For "Dark" creatures that fail to be useful (*GF* 211), there are Defense Against the Dark Arts classes. Grindylows, red caps, and hinkypunks are depicted as if they harm humans out of sheer malice (*PA* 318). Boggarts exist to hide in furniture and confront humans with their worst fear; their "*modus operandi*," as Tracy Bealer puts it, is "to infiltrate the darkest and most eerie places in a human's own home and transform into their greatest fear upon sight" (39). "Nobody knows what a boggart looks like when he is alone" (*PA* 133); Alastor Moody gets a good look at one with his magical eye but does not share the secret, and, frankly, no one cares (*OP* 169). The boggart used as an experimental subject in Remus's class "exploded, burst into a thousand tiny wisps of smoke, and was gone," literally blown to smithereens to mark a successful class (*PA* 139). "Among the foulest creatures that walk this earth," dementors are little more than anthropomorphic embodiments of depression and dementia (187). The eyeless creatures are also described as if the sole reason for their existence is to prey on humans: "They infest the darkest, filthiest places, they glory in decay and despair, they drain peace, hope, and happiness out of the air around them. . . . If it can, the dementor will feed on you long enough to reduce you to something like itself . . . soulless and evil" (187).[2]

Various animals are also systematically conscripted as experimental subjects in classrooms to test amateur potions of questionable safety and to be transfigured into an object or something in between. Do the rabbits, owls, and hedgehogs transfigured into bunny slippers, opera glasses, and pincushions not die in the process (*CS* 284; *GF* 233)? These questions are not meant to be asked. Their Transfiguration exam entails turning a teapot into a tortoise— "It's alive," Viktor Frankenstein might declare—but one student finds that theirs "still had a spout for a tail, what a nightmare," and another comically queries whether their experimental subjects were "*supposed* to breathe steam"

(*PA* 317). In Charms class, students cause teacups to sprout legs; Ron, ever the least competent of the trio, produces a teacup that "grew four very thin spindly legs that hoisted the cup off the desk with great difficulty, trembled for a few seconds, then folded, causing the cup to crack into two" (*OP* 679). Does it hurt? What is their experience? These magical mishaps exist to titillate and amuse. None of these encounters register as tests of the characters' (or the readers') capacity for respecting nonhuman life or sentience.

In *Goblet of Fire*, Crouch-Moody's spider experiments might be one exception, but the one to call attention to the spiders' plight is, ironically, the disguised Death Eater himself. Everyone laughs at the imperiused tap-dancing spider until Crouch-Moody cuts them short by demanding that they briefly identify with its condition: "You'd like it, would you, if I did it to you?" (*GF* 213). The spiders are mere proxies for bodies that matter: their own. When the fake Moody exhibits the Cruciatus Curse on the next spider, Hermione demands that he stop but not for the spider's sake; "She was looking, not at the spider, but at Neville" (214), whose parents had been tortured to insanity by that curse. For the "horrified" Neville (215), the spider is merely a surrogate for the humans with whom he sympathizes. Similarly, the whole class focuses on how the spider that is hit with the Killing Curse is a stand-in for Harry's parents (216). This is the only instance of class experimentation that the reader is encouraged to question as possibly unethical, and even then, the issue of concern is not arachnid welfare but whether the students are too young to be shown Unforgivable Curses.[3] Meanwhile, in Professor McGonagall's classes, animals are routinely vanished for practice (for example, mice and kittens [*OP* 320, 330]). It is only much later that we learn that vanished objects go "into nonbeing" (*DH* 591). Vanishment is the casual Avada Kedavra of nonhuman experience.

Animals as beasts of burden are routinely used despite the magical—not to mention mechanical and electronic—alternatives that surely exist: thestrals pull student carriages to Hogwarts and owls deliver everything from letters to newspapers to mince pies to brooms.[4] Magical nonhumans are also exhibited for entertainment, like the "fancy [hippogriffs]" that adorn a calendar (*OP* 512), the live fairies used to decorate the Christmas tree at Grimmauld Place and Hogwarts (*OP* 501; *PA* 189), or the salamanders that the Weasley twins feed fireworks to (*CS* 130–31). More humanlike appearances or capacities do not spare nonhumans from usage. Consider the leprechauns and veela, showcased as Quidditch-team mascots in *Goblet of Fire*. The veela's position seems particularly tricky, not least because of the many misogynistic remarks regarding their dangerously dizzying effect on men.[5] Goaded by the leprechauns, the veela quickly and easily "lost control," reverting from beautiful human to a bestial state: "Their faces were elongating into sharp, cruel-beaked bird heads, and long, scaly wings were bursting from their shoulders" (*GF* 111). In their human form (or perhaps guise), veela can cheer for and mate with human men but also appear as an exploitable resource. Fleur Delacour even boasts of a wand with her grandmother's veela hair at its core (308), casting veela bodies (and by extension, Fleur's own body) as harvestable.

Keeping the Bar Low

All the uses of nonhuman beings hitherto discussed are significant because they are presented as *in*significant: as prosaic, acceptable ways in which nonhuman beings can be used without reproach. The question of whether such uses should be considered ethically acceptable need never be asked in part because we have such patently worse characters to compare the "good" guys to. Through the contrast, the "good" characters' treatment of nonhuman beings escapes challenge.

For one, *Harry Potter* marks "bad" characters by a cultural shorthand: they do not "like" animals. From Aunt Petunia (who "hated animals" [*PA* 23]) to Dudley Dursley (who drove over the neighbor's dog with a toy tank, traded a pet parrot for an air rifle, and threw a tortoise through a greenhouse roof [*SS* 37, 38]) to Professor Umbridge (who recoils from Fang's affections [*OP* 435]) to the young Tom Riddle (who hung a fellow orphan's rabbit from the rafters [*HBP* 267]), a character's aversion to or disdain for animals puts readers on immediate notice that the character is "bad." This would seem a clear message that "good" characters "like" animals, which presumably entails anything from welcoming their affection to not killing them directly—but none of the previously discussed uses (in sumptuous feasts, for potions and wands, as experimental subjects) appear relevant to determining whether someone "likes" animals.[6]

The Death Eaters who treat all nonhumans as vermin are obviously "bad," setting the bar low for what can be considered "good" treatment. Walden Macnair satiates his desire to kill through his job as the ministry executioner of "Dangerous Creatures" (*PA* 218). The Malfoys are depicted as the worst masters a house-elf can have, reminding the pitiful Dobby to punish himself "extra" and forcing him to wear a degradingly filthy old pillowcase as a "mark" of his "enslavement" (CS 14, 177). The werewolf Fenrir Greyback "might be allowed" to don their robes "when [the Death Eaters] wanted to use him" but not the prestigious Dark Mark that denotes Voldemort's inner circle (DH 453). The relationship is purely transactional and exploitative, as Greyback is reminded when he begs for entry at Malfoy Manor and Narcissa Malfoy pretends to not even recognize him (456). Dark-wizard sympathizers, the Black family garishly mounted the heads of house-elves murdered when they became "too old to carry tea trays" and decorated their foyer with a troll's leg umbrella stand (OP 113, 61).

Many non–Death Eaters espouse similar species-supremacist views and are also explicitly critiqued. The Ministry of Magic's Fountain of Magical Brethren is exposed as a "lie" that this society tells itself (OP 834): the gaudy fountain—featuring a "noble-looking wizard" as the tallest figure, followed by "a beautiful witch," around which gather a centaur, a goblin, and a house-elf, "all looking adoringly up at the witch and wizard" (127)—advertises a society in which witches are secondary to wizards and nonhuman magical beings comprise an admiring, supporting cast. The fantasy proffers moral justification for the hierarchical structure that puts the powerful elite (wizards) on top of those who appear to naturally belong to and choose their inferior position. When Harry takes a closer look at the fountain, however, he realizes that the wizard's face "looked rather weak and foolish," that the witch "was wearing a vapid smile like a beauty contestant," and that neither goblins nor centaurs would possibly "be caught staring this soppily at humans" (156). Those who espouse the fountain's fantasy—the Minister of Magic Cornelius Fudge and his undersecretary Dolores Umbridge—are Harry's main antagonists in Order of the Phoenix. The elected leader of the English wizarding world for most of the series, Fudge suspects Madame Olympe Maxime of murdering Barty Crouch Sr. based solely on her being a half giant and is comfortable presiding over the execution of Buckbeak, a hippogriff, more to appease a powerful lobbyist than out of any real conviction that Buckbeak is dangerous (GF 580; PA 125). In her governmental position, Umbridge writes legislation to exclude and oppress werewolves, who are considered part human,[7] causing the sympathetic Remus undue hardship (OP 302). As Hogwarts High Inquisitor, she insistently speaks to the half giant Hagrid "as though she was addressing somebody both foreign and very slow" and makes it her mission to sack him (447); she also declares centaurs "filthy half-breeds," "beasts," and "uncontrolled animals" (755). These species-supremacist characters are vile, appalling—their introduction a shocking turn for the young reader as Harry realizes that those institutions that ostensibly exist to protect their society are not interested in protecting some of the people Harry has come to love.

Even some "good" characters espouse the same prejudices, however, which partly excuses such attitudes. Provincial and conservative, Molly parrots her society's fear and prejudice against werewolves despite her long-standing positive relationship with Remus. When her hospitalized husband shares that on the nearby bed is a man bitten by a werewolf, her impulse is to wonder if the patient ought to be removed for public safety (*OP* 488). Ron, who has absorbed many of his mother's prejudices, is quick to parrot what "everybody knows" about this or that nonhuman: "They're just vicious, giants . . . it's in their natures, they're like trolls . . . they just like killing, everyone knows that" (*GF* 430). Ron also tells us that trolls are stupid and goblins, untrustworthy (*SS* 173; *DH* 506). Both characters continue to espouse and repeat species prejudices, granting exceptions to a *nice* werewolf and a *half* giant. Neither is strongly rebuked, and their views still appear better than the Death Eaters'. When Remus resigns from his teaching position, it is in anticipation of all the parents who would write in objection of a werewolf teacher (*PA* 423), perhaps the same people who later pen poison letters to Hagrid when his giantess mother is exposed (*GF* 544). As Jessica Mitzner Scully notes, despite his enlightened observations about the fountain, Harry "imagines Hermione's outraged reaction without experiencing such a response himself. His own reaction is to simply grin and empty his money bag into the pool" (99). We understand that Dumbledore is uniquely virtuous because, in contravention to these mainstream views, he admits "anyone" to Hogwarts "s'long as they've got the talent" (*GF* 455), regardless of parentage.

The notion that anti-giant prejudice must be wrong because it is the foul characters that hold such views is also contradicted by the fact that Umbridge's stereotypes appear to be confirmed by the series' depiction of giants. Despite being at least sixty-three years old, the half giant Hagrid is outwitted by and has to be repeatedly bailed out by three kids (as young as eleven in *Sorcerer's Stone* [193, 237]), easily manipulated by masked strangers in pubs (265), and unable to even grasp when he is being humiliated by Umbridge (*OP* 448).[8] His memory seems spotty, his command of standard English is poor, and his vocabulary is limited.[9] He cannot even spell "Voldemort" (*SS* 54). Umbridge is not wrong in noting that he *"has . . . to . . . resort . . . to . . . crude . . . sign . . . language," "appears . . . to . . . have . . . poor . . . short . . . term . . . memory,"* and *"shows . . . signs . . . of . . . pleasure . . . at . . . idea . . . of . . . violence"* (*OP* 447). When we meet Grawp, a full giant, we get further confirmation that giants are dim, use extremely rudimentary language, and casually engage in violence. Hermione correctly asks, "Who is he?" but "Harry found this an odd question. . . . 'What is it?' was the one he had been planning on asking" (690). The paragraph goes on to describe "the back" rather than *his* back and "the legs" rather than *his* legs, which Harry compares to "sledges" (693). Finally encountering his face, Harry can only revert to more objects as descriptors: "a great stone ball," with "yellow teeth the size of half-bricks," "knuckles as big as cricket balls" (695). Similarly, Harry may treat Hagrid as a fellow human and wizard, but the text often begs us to demur: when he is first introduced, he is described as "[looking] simply too big to be allowed"; his hands are compared to "trash can lids," his booted feet, to "baby dolphins" (*SS* 14).

Hagrid is also the mouthpiece for an abridged history of wizard-giant relations that paints wizards in a flattering light for what could be considered genocide through direct extermination and expulsion. Employing the pronoun "we" to refer to humans and "they" to refer to giants, Hagrid describes their decimated numbers as largely self-wrought: "They've bin dyin' out fer ages. Wizards killed a few, o' course, but mostly they killed each other, an' now they're dyin' out faster than ever" (*OP* 426–27). The "o' course" and "a few" downplay the wizard killings; What do they matter when giants are "mostly" killing each other? Some pages later, Hagrid clings to the idea that giants are inexorably dying out but with some contradiction: "They were dying out anyway, and then loads got themselves killed by Aurors" (*GF* 430). "Loads," not just the "few" that he earlier said, but his language also suggests that giants are committing suicide by Auror. Hagrid sounds no different than his persecutor Rita, who writes in the *Daily Prophet*, "Bloodthirsty and brutal, the giants brought themselves to the point of extinction by warring amongst themselves during the last century" (439). He does not seem to grasp what Dumbledore has said, that the giants would not have self-decimated if wizards had not driven them to live "bunched up together" (*OP* 427); instead, he regales the trio with the story of his encounter with an encampment of giants that confirms the idea that giants entertain themselves by killing each other.

Similarly, goblins conform to stereotypes and appear to bring their mistreatment onto themselves. The unattractive species is depicted as a necessary

evil, to be tolerated and controlled but not, as Griphook notes, to be protected or respected (*HBP* 394). As Christina M. Chica describes, "Wizards
acknowledge Goblin racial superiority over enslaved or banished magical
others but frame them as morally inferior to Wizards" (81). In the texts, one
is described as being "about a head shorter than Harry," with "a swarthy,
clever face, a pointed beard, and, Harry noticed, very long fingers and feet"
(*SS* 72). In the movies, they are rendered more monstrously: barely two feet
tall, with long hooked noses, slanted eyes, and sallow, mottled skin. Unlike
house-elves, goblins "stick up for themselves" and are "quite capable of dealing with wizards" (*GF* 449)—a fact that engenders fear rather than respect.
We do not know much of human-goblin relations in history except that they
engaged in one of many rebellions in 1612 and that "goblin resistance [was]
not merely a single event, but a way of life" (*PA* 77; Horne, "Answering the
Race Question" 90). We would not say someone "rebels" against us if we did
not feel entitled to their loyalty, obedience, and subjugation. As justification for wizarding distrust of goblins, Ron points to their violent resistance:
"Goblins aren't exactly fluffy little bunnies, though, are they? . . . They've
killed plenty of us. They've fought dirty too" (*DH* 506).[10]

In *Deathly Hallows*, Harry is confronted with the unsettling possibility
that the Founder of his beloved House might have stolen the goblin-forged,
ruby-encrusted sword for which he is known.[11] Wrestling with this "unpleasant" idea—"he had always been proud to be a Gryffindor; Gryffindor had
been the champion of Muggle-borns, the wizard who had clashed with the
pureblood-loving Slytherin" (*DH* 507)—Harry finds one of the cornerstones
of his identity imperiled. His immediate reaction is to suspect all goblins of
duplicity: "Maybe he's lying. . . . How do we know the goblin version of history's right?" (507). Without further delving into this question, we see that
Harry resolves to deceive Griphook into believing that they will hand over
the sword as soon as he helps them break into Gringotts. Partly honest and
duplicitous, Harry's solution is the middle way between Hermione's insistence
in proceeding honorably and Ron's idea to lie and then "scarper" (507). The
reader, like the trio, is put in the position of concluding that "the betrayal of
one goblin [is] worth the emancipation of all goblins and magical beings"
(Scully 112) because, as Harry reasons, "What choice did they have?" (508).
They could have offered him Aunt Muriel's tiara, which Griphook had also
eyed; instead, the one called upon to pay the price for the "greater good" is
the goblin.

Over the next few days, Harry comes to "[realize] that he did not much like the goblin," finding that Griphook is "unexpectedly bloodthirsty, laughed at the idea of pain in lesser creatures and seemed to relish the possibility that they might have to hurt other wizards to reach the Lestranges' vault" (*DH* 509–10). The narration also emphasizes Griphook's Otherness when it comes to diet. While Fleur is the one to insist on his joining them at table, the narrator chastises him for "[joining] them at the overcrowded table" and "[refusing] to eat the same food, insisting, instead, on lumps of raw meat, roots and various fungi" (510); his diet is an insult to human sensibilities. Why is the meat described unattractively as "lumps"? Why is Bill Weasley's "bloody" "meat" not called out in like manner?[12] Why refer to "roots" and "fungi" as if humans do not eat root vegetables or mushrooms? The text presents Harry as if he is coming to understand through experience that wizarding prejudice against goblins is not, after all, misplaced, but they conceal their "distaste" because they need him to break into Gringotts (510). When Griphook goes on to double-cross the conspiring double-crossers, our sympathy is guided toward the trio, particularly when Harry is shown saving the goblin only to have Griphook scramble on him, "holding tightly to a fistful of Harry's hair" to escape the burning treasure (540). Griphook could be said to be acting in self-defense by scarpering with the sword; however, by this point, he has confirmed wizarding society's negative opinion of goblins. In Jackie C. Horne's reading, Rowling "allows Harry off the hook for deceiving Griphook by making Griphook betray Harry first" ("Multicultural and Social Justice" 38). Just as Harry cannot "'like' the goblin, as a multicultural antiracist must" (Horne, "Answering the Race Question" 95), neither can we.[13]

Goblins and centaurs are also portrayed unflatteringly for resisting wizarding supremacy. In asserting that he will disown any wizarding master, Gornuk sounds instantly "less human" (*DH* 296): a nonhuman that does not submit to human rule is, according to the text, more monstrous. Compared to the house-elves' willingness to dedicate their lives to serving human masters, goblins are rendered unattractive by their expectation that humans negotiate with them in terms of equality. This expectation is experienced by the wizarding community as offensive: an inferior species' failure to recognize what is rightfully due to the human species. The other nonhuman group known for espousing species dignity in the series, centaurs also object to subservience to humans and are represented negatively as a result, "[dismissed] . . . as inherently aggressive" (Scully 101). Their separatist stance "does not mean

... that they do not have to contend with the consequences of being viewed as morally or epistemologically inferior" (Chica 81). While most of the centaurs disapprove of Firenze for allowing Harry to ride him like "a common mule" (*SS* 257), it is Firenze who appears the most sympathetic for degrading himself in service of our hero. The separatist centaurs even turn into potential child murderers in *Order of Phoenix*—the same year that Firenze finds himself elevated to Divination professor at Hogwarts.[14]

A troll is "a horrible sight," with "skin . . . a dull, granite gray, its great lumpy body like a boulder with its small bald head perched on top like a coconut," and terribly malodorous (*SS* 174). The word "troll" also denotes the lowest possible grade at Hogwarts; a dunce of a student risks nominal expulsion from the human species (*OP* 311). The garden gnomes discussed at the outset—"small and leathery looking, with a large, knobby, bald head exactly like a potato" (*CS* 37)—are some of the first magical nonhumans that Harry encounters, where Harry's compassionate instinct is immediately supplanted by his acceptance of prevailing anthropocentric norms. A bite erases the fact that the Weasleys eject these creatures solely because they can and desire to do so and despite the clear evidence that gnomes are capable of human language, reason, and some measure of civil society.[15] Overwhelmingly, despite what can appear as tolerant, benign messaging, nonhuman beings are, if not systematically consumed or exploited, treated with a rightful wariness that sets them apart and below humans.

Humaneness as the Means to an Anthropocentric End

Against this backdrop of widespread, prosaic consumption, exploitation, and suspicion of nonhumans, the ethics of which are largely unchallenged, the texts nevertheless unironically present Harry as a liberator of captive nonhumans. The repeated motif suggests that nonhuman captivity is wrong, but this message is, in turn, grossly undercut. The contradictions are so severe that they beg the question of why: Was Rowling conflicted, hypocritical, or simply sloppy?

In the earliest pages of the first book, a boa constrictor at the zoo draws the reader's sympathies as the object of Dudley's harassment. Tapping on the glass, the bully insists that the snake satisfy his sense of what the "largest snake in the place" should be like (*SS* 27). This scene portrays Harry as uniquely and surprisingly sympathetic to the captivity of a nonhuman being: "He wouldn't have been surprised if it had died of boredom itself—no company except stupid people drumming their fingers on the glass trying to disturb it all day long" (27). He goes on to relate with the nonhuman that is being bullied by his own lifelong tormentor. While Dudley treats the snake as an entertaining object, Harry engages it as a subject with feelings and experiences worth knowing.[16] He even uses magic to liberate the snake from his glass enclosure. In Catherine Olver's words, "Harry enters the magical world by vanishing a zoo's glass barrier between human viewers and an animal object of their gazes, poignantly promising more equal relationships between humans and animals in the magical world" (191).

Yet the episode with the boa does not ultimately argue against zoos or animal captivity. There is no sympathetic observation of other zoo animals nor any remark suggesting that Harry believes that animals do not belong in the zoo, which he was so looking forward to visiting (SS 22). Rather, the episode primarily serves as a metaphor for Harry's living conditions. Harry directly compares the snake's captivity to his own when he considers that the terrarium must be "worse than having a cupboard as a bedroom" (27). Just as Dudley taps insistently at the tank, so Aunt Petunia can, as Harry's "only visitor," be found "hammering" on his cupboard door to wake him (27). The film version has Harry reading the sign explaining that the snake was "bred in captivity" and saying, "Ah, that's me as well." Describing the snake's captivity allows the text to maintain a lighthearted tone as it belabors the cruelty of Harry's housing situation by suggesting, in effect, that it is inhuman(e)—not fit for humans. Readers are meant to think how horrible it is that Harry finds so many commonalities with the captive snake. We are not, however, meant to think that the terrarium is not good enough for the snake.

By and large, nonhuman captivity is accepted by the texts; the tone merely shifts when such captivity can serve as a metaphor for Harry's captivity, and this tonal shift can be misread as a prohumaneness message. The real problem, according to the series, is not that animals are treated as animals but that Harry might be treated like an animal. Molly Weasley chides her curious children for ogling famous Harry Potter because "the poor boy isn't something you goggle at in a zoo" (SS 97), tacitly confirming that nonhuman animals may be. Locked in his bedroom in Chamber of Secrets, Harry explicitly compares himself to a zoo animal, dreaming that he is "on show in a zoo, with a card reading UNDERAGE WIZARD attached to his cage. People goggled through the bars at him as he lay, starving and weak, on a bed of straw. . . . Then the Dursleys appeared and Dudley rattled the bars of the cage, laughing at him" (23). Much of the abuse Harry suffers from his adoptive family is framed in such terms: his cousin Dudley's "favorite sport" is "Harry Hunting" (*SS* 31); Aunt Petunia dyes Dudley's old clothes gray for his school uniform, leading Harry to dread appearing at school "wearing bits of old elephant skin" (33); Uncle Dursley installs a cat flap on his locked bedroom door to feed him (*CS* 22); Aunt Marge gifts him a box of dog biscuits and compares him to an "underbred," "mean, runty" dog that should have been drowned at birth (*PA* 18, 27); the prospect of returning to Privet Drive means, to Harry, going "back to being treated like a dog that had rolled in something smelly" (*CS* 5).

Moreover, despite his identification with this snake's condition, Harry never actually intends to liberate it; he does so only in a flash of anger because Dudley punches him (*SS* 28). (In the movie, Dudley shoves him to the floor.) As he says in retrospect, "I sort of set it free without meaning to" (*CS* 195). His vengeful anger against Dudley propels the magic, so it makes sense to say that Harry's main intent had been to make something bad happen to Dudley: and indeed, the slithering snake, "playfully" snapping at heels, reduces his bully to a blubbering coward (*SS* 29). (In the movie, Dudley also ends up captive behind the glass when it spontaneously reappears.) In freeing the snake, Harry effectively frees himself to, for once, strike back against his bully: "Hadn't he got his revenge, without even realizing he was doing it?" (58). This episode makes nonhuman liberation the collateral benefit of a human end, not the human's primary motive—a pattern that we will see several more times.

As the zoo-snake incident suggests, even when Harry exhibits interest in nonhuman welfare by extending himself to save or free a nonhuman being, his interactions with them remain at least partially instrumental and have no impact on the systematic control and exploitation of nonhuman species. The texts emphasize the comforting narrative that putting human interests first will happily coincide with the interests of nonhuman beings.

Consider the vastly inconsistent treatment of dragons in the series. The Gringotts dragon is presented as a victim of goblin cruelty, rendered sympathetically by narrative attention to its abused body—its underground prison has turned its scales "pale and flaky" and its eyes "milkily pink" and "partially blind" (*DH* 535). Griphook explains that the dragon has been conditioned to associate the sound of clangers with the pain of hot swords, which, in the film,

Hermione declares "barbaric." No one has any plans to liberate the animal, however, until they find themselves trapped in the bank, and Harry directs the trio to hop onto the dragon. Dramatically, they help their getaway vehicle break its way out. Several sentences are devoted to paying attention to the blind dragon's relishing of its newfound freedom—the fresh air, the joy of flight, the gulps of water—signaling that the trio has done something good. However, this liberation is only the result of a fit of "inspiration, or madness" on the part of a human who desperately needs a way to escape the bowels of the heavily guarded bank (541). As with the zoo snake, Harry's primary intent is never to liberate a captive animal but to exploit the animal's power for his own ends. After they jump off the dragon, Hermione worries about how it will cope—a concern that Ron dismisses as silly because "it's a dragon . . . it can look after itself" (548). Yet when recounting their exploit, Ron chooses humane-sounding language that grossly misrepresents their and the dragon's agency in the escape, claiming they "released it into the wild" (573). This dramatic episode furthers the conceit that the hero's anthropocentric ends will also happen to benefit a deserving nonhuman creature.

In contrast, the Hungarian Horntail from *Goblet of Fire* is rendered as an unsympathetic villain requiring vanquishing by the same human(e) savior. When presented as an "it," the dragon is a "vicious thing" with "evil, yellow eyes" (*GF* 328, 353), "its back end's as dangerous as its front" (328). She/her pronouns are used almost exclusively when the text needs to remind us she is a mother; to ensure combative dragon foes, the Triwizard Tournament organizers intentionally procured "nesting mothers" to hide a golden egg among their real ones (328).

When Harry first sees her in the forest, he notices her eyes "[bulge] with either fear or rage, he couldn't tell which" (*GF* 326), which implies at least an effort to decipher her emotional state, but it is interesting what the two interpretive options lay bare. If the dragon is feeling "fear"—because she has been drugged, awakened to find that she has been towed to a strange location with her eggs, and stunned by her "keepers" (327)—he would have to pity her to maintain his humane persona. However, if he decides that the dragon is feeling "rage," Harry could position himself as acting in self-defense. The next day, she wakes in a pit, chained in front of a mass of humans, only able to "[crouch] low over her clutch of eggs" to protect them from who knows what (353). The mother is then harassed by a human concerned only with his self-appointed mission to be a "champion," but readers' sympathies are directed toward Harry—ill-prepared, underage, and thrust into the tournament against his will. The narrative focuses on Harry's cunning use of diversion to coax the dragon into not being "too protective of her eggs" (355), which, coming from the Boy Who Lived Only Because of His Mother's Sacrifice, is an assessment that suggests that nonhuman beings should be held to a lower standard of "motherly" instinct.[17] Viktor is "the best after" Harry because he scores points hitting his dragon in the eye but gets points docked when the pain causes the dragon to go "trampling around in agony and squashed half the real eggs" (359)—an interesting moment to not refer to the eggs as *hers*. Against this dragon, Harry is the classic male adventurer, a veritable St. George slaying the fabled dragon. At the same time, the dragon then stands in as the overly protective mother figure that the boy can allegorically vanquish to mark his growing up.[18]

Harry's encounter with the Horntail also highlights the idea that we regard as monstrous those beings of which we are afraid and that the one tried and true way we manage that fear is to establish dominance. Empowered by his broomstick, Harry soars high enough so that the dragon "shrank to the size of a dog," reducing the monstrous to a pet—a position that brings Harry "back where he belonged" (*GF* 354). After he outwits the dragon, he concedes, gazing at the small model of the Horntail by his bedside, that perhaps "*Hagrid had a point . . . they were all right, really, dragons*" (367). Meanwhile, the unidentified dragons that become potion ingredients, wand components, and Bill Weasley's dragon-hide boots are of no ethical concern. It eludes Hagrid that the dragon steak he uses on his bruised eye could have come from Norbert, his erstwhile pet (*OP* 422). The use to which nonhuman beings can be put has little to do with what wizarding society pretends: that this or that species is more deserving of respect or protection because it is useful, innocuous, intelligent, capable of feeling, or cute. Instead, *one* dragon among countless others is liberated.

The zoo boa and the Gringotts dragon are set up as sympathetic subjects of Harry's rescue, but he receives the bulk of his moral credit for liberating Dobby from the Malfoys' abusive ownership. At the end of *Chamber of Secrets*, Harry contrives to free Dobby after hearing the house-elf "squealing with pain all the way along the corridor" from Lucius Malfoy's gratuitous kicks (337). Dobby's liberation is posited as being directly inspired by Harry's instinctive empathy, but the nonhuman's freedom remains an insufficient end in itself: Dobby's freedom humiliates Lucius insofar as the teenager successfully hoodwinks him into losing a slave and status symbol. Elaine Ostry goes so far as to describe Dobby's liberation as "only [incidental]" to Harry's purposes (96). Moreover, Dobby effectively earned his freedom; Brycchan Carey rightly argues that Harry's "motivation is explicitly that of personally rewarding Dobby for his individual good behavior" (104). As with the snake, whose mysterious liberation brought Harry a measure of revenge against his bully, Dobby's liberation benefits Harry—again linking anthropocentric objectives to the humane urge. Harry is declared the "defender of house-elves" (*DH* 734), though he has, at best, defended a single elf.

After a lifetime of abuse in a Death Eater household, Dobby's expectations are abysmally low, so he is exponentially grateful to Harry for merely being nice. Gushing of Harry's "greatness" and "goodness" at every opportunity (*CS* 15), Dobby fawns over Harry; his "slavish adoration of Harry is played for laughs and underscores his essential slave nature" (Ostry 96). After Harry helps him attain freedom, Dobby devotes himself to aiding Harry in the Triwizard Tournament, helping him find the Room of Requirement in *Order of the Phoenix*, and spying on Draco in *Half-Blood Prince*. This is, perhaps, the ultimate human fantasy: that the freed nonhuman would use their new-found agency to choose again to be subjected to a deserving new master.[19] In turn, the master can feel virtuous while enjoying the benefits of species hierarchy: "Dobby is a free house-elf," he declares, free to "obey anyone he likes and Dobby will do whatever Harry Potter wants him to do!" (*HBP* 421).

As a character, Dobby resembles a loyal and overeager pet, and while Harry grows to become grateful for his loyalty, their relationship is deeply asymmetrical. In *Goblet of Fire*'s Christmas, Dobby gifts him a pair of hand-knit socks, and Harry is taken by surprise that Dobby thinks they are on gift-exchanging terms. Scrambling, he tosses Dobby an old pair of mustard-yellow socks, for which Dobby is (as usual) excessively grateful. This is the same pair of used socks that Harry received from Uncle Vernon for his tenth birthday, representing how little the Dursleys ever cared for him. In turn, the socks that Dobby has lovingly handknitted for Harry, featuring motifs tailored to his Quidditch obsession, are underappreciated: Harry soon declares that his other presents were "much more satisfactory than Dobby's odd socks" (*GF* 410). It is not until Dobby provides him with concrete help—the gillyweed that helps him succeed in the second task of the Triwizard Tournament—that Harry truly feels motivated to buy him socks as a thank you. Effectively, Rowling never shows Harry giving for nothing, suggesting that this is how things ought to be. Comparatively, Ron's spontaneous offer of his Christmas sweater and socks is actually more friendly and generous. When Dobby comes to warn Dumbledore's Army of Umbridge's raid, Harry does prove grateful and considerate as he whisks him out of the room—which again can be read as kindness for services rendered.

By the end of the series, Dobby gives the proverbial ultimate gift to save the heroes in their hour of direst need. The burial scene is often offered as proof of Harry's respect for nonhumans because he insists on burying Dobby "properly." To Harry, this entails digging the grave manually, and "every drop of his sweat and every blister felt like a gift to the elf who had saved their lives" (*DH* 478). Again, Harry's choice to dig is not nothing, but the text aggrandizes Harry's choice; instead of taking it for granted that when someone dies for you, taking care with their body is the least you can do, his actions are presented as a *gift*. The series makes much of the idea that the ability to experience the pain of love lost is a "part of being human" (*OP* 824)—appropriating these fine feelings exclusively for the human species— but experiencing this degree of grief for the loss of a (mere) nonhuman is deemed extraordinarily generous. Harry's gestures again appear unusually virtuous by the stipulated context of other wizards' horrifying treatment of nonhumans, encouraging readers to notice only that he could have done less rather than wonder why he did not do more. The text then deploys another nonhuman to label Harry's behavior special: the proudest, most suspicious goblin pronounces him the only wizard who would "not seek personal gain" (*DH* 488). Griphook makes it clear that he would not have agreed to help them break into Gringotts had he not witnessed Harry's burial of Dobby.

Again and again, Harry is amply rewarded for the behavior he under-takes primarily for or with immediate rewards. In *Prisoner of Azkaban*, Buckbeak's rescue is framed as a collateral benefit to saving Sirius: like the Gringotts dragon, the hippogriff is the necessary vehicle on which to achieve a human rescue. Interpreting Dumbledore's cryptic hint that more than one life might be saved by their time travel, Harry announces that they should save Buckbeak, to which Hermione replies, "But—how will that help Sirius?" (*PA* 396), suggesting that to Hermione, time traveling to save Buckbeak could only make sense as part of the plan to save a human.[20] In *Half-Blood Prince*, Harry attends Aragog's funeral—not because he cares at all about the spider or even respects Hagrid's feelings about his friend of fifty-odd years. Harry is described as feeling some sympathy for Hagrid, but he would not have risked detention to attend the funeral had there not been an anthropocentric goal—attaining Professor Slughorn's memory about Voldemort (*HBP* 471).[21] The text itself does not take Hagrid's grief seriously; Aragog's funeral lacks any of the dignity afforded Dobby's. The language not only continues to ridicule Hagrid's inability to recognize the acromantula's monstrosity but also speaks indelicately of the "rather horrible, crunchy thud" the repulsive corpse makes when Hagrid rolls it into the grave (484). For showing up to something that even the text signals is ludicrous, Harry is rewarded with Professor Slughorn's secrets and Dumbledore's praise.

Moreover, not all captivity seems to rise to the level of sympathetic portrayal. In Care of Magical Creatures classes, nonhumans are held captive and subjected to the ogling and manipulation of a crowd of teenagers without textual reproach. The bowtruckles are casually described as "captive" (*OP* 322); the hippogriffs "didn't seem to like being tethered like this" (*PA* 115). In the next book, Hagrid "managed to capture two unicorn foals," taking advantage of the fact that "babies" are more "trustin'" (*GF* 484)—and it is presented as a win, for he one-ups the substitute teacher, Professor Grubbly-Plank, and even impresses the Slytherin Pansy Parkinson. Even if the nonhumans are described as not liking it, the text does not signal that their preferences are relevant. Because these captives are not needed as metaphors for Harry, their restraints are not represented in a way that elicits readerly sympathy. It might be fair to say that in *Harry Potter*, captivity is only "wrong" when it is done by "bad" characters (the Malfoys, the Gringotts goblins, perhaps the Muggle zookeepers).

Lastly, Hedwig, another animal character whose narrative arc includes spates of captivity, leads a life that is fairly confined. As Dendle puts it, "Though she enjoys Harry's attention, [Hedwig] is hardly allowed to live a life of freedom and dignity" (169). Even when Hedwig is present in a scene—such as in the Hogwarts train car—she is "disappeared . . . discursively absent," because "the text's representation of nonhuman characters serves merely to further develop human characters" (Hayles 195). Their mutual affection is established, but their relationship is also asymmetrical. While Hedwig is described as Harry's "only friend" at the Dursleys' (*OP* 43), he values her primarily—as he thinks shortly after her death—because she constitutes "his one great link with the magical world" during his holidays on Privet Drive (*DH* 67). At Hogwarts, where he has his human friends, she "sometimes" seeks him out for affection (*SS* 135), but he seeks her out only to send mail.

As with the zoo boa, Hedwig's captivity matters only when it can serve as a metaphor for Harry's confinement under the Dursleys. In the second book, Uncle Vernon padlocks Hedwig in her small cage, rendering her bored and restless, unable to "stretch her wings for ages" (CS 28). It is a massive understatement of the harm of close confinement to such an animal, but it is not nothing: our attention is at least momentarily drawn to the welfare of a nonhuman character. Yet this focus on Hedwig is primarily meant to draw our pity for Harry: this is the same summer that, as punishment, he is caged in his bedroom—windows barred, door locked, with a cat flap installed for meals. The following scene describes their linked condition on day three, when, with his "insides . . . aching with hunger," he drank his "stone-cold" soup and "tipped the soggy vegetables at the bottom of the bowl" into Hedwig's "empty food tray" (22). Not comprehending his sacrifice, "she ruffled her feathers and gave him a look of deep disgust" (22). With Hedwig as Harry's double, amplifying the sense of abuse, pity for the owl extends pity to her master. Moreover, by casting his dilemma in such stark terms—Will this teenager choose to starve for his owl?—the narrative begs readers to admire his choice as exemplary and rare. For this to rise to the level of admiration, this scene requires that we think it likely, and to some degree acceptable, that Harry might keep his paltry food allowance entirely for himself—that he might *not* share with the animal that has been rendered captive solely for his service. The it's-just-an-animal mentality is the backdrop against which his sharing food seems special or unusual.

The pathos of the scene also obscures the question of why Hedwig is there at all. At the very least, facing these abusive summers and knowing how Hedwig would also suffer, Harry could have sent her to Hogwarts or Ron's, as he readily does in *Prisoner of Azkaban* for the selfish reason of earning his uncle's permission to visit Hogsmeade (21). After all, Hedwig does not need his care, nor can she even rely on it. Though he occasionally buys owl nuts, Hedwig primarily feeds herself and is obviously expected to do so while she delivers his mail to far-off locales, even to "tropical" places in the "south" (GF 24). Narratively, Rowling could have achieved similar pathos by describing Harry as choosing to give up his one source of positive companionship at Privet Drive.

Consider, too, why Hedwig is caged on every journey on the *Hogwarts Express*. She can certainly fly to the school on her own, but Rowling repeatedly includes her, caged, to comically add to Harry's troubles. In *Sorcerer's Stone*'s King Cross scene, Harry "[attracts] a lot of funny looks, because of

Hedwig" (91). In *Chamber of Secrets*, after Dobby blocks entry to Platform 9¾, the way Hedwig's cage "bounced onto the shiny floor, and she rolled away, shrieking indignantly" again offers us her captive discomfort to amusingly highlight Harry's problems: "Hedwig . . . was causing such a scene that there was a lot of muttering about cruelty to animals from the surrounding crowd" (68). Although Hedwig was mercifully allowed to fly free next to the Ford Anglia on their earlier ride from Privet Drive to the Burrow (28), for their alternative commute from King's Cross to school on the Anglia, she is inexplicably kept in her cage in the backseat (70). She could have been the one to show them the way, but instead, her discomfort provides another laugh during their violent encounter with the Whopping Willow (75–76). Unlike the caging at Privet Drive that second summer, all these other scenes of Hedwig's caging are not written to trigger sympathy for the owl—quite the opposite. As these moments are not needed to serve as metaphors for Harry's captivity, her caging serves to ground Rowling's humor.

At no point has this cage offered her safety; it has been a prison and an endangering restraint. Poignantly foreshadowing her death in the final book is the moment in *Half-Blood Prince* where Harry cages her and it is described as a positive experience: he "shut his snowy owl, Hedwig, safely in her cage" (44).[22] For an animal that cannot get lost, the very idea of her needing to be caged for her safety is ludicrous. But she has to be caged under this pretense of care so that, for Harry's final departure from Privet Drive in *Deathly Hallows*, she can be killed, setting the last novel's darker tone.[23] Alastor Moody goes through the contrivance of producing seven replica stuffed owls in cages for the "high-risk sortie" (Dendle 170), during which she—caged, unable to fly away—is cursed in the crossfire. Harry's captivity of Hedwig literally gets her killed, but the text does not write it that way, instead lulling us into reading the circumstances as a tragically inevitable loss that, again, increases pathos for Harry. During her life, no one asks if Hedwig needs or desires other companions or if Hedwig should be freed from service. When he learns of her death, Hagrid says consolingly that she "had a great old life" (*DH* 67), which—given what we know of her life—conceives of an owl's capacity for a great life as being largely centered around human service.

Thus, in *Harry Potter*, nonhuman benefit is always tied to human self-interest. Each instance of rescue or liberation across the series requires the nonhuman's freedom to be, at best, a collateral benefit to an anthropocentric end. This is not so much a critique of the characters but rather a critique of the author, who considered such a linkage essential. Though happy to tap into the discourse of humaneness to embellish her "good" characters, to Rowling, saving or helping nonhumans could never be the end itself. The generous reading would be that Rowling seeks to sell a humane message by promising readers sweet rewards. However, as the next section discusses, it is more likely that Rowling's position is that nonhumans should never be our primary concern.

Being Too Sorry for the Nonhuman

It is not only that Harry does little for nonhumans to so much acclaim or even that every such favor is tied to, if not contingent on, anthropocentric ends: the series also makes it clear that it is undesirable to attempt to care or do any more for nonhumans or to do so without self-interest. To reinforce the limits that Harry continually performs, the texts present us with two models of excessive concern or attachment for nonhumans: Hagrid and Hermione.[24]

Hagrid is "one of the main ambassadors to the world of magical creatures" (Dendle 165), and while he is presented sympathetically, the texts also signal to the reader that his softness is a form of feminine weakness. The overall message is that while Hagrid is well intentioned and worth befriending, it is undesirable to *be* like him. Hagrid is one of those "nutters" for whom the book *Men Who Love Dragons Too Much* is intended (*GF* 338): his dearest wish is to keep a dragon for a pet—a dream briefly realized in *Sorcerer's Stone* with an illicitly acquired dragon egg. Identifying himself as Norbert's "mummy"—an emasculating choice in a series that undercuts mothers—Hagrid gushes over the "*beautiful*" baby dragon, apparently oblivious to its monstrousness: "Isn't he *beautiful*? . . . Bless him, look, he knows his mummy!" (*SS* 235). Singing it lullabies, "[going] on about it" (237), packing it a teddy bear "in case he gets lonely," and sobbing when he has to give it up (240), he appears as besotted, obsessed, and unable to recognize the reality that the rest can plainly see. In *Chamber of Secrets*, this excessive concern for nonhumans even fuels Harry's suspicion that Hagrid had been the first to open the chamber out of misplaced pity: "He'd probably thought it was a shame that the monster had been cooped up so long, and thought it deserved the chance to stretch its many legs; Harry could just imagine the thirteen-year-old Hagrid trying to fit a leash and collar on it" (249).[25]

The Monster Book of Monsters, Hagrid's textbook assignment, serves as a metaphor for his philosophy of reform and redemption of the monstrous. Every student reacts with fear to the toothy book and resorts to restraints (belts, ropes, binder clips, bags [*PA* 112]). To everyone's surprise, however, the secret to opening the book safely is "ter *stroke* 'em," which Hagrid explains "as though this was the most obvious thing in the world" (113). He demonstrates: when Hagrid "ran a giant forefinger down its spine, . . . the book shivered, and then fell open and lay quiet in his hand" (113). Motivated by the same belief in his ability to redeem monsters via affection, Hagrid forces his half brother to live in the Forbidden Forest and be "civilized."[26] When the centaurs who reside in the forest object, describing it as "our forest," Hagrid "angrily" retorts, "I'll have less of the 'our' forest, if it's all the same ter you. It's not up ter you who comes an' goes in here—" (*OP* 698). The centaurs rightly retort that it is not up to him, either; Hagrid has abrogated this right for himself. Having been abandoned by his giantess mother and keenly afraid of anti-giant prejudice, Hagrid is on a mission to mother creatures that others see as monsters. The runty Grawp was being pitiably "kicked around" by the larger giants (692), but Hagrid is motivated to redeem Grawp because his half brother was also abandoned by their mother. Loving on Norbert and other "monsters" is a form of self-love, making Hagrid's excessive interest appear the unhealthy byproduct of his own trauma.[27] Even in the Battle of Hogwarts, as Hagrid is carried away as "prey" by acromantulas (his beloved Aragog's descendants), he cries out, "Don't hurt 'em, don't hurt 'em!" (*DH* 647). Thanks to the ungrateful spiders, Hagrid ends up in Voldemort's clutches. The lesson is clear: excessive concern for nonhumans can lead you to your doom.

Hermione's approach to the house-elves appears "over-cerebral and dogmatic" (Dendle 165), but her motivations come from the same place: unchecked empathy for the nonhuman Other. Moved by witnessing Winky's mistreatment by ministry wizards, Hermione is then shocked to learn that Hogwarts is serviced by enslaved house-elves. In *Goblet of Fire*, Hermione begins her crusade by establishing S.P.E.W. to fight an injustice that not even its purported victims care to fight against. Her original name for the organization, Stop the Outrageous Abuse of Our Fellow Magical Creatures and Campaign for a Change in Their Legal Status (*GF* 224), was more ambitious in calling out abuse—and claiming outrage, kinship with house-elves, and a demand for abolition—but her goals remain lofty, with "short-term aims" ("secure fair wages and working conditions") and "long-term aims" ("changing the law about non-wand use, trying to get an elf into the Department for the Regulation and Control of Magical Creatures") (225).

While some readers may argue that Rowling means for Hermione to be taken seriously, I agree with Scully's skepticism (105). A satire of animal-protection societies, Hermione's "organization" appears a ridiculous army of one, with an embarrassing acronym and grandiose "manifesto" (*GF* 224). The texts could have portrayed her indefatigable efforts as admirable, but instead, she is a joke: "She had . . . taken to rattling around the Gryffindor common room every evening, cornering people and shaking the collecting tin under their noses" like a pushy panhandler (239). Moreover, the Hogwarts house-elves roundly reject her proselytizing. When she leaves clothing items around for elves to accidentally free themselves, they react with anger and refuse to clean their common room; her poor knitting skills also become a running gag. For their part, adults are also uninterested. Arthur cuts her off from speaking in Winky's defense, insisting "now is not the time to discuss elf rights" as he shepherds them from the scene (139), leaving Winky at the mercy of wizards intent on railroading her for a crime she did not commit. While Hermione earnestly argues for Kreacher's better treatment, she receives no approbation or reward; Sirius also repeatedly cuts her off while she is speaking on the topic of Kreacher (*OP* 110, 303). True to character, Remus listens to her "talking very earnestly about her view of elf rights" (170), but Rowling "doesn't allow us to hear Lupin's reply" (Horne, "Multicultural and Social Justice" 87), so the moment exists to further her portrayal as a zealot. To her disappointment, even Hagrid insists that liberating house-elves would be an "unkindness" (*GF* 265). And while Dumbledore criticizes many supremacist prejudices and is nice enough to hire and pay the freed Dobby, it remains the glaring case that Hogwarts is staffed by hundreds of slaves. In *Harry Potter*, it is never the right time to discuss elf rights.

Spared from tarnishing his image as the great defender of house-elves, Harry does not take a firm position either way but "seems utterly uninterested in universalizing this principle of freedom to any other elves" (Dendle 168). While he is shown to be very sympathetic to Dobby's condition on their first meeting and briefly sympathizes with the house-elf Voldemort framed, he never considers their enslavement to be wrong. Instead, he "[wonders] vaguely how many elves had now been set free whether they wanted to be or not" and devotes no more time to ethical questions (*OP* 279–80), sharing "exasperation" with Ron every time Hermione raises the tedious issue (*GF*

225). While Hermione is unable to witness house-elf servility without feeling empathy (she refuses the extra food, "with a pained look at the way the elves kept bowing and curtsying"), Harry is ready to enjoy their services and fill his pockets with the food they provide (382).[28] Learning that Kreacher also sleeps in a cupboard does not trigger any identification nor does his sympathy twitch when Sirius casually jokes that "he might have crawled into the airing cupboard and died. . . . But I mustn't get my hopes up" (*OP* 505). Even when he becomes a slaveowner himself, inheriting Kreacher, he does not consider the ethics of house-elf slavery. When, in *Half-Blood Prince*, he bemoans not having "an office full of Aurors at his command" to set a tail on Draco (418), he remembers that he does, in fact, have an elf at his disposal. As he calls on the slave that he had vehemently insisted he did not want and who obviously loathes and rejects him, he thinks, "How could he have forgotten, why hadn't he thought of it before?" (419).[29] Earlier, Harry appears kind when, "frowning," he queries why Winky was forced to stay in the box at the World Cup when she is afraid of heights, but he is now untroubled when Kreacher points out that he obeys Harry's orders only "because Kreacher has no choice" (*GF* 99; *HBP* 421). Now his only concern is to hide his slave usage from Hermione so as to avoid her lecture (*HBP* 451). At one point, Harry asks when Hermione will "give up on this spew stuff" (*GF* 320), suggesting that he is waiting for the blessed day when he will no longer have to hear her nagging.

Ever the lesser person in contrast to Harry,[30] Ron bears the brunt of voicing the primary argument against S.P.E.W.'s mission: that house-elf enslavement is ethically unproblematic because they like it. This reflects the "pervasive belief among the wizarding community that house-elves prefer a life of servitude over freedom; however, house-elves have never experienced agency or freedom" (Rao and Gorecki 281). Upon learning that she has been covering hats with trash to try to force manumission, Ron criticizes Hermione's scheme. He even removes the rubbish, ironically engaging in more action to keep them enslaved than he ever has or will ever engage in for their welfare or freedom.

The construct of the "happy" house-elf is further propagated by the fact that the house-elves are not ever shown to be working in a way that we would read as hard. As Ron puts it, what they provide is "good service" (*GF* 377). We only see them carrying food from one place to the next, rather than struggling with heavy loads, toiling over hot cauldrons, or roasting the one-hundred-plus turkeys for the *Goblet of Fire* Christmas feast (410). According to the Weasley twins, the Hogwarts house-elves "think they've got the best job in the world" (239), and the texts suggest that, indeed, it may not be so bad to be a slave as long as one's master is "kind."[31]

The same "happy" trope is evident with Pigwidgeon, Ron's diminutive owl. When he grabs the bird out of the air, clutches him in his fist, and waves him about, the description is of what we would consider rough treatment, but the owl "hooted more happily than ever as he soared through the air" (*GF* 406), so we do not. Ron also speaks to him rudely ("Stupid little feathery git!" [405]) and frequently throws him out of the window to deliver mail that is too heavy for him while Pigwidgeon gleefully hoots on (364). Pigwidgeon, too, thinks he has the best job in the world. It comes off as consensual sadomasochism: the owl appears happy, so Ron does not appear abusive even as he engages in what appears as abusive behavior. While the goblins, who "stick up for themselves" (449), and centaurs, who refuse to be mules, lose the sympathy of potential human allies, those nonhumans who do not stick up for themselves are taken to accept their enslavement. The subaltern's apparent happiness effectively erases inequality and injustice.

Happiness and justice differ—and can conflict, as fair treatment may or may not bring happiness.[32] While Hermione is not wrong to describe house-elves as "uneducated and brainwashed" (*GF* 239)—they are quite literally bred to service, bound by magical contract, subject to ministry discipline for failing to abide by their lot, and subject to intense pressure to believe that any disobedience is the mark of being "bad"—it is also true that the vast majority of house-elves are, likely as a result of all these factors, happy to be enslaved. Their happiness is the product of grievous manipulation and oppression, yet it is an incontrovertible reality that if magical society were to grant house-elves the right to choose, the vast majority would choose as they have been reared and directed to choose. Readers can, of course, take Hermione's side on the issue, but the texts nudge readers away from doing so. Scully is right to say that "ultimately, although Hermione raises the possibility of brainwashing, the novels themselves don't seem to dispute the idea that the elves really *are* naturally happy servants" (105). Hermione appears obtuse—even selfish—in ignoring what the house-elves say they want. Dobby is positioned as "weird" (*GF* 265)—an exception to a general rule—and the text suggests that he is uniquely motivated to be free because of the Malfoys' unusual cruelty.

Harry might have saved only one elf, but for all of Hermione's earnest efforts to save them all, she fails to save even one. It is Harry's way—liberating individual animals on a case-by-case basis and only when a human end is achieved by the animal's liberation—that appears productive and useful. Keeping the fight "on a personal level," which Horne describes as a "multicultural approach" ("Multicultural and Social Justice" 25), Harry chooses one more house-elf to be nicer to, and—yet again—his efforts reap him great rewards: a "dramatically different" Kreacher now happily scrubs down Grimmauld Place, serves Harry's favorite foods, and refers to him as "master Harry" (*DH* 225). Kreacher not only returns to happy servility but also marshals the Hogwarts house-elves to fight in his master's name in the Battle of Hogwarts (734), and even as the series comes to a close, we find Harry "wondering whether Kreacher might bring him a sandwich" (749). Our humane hero remains a slaveowner, as does Hogwarts, affirming that abolition—much less equality—have never been the series' goal.[33] For her part, Hermione "must forget about S.P.E.W.... because collective political action is treated in these books as a dull topic, difficult to sustain, and less compelling than narrower concerns of family and romance" (Byler 130).

Extermination and sadistic abuse, which are the purview of Death Eaters, is firmly unacceptable, but that is how low *Harry Potter* sets the bar for the treatment of nonhuman Others. At the same time, the texts go to great narrative lengths to celebrate Harry's meager efforts at every turn and render ridiculous any deeper concern or attempts to reform systemic issues. Dendle conjectures that "by the end of the series, the author has simply lost interest in the concerted political sympathy she was at such pains to rally for elves in the fourth book" (165), but it is more accurate to say that systematic change is anathema to Rowling's vision in *Harry Potter*.

Resistance Is Futile

To the stalwart anthropocentrist, some measure of nonhuman resistance is actually welcome. The Other's violent resistance can conveniently justify more violent measures that are then framed as righteous reprisals. Consider this paradox: Harry comes to enjoy the expelling of the gnomes that contribute to the garden's disorder, but he also thinks that the "overgrown" Weasley garden is "exactly what a garden should be" (*DH* 107; *CS* 36)—and, when the garden is marshaled into tidiness for the *Deathly Hallows* wedding, he "thought that it looked rather forlorn without its usual contingent of capering gnomes" (*DH*

107). To him, the ideal garden offers a live battleground between humans and nature, providing ongoing opportunities for reasserting control rather than a fait accompli. Thankfully, because of Arthur's "too soft" attitude, Harry can expect "they'll be back" (CS 37).

Most instances in which nonhumans object to their treatment at human hands are passed off as comical and charming, perpetuating the idea that their raison d'être is to be used. At best, the ethical issues that the series explicitly raises "[wind] up presenting an uncomfortable obstacle Rowling must navigate as she crafts humorous scenes that often involve the exploitation and sometimes pain of lesser creatures" (Dendle 164). At worst, such scenes argue that a nonhuman's objection can and should be overridden. Neville's toad, Trevor, repeatedly makes bids for freedom only to fail, but we are not meant to care that he is an unhappy captive: they only symbolize Neville's inability to control a mere toad. The bullfrog on which Hermione practices Silencing Charms turns to "glare at her reproachfully" (OP 375), as if what she has done is merely inconvenient. When owls, like Hedwig, turn their backs, nip their masters, or cuff them as they fly away, we are encouraged to read these small instances of resistance as amusing; Hedwig's grouchiness gives her a bit of character and is never meant to be taken as a serious bid for freedom or rights.

The as-yet-unreformed Kreacher's passive-aggressiveness to Sirius is another example. Bound in slavery to a master he loathes, Kreacher resorts to pantomiming the behavior of a "good" house-elf. For example, he purposefully acts as if he is too old and feeble to greet his master's guests. When the Weasley twins intentionally call his attention, Kreacher "[gives] a very pronounced and very unconvincing start of surprise," claiming that he "did not see Young Master" but then audibly adding his illicit thoughts: "Nasty little brat of a blood traitor it is" (OP 108). Confronted by his master, Kreacher "[flings] himself into a ridiculously low bow" and claims he is "cleaning" as a cover for his forbidden feelings (109). With the reassurance that he remains bound in slavery, the Weasley twins find Kreacher's resistance comical.[34]

Although designed as a joke, Hagrid's blast-ended skrewts perhaps offer a glimmer of hope as models of nonhuman resistance. For one, they are viscerally unappealing, satisfying none of our typical aesthetic preferences: "deformed, shell-less lobsters, horribly pale and slimy-looking, with legs sticking out in very odd places and no visible heads" (GF 196). Assaulting multiple senses, they emit a "very powerful smell of rotting fish" (196). Draco asks if there is any *"point"* to the skrewts: "Why would we *want* to raise them? . . . I mean what do they *do*?" (196). Are the skrewts to be cared for as "pets that can burn, sting, and bite all at once?" (197). Yet it is not only a "bad" character who asks this question: Hermione rebuts Draco by insisting that even if not "pretty," the skrewts might still be "useful," reflecting the same anthropocentric view (197). (According to our house-elf welfarist, however, "the best thing to do would be to stamp on the lot of [skrewts] before they start attacking us all" [198].) Harry, too, echoes this logic when "for the life of him he could not see what [Neville] would want" with his Mimbulus Mimbletonia, an animalized little plant, and asks, "Does it—er—*do* anything?" (*OP* 186, 187). It is therefore no surprise that the least kind of the trio, Ron, asks the same question of flobberworms, "some of the most boring creatures in existence": "Why would anybody *bother* to look after them?" (*PA* 142).[35] All nonhuman creatures bear the burden of proving they have a "point"—a human use—to motivate human "care."

Within this anthropocentric value system, the skrewts seem to completely resist being "useful": it appears that neither their labor nor their parts can be used. Hagrid does not appear to have considered any practical point for breeding this new species, but he is still pursuing his own interests: he thought the skrewts would be "fun" (*GF* 439). Yet they also reject Hagrid's attempts to care for them as pets. Despite his best efforts, he cannot identify what to feed the creatures; they do not even seem to have mouths. As the skrewts begin to kill each other at an alarming rate, Hagrid struggles to even keep them alive (264). The class is tasked with taking them for a walk, but their very bodies defy his wishes as it is not even clear where the leash would go—"the sting, the blasting end, or the sucker?" (294). Hagrid also attempts to induce the skrewts into hibernation by having the class manipulate them into "boxes lined with pillows and fluffy blankets" and then nailing the lids shut (368); the bedding reads like care, but the nailed lids show how he is forcibly projecting his desire to "care" onto them. The skrewts break out; they simply do not care to be cared for.

Yet even the skrewts will, eventually, be boxed in: one of the survivors becomes a Dark creature, deployed as part of the Triwizard Tournament to challenge teenagers to showcase their skills. There is no escape, even for the least cooperative and most separatist of species. In the all-encompassing logic of *Harry Potter*'s anthropocentrism, resistance is futile. Thus, representations of resistance that show that humans are not always in full control of the nonhuman may not mount a forceful challenge to the construct of the liberal human(e) subject.

Conclusion

Dobby's death, like Hedwig's, serves a critical narrative function whereby the loss of the Other is contrived to further the construct of exceptional human virtue. Proverbial sacrificial lambs, the beloved nonhuman characters are killed off so we may congratulate ourselves for our grief. In shedding tears for Dobby or Hedwig and in celebrating the liberation of select sympathetic nonhumans, readers are given opportunities to feel the "right feelings"— to feel interspecies empathy, perhaps even surprising themselves at the depth of their feelings for mere nonhuman characters—and then to congratulate themselves as if they have passed a moral test. I credit Rowling for making two nonhuman characters matter so much to us as to make us weep at their deaths, even as it is also problematic that they had to die that tragically to engage our empathy and disappointing if—like Harry digging that grave and counting every drop of sweat—we make too much of our tears.

Paradoxically, this capacity for humaneness is presumed to be *part* of being human but never required to motivate us to action. *Harry Potter* merely beseeches us to not actively persecute, hurt, or kill nonhuman Others—and perhaps to speak to them kindly. While Harry (and his mentor Dumbledore) are held up as unusually virtuous, the series makes clear that humans are nevertheless not in danger of losing their status as "good" for failing to rescue, protect, or care for nonhuman Others. My point is not that Harry does not "care" enough about Hedwig, Dobby, or the rest but rather that the text repeatedly sets meager limits for how much a hero should care: never primarily, never in terms of equality, never prioritizing the nonhuman, and—while perhaps saving a select few—never questioning the systemic subjection of countless others. *Harry Potter*'s heroism does not entail a wholesale rejection of empathy but rather the development of the paradoxical ability to both feel empathy *and* cease feeling empathy in order to put human concerns first.

CHAPTER 4

WHY WORK?

Magic, Technology, and the Value
of Manual Labor in *Harry Potter*

But for heaven's sake—you're *wizards*! You can do *magic*!
Surely you can sort out—well—*anything*!

—*HALF-BLOOD PRINCE*

Dobby likes freedom, miss, but he isn't wanting too much,
miss, he likes work better.

—*GOBLET OF FIRE*

With his limited knowledge of the magical world, the Muggle Prime Minister in *Half-Blood Prince* expresses what would likely be anyone's assumption if we were told that magic exists: that if it were possible and real, magic would solve all our problems. Cornelius Fudge, at this point ex–Minister of Magic, regrettably informs him that limitless magical potential does not help in the case of war, at least not when "the other side can do magic too" (*HBP* 18), but the Muggle's assumption would otherwise be fair. The magic described in the series would seem to confer limitless potential to, say, resolve the energy conundrum and escape the climate crisis or, at least, avoid everyday inconvenience and discomfort. This potential is why the Ministry of Magic's most important function is, according to Rubeus Hagrid, to maintain the International Statute of Secrecy: because if the Muggles knew that magic was real, "everyone'd be wantin' magical solutions to their problems" (*SS* 65).

In sci-fi and fantasy, technology and magic often function in similar ways, fundamentally structuring how a society functions—particularly in relationship to work. Supersonic aircraft and enchanted broomsticks, remote controls and wands, both technology and magic ostensibly offer alternatives to physical exertion and enable otherwise impossible feats. *Harry Potter* "thoroughly, persistently, and consistently [blurs] the line between technology and magic" (Sheltrown 48). "Just as Muggles have created dishwashers, mass transit, and telephones or videophones through science, so the wizards have used magic to create the same conveniences," saving themselves time, energy, and effort (A. Doughty 54). Although our technology is described from the wizarding point of view as "substitutes for magic" (*GF* 548), the inverse is truer. In Muggle Studies class they must "Explain Why Muggles Need Electricity" (*PA* 250), but why do wizards and witches need magic? To wit, it is because they do not know how to harness electricity.

Unsurprisingly, there is a parallel between our contemporary ambivalence toward advanced, labor-saving technology and Rowling's attitude toward magic in *Harry Potter*. While bringing convenience and comfort, our technology-saturated lives have fueled social anxieties about its hidden harms. Today, we fear that overreliance on technology leads us to ruin of body, mind, and spirit; most science fiction films portray hypertechnological dystopias that we are invited to compare with our own condition, and calls to "unplug" are a staple of health and wellness advice. Under threat is, apparently, our work ethic: if we do not *need* to do anything, so the fear goes, we would lose motivation to do anything at all. We do not walk when we can take a car nor remember phone numbers or calculate tips when our phones do it better. Rowling echoes these same fears and asserts that her characters should not be, as Molly says, "[WHIPPING THEIR] WANDS OUT FOR EVERY LITTLE THING" (*OP* 84). Indeed, according to *Harry Potter*, you should not only "never trust anything that can think for itself *if you can't see where it keeps its brain*" but also be wary of becoming "too fond of or dependent" on any magical technology (*CS* 329; *DH* 105).

Elizabeth Teare finds that "most critics who have weighed in on the Harry Potter phenomenon to date have placed the books firmly in the Luddite tradition of children's fantasy" (337). For example, Nicholas Sheltrown conjectures that *Harry Potter* is "perhaps . . . , at its core, a morality tale about technology" (58)—a warning that it is dangerous for humanity to overly rely on it, and this warning has resonated with many readers. While supportive of what they see as one of the morals of the series, however, none of these critics take a Luddite's firm antitechnology stance. "To be categorically anti-technology is idiotic," declares Joel Hunter, mincing no words (116). Many seem to tacitly believe that, on one side of a clear line, there is legitimate usage and, on the other, there is overuse, overreliance, and the "frivolous" (Oakes 121), and many applaud where Rowling draws the line. However, there is a tendency to read into *Harry Potter* a more antitechnology position than the texts warrant, which speaks to many readers' projected desires—as well as the texts' willingness to invite these projections.

However, *Harry Potter* is not a straightforward morality tale about technology. The chapter's first section responds to a tendency in *Harry Potter* studies to interpret the series as if its version of magic portrays a profoundly different and salutary alternative to Muggle technology. While Rowling purposefully taps into readers' anxieties about technology's propensity to fuel consumerism and inspire dependency, *Harry Potter*'s magic should be, by its own terms, no better able to deter its users from consumerism or overreliance than contemporary technologies can.

That said, many of Rowling's characters do appear to model restraint, apparently resisting the temptation to use magic to solve their problems. The second section discusses Rowling's imposition of material lack on some of her characters, which some critics cite as an example of Rowling refusing to let her characters overuse magic. However, Rowling's reasons for not allowing her characters to magic their way out of poverty or need likely have less to do with concerns for magical overuse and more to do with an attachment to problematic class stereotypes and a reliance on material suffering as a trope to propel character and plot development. The austerity she imposes on the characters is contradictory, even nonsensical, but allows her to lean on discourses of class and "hard work" to define her characters and advance the plot.

The third and fourth sections discuss where Rowling's apparent concern for technological overuse does seem to overlap with some of her readers' anxieties. In presenting a pastoralized ideal in which it appears that technology can be safely wielded without overuse, however, the texts effectively conceal who must still perform nonmagical work and why, producing a fantasy in which displaced costs are borne by nonmale and nonhuman Others. To a large extent, her magical world succeeds in using less magic by conscripting nonhumans as magical slaves. In addition to nonhuman labor, the series requires housewives to engage in hypervisible, hybrid labor as a gendered spectacle of love.

Technophobia and Magic

We can readily see that *Harry Potter* overtly critiques the consumerist aspect of technological advancement. In his essay, Hunter addresses an audience that, in his opinion, was far too wont to chase after the newest technology: "The bewitching charm, the 'gee-whiz' attraction of gadgetry functions like an Imperius curse" (114). When Harry and the Weasley children visit Arthur at St. Mungo's Hospital, they are nearly bowled over by "a gaggle of [Muggle] shoppers plainly intent on nothing but making it into a nearby shop full of electrical gadgets" (*OP* 483). In the opening of the third book, the Dursleys loudly call attention to their new company car so that the neighbors might hear (*PA* 3). Dudley Dursley pitches a fit because he receives only thirty-seven birthday presents, two less than the previous year (*SS* 21). A second bedroom houses his considerable collection of items—from a video camera to a birdcage to a working tank, "nearly everything . . . broken" (37)—instead of providing a room for his cousin Harry, who sleeps in a cupboard. The Dursleys seem to buy for Dudley without purpose except to flaunt, and most of the items are unused or carelessly broken.

Alas, consumerism always appears to be someone else's bad habit. As Teare points out, the series' heroes also "love to buy": "The virtuous Dumbledore apart, the wizard world is much like ours: highly commercialized and obsessed with its technologies" (341, 339).[1] Harry and his friends are gleeful consumers of toys and collectibles, eagerly partaking in all the commercial opportunities offered by Diagon Alley and Hogsmeade without textual reproach. As the magic of some charmed objects seems to wear off (*HBP* 449), requiring frequent repurchase, magic and consumerism go hand in hand.

At times, it seems as if the texts contrive to let Harry have high-tech magical things while protecting his portrayal as a superior boy. At the Quidditch World Cup, for example, Harry gravitates toward the most high-tech purchase possible, the one-time-use, ten-Galleons-each Omnioculars (*GF* 93), but the moment makes him appear generous, rather than greedy for the cool technology, because he buys an additional pair for Ron and Hermione. In *Prisoner of Azkaban*, like the excited crowd gathered outside the shop, Harry longs to buy the cutting-edge, international-standard Firebolt, which is described as superior to his current broomstick, the Nimbus Two Thousand (52), which, in turn, puts the older and cheaper Comet 360 to shame (*SS* 165). "He had never wanted anything as much in his whole life" (*PA* 51–52), but he resists, which makes him appear both fiscally responsible and able to resist technology's siren call. Nevertheless, "he returned, almost every day after that, just to look at the Firebolt" (52), and soon receives his heart's desire through the contrivance of an anonymous gift. His fancy Nimbus had also been a gift, and it is hard to understand why Professor McGonagall, Dumbledore, or Hogwarts would have felt called upon to purchase his Nimbus for him given his inherited wealth except so that Harry could avoid the taint of being the purchaser of such a significant Quidditch advantage. Conveniently, his equipment is now upgraded at no cost to either him or his nonconsumerist persona. Owning the latest and best broomstick increases Harry's popularity—an eager group of students gathers to ogle and touch the Firebolt (257)—and enables further Quidditch victories, but he is never criticized for his obsession with brooms.[2]

In addition to consumerism, some critics raise the concern that we might lose an avenue for self-identity as the feats we achieve through technology may not feel as if they can be claimed as truly our own. In *Enough: Staying Human in an Engineered Age* (2003), Bill McKibben argues that advanced technologies such as genetic engineering and nanorobotics would be profoundly detrimental to our sense of humanity. One of the prominent voices of this concern, McKibben says that "*we stand on the edge of disappearing even as individuals,*" perched on the precipice of living lives of total "meaninglessness" (46). Indeed, "no one *needs* to run in the twenty-first century," but one might still take it up as "an outlet for spirit, for finding out who you are, no more mandatory than art or music," but technology such as bioengineering would take away our ability to feel like our achievements in running, or any other exertion, are "ours": "It's not the personal *challenge* that will disappear. It's the *personal*" (7). With the loss of the *personal*, McKibben argues, we would lose the ability to derive a sense of self-worth through competition— we will "lose *racing*: we'll lose the possibility of the test, the challenge, the celebration that athletics represents" (6). "The point has to do with seeking out my limits, centering my attention: finding out who I am" (48).

McKibben does not seem to have strong qualms about this competitive I, I, I mindset, nor does he fundamentally challenge our current comfort with feeling individual, personal achievement with the support of our current technologies—be they fitness watches, ergonomic sneakers, gel packs, massage guns, supplements, or medical care—because these technologies have not denied us the narrative of "*I* did that." While he recognizes that his preference for hyperindividuality and self-definition through competition is the product of the world that we have created, and even though these cultural drives are tied to the same world-destroying rapaciousness that he might have otherwise decried, McKibben seems to also cling to this worldview as "the very last weight holding us to the ground," without which "we will float silently away into the vacuum of meaninglessness" (47). There are neurochemical, psychobiological explanations that support the argument that ease leads to a loss of motivation,[3] so his fears are not unfounded. But I question whether, in this world where we must "produce . . . context for ourselves" (46), this competitive "*I*-did-that" mindset is truly the last weight we *want* holding us to the ground. Ultimately, McKibben seems unable to imagine an alternative way for modern, secular life to have meaning that is not grounded in a self-concept of hyperindividuality and the false belief that technology does not already mediate every aspect of our existence.

In a similar vein, Hunter urges *Harry Potter* readers to learn from the series to "refuse the technological imperative, disestablish the technological society, and return technology to its role as servant to human flourishing" (130). Here, we see again the moralizing language of resisting temptation and the anthropocentric urge to reclaim power from technology, to reestablish the "right" relationship by placing humans back in control. Hunter identifies the series' villain, Voldemort, as the "[embodiment of] the technological spirit in its purest and most explicit form" for wanting to use magical technology to conquer death itself (122).[4] This is, in part, correct: Voldemort *is* extremely covetous of power. Yet the narrative of achieving power independently from magical technology is actually also quite Voldemortian. "I have experimented; I have pushed the boundaries of magic further, perhaps, than they have ever been pushed," the Dark Lord boasts, with an emphasis on the "I" (*HBP* 443). Is it not Voldemort who first eschews the Sorcerer's Stone because "he would have found the thought of being dependent" on its elixir "intolerable" (502)? Is it not Voldemort who, by *Deathly Hallows*, masters the ability to fly without the need of a broom?

In fact, Voldemort's independence from much magical technology is rather unique; he appears to only ever use a wand and his Horcruxes. Wizarding society is otherwise extremely enmeshed with its magical technologies, the vast majority of which are much more powerful than our own and go without textual critique. While Dumbledore does pay a dear price for his youthful pursuit of the Deathly Hallows—arguably, the most powerful technology of the series—most of the wizarding community's day-to-day depends on a large variety of magical or magic-powered technologies: not only wands but also broomsticks, the Sorting Hat, the Goblet of Fire, the Weasleys' mangle, Xenophilius Lovegood's printing press, the flying Ford Anglia, Sirius's motorcycle, Omnioculars, Sneakoscopes, Pensieves, secrecy sensors, self-stirring cauldrons, and everything in their joke shops.

Moreover, magical people's capacities and abilities depend in large part on the quality of their technology. This is most evident with brooms, as earlier discussed: in the very unlevel playing field that is Quidditch, the quality (and price) of the broom directly impacts ability. Harry's Nimbus Two Thousand "was easily the best broom; Ron's old Shooting Star was often outstripped by passing butterflies" (*CS* 46); the Gryffindor team rightfully worries when they learn that the entire Slytherin team has been upgraded to Nimbus Two Thousand and Twos (112); Ron does not even dare to try out for the team until he gets a "decent broom" (*OP* 271); and, as earlier mentioned, Harry's Firebolt is universally recognized as giving him a unique edge, thanks to its "UNSURPASSABLE BALANCE," "PINPOINT PRECISION," and "ACCELERATION OF 150 MILES AN HOUR IN TEN SECONDS" (*PA* 51). Noticeably, no one asserts that Harry's achievements on the field are not his own nor qualifies his Snitch snatches with an asterisk. The series repeatedly hypes up his talent and nerve so that we can discount the technological inequalities and give him all the personal credit for being the best at flying. (Notably, though they can almost all use brooms to fly, only of Voldemort is it said that *he can fly* [*DH* 72].)[5]

For many, self-empowerment on the level of "I" seems to be the point of eschewing technology. Noel Chevalier praises *Harry Potter*'s magic as an imagined alternative to how modern technology "has fragmented the natural body to the point that manipulation of nature, even communication between humans, cannot take place unmediated by it" (408). Compared to technology, magic allows the characters to exert control over "nature" through more "natural" means: "Rowling's conception of magic reinscribes control over nature in language (use of charms and spells) and in combination of natural objects (substances used to make potions)" (408). In Rowling's apparent uto-pia, "the body reclaims its own ability, unmediated by technology, to exert influence over nature, which technology has taken away from it" (408). To reach his interpretations, however, Chevalier has to dismiss the obvious par-allels between modern technology and their wands and charmed objects. By declaring that "things work in the wizarding world without technology," he concludes that "it makes no difference" that much of their magic operates with largely the same uses and effects as technology (408). Such a reading seems to be motivated by a desire to feel that one could *directly* manipulate nature without technology—to feel power, control, influence, and thereby meaning.

Apparently driven by the same sense of disempowerment in the face of technology, Oakes focuses on magical *talent* as a way to relocate the font of power in each and every user. "Where we have created devices external to our beings that accomplish tasks for us," she contrasts, "witches and wizards learn to control certain forces with their own minds and talents" (Oakes 120). Oakes celebrates the fact that, in *Harry Potter*, "any average witch or wizard has powers *within his or her own knowledge and control* that outstrip those of even the cleverest, most McGuyver-like Muggle, without *relying* on electricity, nuclear power, digital technology, or even a pocket lighter" (120, emphasis added). In this language, we can see that Oakes relishes the idea of magical people containing the magical talent that makes their technolo-gies work. Rowling's wizards and witches could, in Oakes's opinion, claim personal, I-did-it-myself credit for what they achieve through magic instead of giving credit to the "external devices"—devices of which, it seems, some of us are profoundly jealous and resentful. While not denying the parallels between Muggle and magical technologies, Oakes's conclusions depend on ignoring magical people's complete dependence on a wand—the indisput-able sine qua non of reliable spellwork.[6] As children, Tom Riddle and Harry Potter can make things happen without wands, but this pales in comparison to what they can do with a wand, as Harry rediscovers when his own wand is broken in *Deathly Hallows*: he feels "fatally weakened, vulnerable and naked, as though the best part of his magical power has been torn from him" (350). At least theoretically, any magical person with a seven-Galleon wand already owns every technology—it is a powerful technology that can be used to make infinitely more technology by the enchanting of virtually anything and *any-one* else. But without it, no matter how powerful their minds or talents, they are no more able to reliably manipulate their environment than any Muggle without their gadgets and devices. As the unfortunate Muggle-borns experience under Death Eater rule, without a wand, they can only be beggars (525).

Many who fear the advancement of technology also worry that with each advancement comes a loss of knowledge or skills: with calculators, learning math feels superfluous; with typing, good handwriting becomes a relic of the past; with transportation technology, bodies seem to atrophy. This effect is generally indisputable. Rowling's magic would theoretically give rise to the same effects—and so does not inherently offer an advantage—yet some critics celebrate her fantasy alternative as if it does. As with Muggle technology, magic-driven technology functions without the user necessarily knowing how the technology works to produce the desired result, just as when we tabulate sums with a calculator, we do not need to understand how to add nor how the calculator does the adding. When using a Spell-Check Quill, presumably one does not need to know spelling to wield it (*HBP* 449). Arthur's "dearest ambition" is "to find out how airplanes stay up" (86)—something that your average Muggle would also not know, and we can assume that, if asked, Arthur would not be able to explain how magic makes a broom stay up either.

Oakes notes that, in addition to talent, magic requires years of training, which to her redeems it as a form of knowledge (120), yet a Muggle child must also be taught to flip a switch, turn a knob, and push buttons in the right order, and certainly adults need to develop knowledge and skills to use software and, at more advanced levels, to code it. Arthur lacks the understanding and physical dexterity to successfully light a match (*GF* 85), having never needed to do so before that moment. He would probably also fumble with a Muggle light switch. His dependence on magic means he has not developed a slew of swish-and-flick-like motor skills that we take for granted and do not consider "knowledge" gained by "training."[7] Oakes also does not account for the difference in educational systems: at Hogwarts, many of their classes cover what we might call basic or practical skills, such as turning on a light (Lumos) or activating a spout (Aguamenti) or dusting some dirt (Tergeo). If our K–12 covered car maintenance, computing and coding, HVAC maintenance, electrical engineering, and plumbing, we would not feel, as Oakes bemoans, "inept, unprepared, or at worst, stupid" when our air conditioning breaks down or the alerts flash in our cars (119). As for spellcasting, while it is mostly true that "you cannot just know the spell . . . you have to study it, practice it, and perfect it" (Appelbaum 39), there are notable instances when this is proven false—at least, when convenient for Rowling's plot. On first try, Harry pulls off the highly impact-ful Levicorpus and Sectumsempra spells he finds scribbled on the margins of the Half-Blood Prince's Potions textbook despite not having any instructions on what specific motions to make with his wand and not knowing what they would do (*HBP* 239, 522). In fact, when casting Sectumsempra, Harry simply "[waves] his wand wildly" (522). Even in the case of those spells that seem to take him a lot of practice—Accio, Expecto Patronum—the text emphasizes more his insufficient focus rather than what we would call skill, knowledge, or understanding.

Many also seem to fear and resent the possibility that technological usage renders users into automatons, compelled by the addictive appeal of technology to click, tap, and watch, and yet again, Harry does not seem immune to this. As noted, he is fairly obsessed with flying and his broom. Holding the Marauder's Map for the first time, he reflects on how it is certainly a powerful item that he should distrust—as Arthur had counseled—because one cannot see its brain, but Harry finds himself responding to the Marauder's Map as if compelled to "[follow] orders" (*PA* 194). Yet the texts do not critique his relationship to these addictive technologies. When his Nimbus Two Thousand is rendered into splinters by the Whomping Willow, he "felt as though he'd lost one of his best friends" (183). In fact, a list of "all his most prized possessions" comprises three powerful magical technologies: the Invisibility Cloak, his Firebolt, and the Marauder's Map (*GF* 39). The album of his parents' photos does not make the cut.

Chevalier also praises how "Rowling reinstates . . . tactility in the wizard's magic" (408), thereby offering a more humanizing experience, but the texts also contest such a conclusion. Though most of the characters do not treat it as such, magic could vitiate most tactility: one's wand could be a universal remote control for every other object in one's environment. Daedalus Diggle remarks on the confounding number of "buttons and knobs" in a Muggle car because most magical technology is operated with a wand and a voice command (or nonverbally, for the adept) (*DH* 37). In the Ministry of Magic, employees in neat rows perform identical wand actions to produce neat stacks of pamphlets to "mesmerizing" effect (248). The film captures the automaton-like feeling of the scene, each person a cog that does not even touch the paper it processes. Shortly after this, we see Pius Thicknesse foregoing virtually all tactility to write a simple note: he "pointed his wand at the quill standing ready in the ink pot. It sprang out and began scribbling a note to Umbridge" (253). In fact, magical life has the potential to be even more radically incorporeal than our own.

Rowling's magic seems to appeal to some critics as a way to have one's pro-verbial cake and eat it—advanced technology without the harmful effects—but this interpretation might hinge more on readerly projections than what the texts bear out. There is nothing inherently better about Rowling's magic that would lead its users to escape the loss of a personal sense of accomplish-ment—or knowledge, skills, or tactility—and as the novels show, the threat of overuse looms as greatly over their existence as our own.

Artificial Austerity Improves Character(s)

In the series, stark class divisions exist that are not merit based but due to inheritance, with no explanation of how previous generations amassed their wealth. In her article, Oakes praises Rowling for not "[resorting] to that easy way out" by letting her characters use magic to, for example, "create gold out of thin air" (120). In not "[allowing] her wizards the Faustian luxury of conjuring up lottery-scale riches" or otherwise not using magic to ease more of the burdens that it ought to be able to ease, *Harry Potter* appears to have created a utopian world where, in Oakes's opinion, "magic makes things easier, but does not go beyond what is necessary into the frivolous" (120, 121). Sheltrown wonders why magic is "not applied more consistently to make material life for wizards and witches better" and concludes that the members of this superior society simply choose not to, wisely realizing that "the over-application of any magical technology or spell will complicate the lives of wizards and witches in unforeseen ways" (58).

Indeed, though they possess wondrous magical powers, wizards and witches still need to go to work in prosaic places like offices, shops, and hospitals because they still need to purchase most things with money. In the series, "money is always a concern and often a worry . . . since expensive accessories of magic—spellbooks, cauldrons, potion ingredients, wands—must be purchased before any magic can be performed" (Teare 340). In fact, all the magical talent in the world would be no help without the "gold, filthy gold" required to buy a wand (*DH* 528).

On its face, their reliance on money can perhaps be explained by some extrapolation. If magical ability depends on innate talent, less talented magical people have to outsource at least some of their needs. Nymphadora Tonks, the clumsy Auror, remarks that she "never quite got the hang of . . . household spells" (*OP* 53), and clearly some characters are more "accomplished" at the same spells than others (*DH* 108)—for which the contrast of Neville Longbottom and Hermione Granger offers regular proof.[8] The Weasley twins sell five hundred Shield Hats to the Ministry of Magic for employees who cannot manage a Shield Charm (*HBP* 119)—a spell they should have mastered as teenagers. Even those who are competent in spellwork are beholden to others to create new spells and magical innovations, as it seems that not many can invent. Consider that, at the same age, Snape was an innovative spell creator and recipe refiner, while Harry was only an able verbal spell caster and adequate recipe follower. If most are basically capable (like Harry, Ron, and even Hermione) and only a very select few are experimenters and successful innovators (in Harry's generation, only Fred and George Weasley),[9] then whoever guards their discoveries could have a lucrative monopoly on their products. Dumbledore, for example, shared the twelve uses of dragon's blood but not how to reproduce his Deluminator (*SS* 103; *DH* 125).

This extrapolation partly explains why some wizards and witches still need to go to work but not why some of them seem to live in want. Somehow significant class divisions persist even though magic should have eased at least the starkest disparities. The class divisions of Rowling's magical society are most obvious in the juxtaposition of the Malfoys as a caricature of the rich and the Weasleys of the poor. Although Ron was not, as Draco Malfoy derisively sings, "BORN IN A BIN" (*OP* 409), the Weasley home—suggestively named the Burrow—is likened to a "large stone pigpen" with rooms piled on so that it "looked as though it were held up as magic" (*CS* 32). While the Malfoys use their inherited wealth to buy friends and influence Ministers (*GF* 101), the Weasleys must empty their bank vault just to buy secondhand educational necessities for their children (*CS* 57). In summary, they "were very nice and extremely poor" (*PA* 9)—perhaps unfairly described as the "epitome of working class" (Clifton 71). Given Arthur's job, the Weasleys should "belong to the middle class," as Julia Park identifies, "but with the taint of too little money and too many children" (186).

In most cases, there is a ready magical solution to their problems that is simply ignored. Their home is always crowded and "cramped" (*CS* 33), as if they have run out of magic to attach extra rooms or passed some sort of bandwidth cap for magical use. Why not use Enlargement or Extension

Charms, as in the case of their magically expanded flying car (66), their borrowed camping tent (*GF* 80), or Hermione Granger's capacious beaded purse (*DH* 162)? Ron's bed has inexplicably "rusty," "creaking" bedsprings (94)—just one of a plethora of minor discomforts that one would not have expected magical people to have to bear but that exist to continually mark their poverty. We are told that the Weasleys "usually wore long robes in varying states of shabbiness" (*GF* 40), even though chairs can be materialized out of thin air (*PA* 228; *OP* 139; *HBP* 615), and Hermione can produce a convincing replica of Slytherin's bejeweled golden locket in a matter of seconds (*DH* 263). Ron Weasley's pajamas perpetually show too much leg (*GF* 335), and much is made of the embarrassment of his having to wear feminine, out-of-style, secondhand robes to the Triwizard Ball, which he can only slightly alter by magic: "He used a Severing Charm on the ruff and cuffs. It worked fairly well; at least he was now lace-free, although he hadn't done a very neat job, and the edges still looked depressingly frayed" (411). Inexplicable limitations consign Ron to public humiliation because magic can only achieve, at best, the effect of a pair of dull scissors. The shame of appearing poor is accepted as the way things are—posited as a problem that only *gold* can solve, not magic. For good reason, Ron angrily declares, "I hate being poor" (546).[10]

The Weasleys' hypervisible poverty is also inscribed on their bodies as shabbiness and uncleanliness. On our first meeting Ron, he has an embarrassing spot on his nose (*SS* 98). The family travels by Floo powder, which seems fiscally and hygienically irresponsible compared to other magical modes of travel, such as Side-Along-Apparition.[11] We are again reminded of their poverty when Molly scrapes the bottom of the powder pot (*CS* 47), portraying them as too poor to keep well stocked with their equivalent of train fare.[12] As with the enslaved Dobby's filthy pillowcase, the "mark of the house-elf's enslavement" (177), which the Malfoys have him wear presumably to make his situation especially abject (compared to the very clean Hogwarts house-elves [*GF* 376]), Rowling visually marks the Weasleys with dirt, even though there is no reason for magical people to be dirty. Similarly, the cinematic Hagrid is first presented to us with a dirty face, marking him as lower class before he can speak a single word of his broken English. In addition to shabby and patched clothing (*PA* 74), Remus Lupin's poverty is also marked by the dust on his belongings. As he uses magic to bring his kettle to a boil, he obtains teabags from a "dusty tin" (154). One wonders why his poverty would prevent him from saying one word to clean the tin. As Beth

Sutton-Ramspeck ably catalogs, the series is vastly inconsistent about using dirt as a signifier (59). While ridiculing Aunt Petunia's obsessive cleaning and complimenting Harry's messiness, shabbiness and dirt are deployed across the series as a degrading shorthand for the poor—a convenient class signifier that exploits a stereotype of the poor as unclean.

Such needless degradation reveals "what a rigid, structured world it truly is," reflecting Rowling's "staunchly middle-class worldview" (Park 180). Although Arthur is head of the Misuse of Muggle Artifacts Office, his workplace space is purposefully lacking—"dingy" and "slightly smaller than the broom cupboard" it abuts with, there is "barely room to move around" (*OP* 132). The ministry ought not to be short on room; it just refuses to give people of his rank the dignity of space. Although every window at the ministry is merely a magical illusion, their office does not get a window: "We've asked, but they don't seem to think we need one" (133). We might conjecture that in an office hierarchy that denies them a magical window, there are likely also rules forbidding any employee from magicking themselves a window, more room, or nicer furnishings—an enforced austerity that produces suffering to give cultural meaning to different work titles. Quidditch World Cup tickets, we are told, cost about "a sackful of Galleons" (*GF* 72), and those with "cheaper tickets" must arrive two weeks ahead of the match, ostensibly to avoid "clogging up" Muggle buses and trains (70). Effectively, the policy is a poor tax, requiring those who can least afford it to miss work and pay a camping fee for two additional weeks.[13] Magic is not allowed to equalize conditions.

People like the Weasleys live without because their society chooses to deny them, and this choice is of course an authorial choice. In a 2000 interview, Rowling was asked why the wizarding world relies on money given what they could conjure. Rowling's reply cited magical "rules" that are not named in the books: "There is legislation about what you can conjure and what you can't. Something that you conjure out of thin air will not last. This is a rule I set down for myself early on" ("World Exclusive Interview"). This revisionist solution to one of the series' open questions also fails to answer it, for it can hardly be trouble to reconjure whatever disappears. But if this legislation did exist, Rowling's wizarding society could well be a dystopia: What sort of society would pass legislation explicitly to prevent people from using their magic to create more material equality?

Lindsay Clifton argues that, given magic, "working-class characters hardly seem necessary" but are included to make the novels more relatable and attractive to readers (67), which seems partly the answer. Rowling's magical society is contrived to amplify conditions of austerity, producing a starker class hierarchy than needs to exist in a world with magic, because such class stereotypes quickly and conveniently define characters as "good" or "bad." Rowling marks Harry's good character in contrast to the Malfoys' flagrantly bad one by their responses to the Weasleys. For example, Draco never misses the opportunity for a joke about the Weasleys' poverty, marking him as "bad." In contrast, Harry first forges his relationship with Ron by being sympathetic to Ron's inability to buy snacks (SS 102). In Teare's view, their income disparity also "[allows] Rowling to comment on the difficulties faced by people who don't have enough money to provide their children with the commodities that trigger self-esteem in capitalist culture" (340–41)—discomforts which are only in small part mitigated by Harry's small occasions of generosity. In turn, Harry is established as a "good" character despite his inherited wealth and without having to give any significant amount of it up.[14] Rowling thus invests significant effort in marking out certain sympathetic characters as poor, keeping them in want in the face of copious magical possibilities, but *not* because she wishes to urge her readers against the overuse of technology. Rather, Rowling maintains stark class disparities in order to define her characters through familiar, and problematic, stereotypes.

In addition to helping massage readers' perceptions of her characters, these discomforts that inexplicably exist despite magic also propel plot points, such as when the "crowded" Weasley kitchen leads Harry to be "crammed beside Ginny" for dinner right after a tense moment of reconnection (DH 90). This moment could only happen in this way because both characters are pushed, by the contrivance of a too-small home, into physical proximity. Similarly, in *Goblet of Fire*, Sirius Black proves his godfatherly devotion by living in a cave subsisting largely on rats (521). These hardships are borne even though traveling vast distances through Apparition for proper food under magical disguise and returning to Grimmauld Place to sleep in a proper bed ought to have been quite easy. (The memory of Sirius "crouching in a cave and living on rats" returns to Harry as part of his negative assessment of Professor Slughorn, who enjoyed a "cosseted existence" while evading the Death Eaters by the much more comfortable expediency of staying in unoccupied Muggle homes [HBP 72].) While it is true that Sirius could not take part in guard duty, his suffering while in hiding is greatly exaggerated in order to render it more believable that Harry would think he went to the Department of Mysteries against Dumbledore's orders. Ron sympathizes with how poor Sirius had not "seen daylight for months" (*OP* 183), even though with a bit of Polyjuice Potion, some Transfiguration, or an invisibility cloak, Sirius could have sunbathed every afternoon. Harry also perversely fails to use the magical mirror to contact his godfather, giving Kreacher the opportunity to trick him. There are many more such examples where the characters ignore magic just to foster sympathy for the "good" characters and advance the plot.

Magic is a central premise of the series—the appeal that brings fans to the cash register—but selectively cast aside so that the narrative can unfold in familiarly Muggle ways, with characters grappling with decidedly unmagical inconveniences and hardships. This is perhaps most readily apparent when unnecessary physical suffering is the narrative basis of a large portion of *Deathly Hallows*, in which Harry, Hermione, and Ron go on the hunt for Horcruxes. The book describes the three main characters living roughly for months, pitching a tent in inclement weather and perpetually lacking food— apparently forgetting that Professor Slughorn modeled a very practical way of hiding quite comfortably from Death Eaters in the previous book. They use the same tent from the Quidditch World Cup, described earlier as "an old-fashioned, three-room flat, complete with bathroom and kitchen" (*GF* 80), but which is significantly less well appointed in book seven, where Rowling has them stewing foraged mushrooms in a billycan (*DH* 277).[15] Although they can Apparate anywhere, they seem to choose the coldest and most inhospitable locations so that the elements could "[add] to their troubles" (292). Much emphasis is placed on their lack of food: subsisting on mushrooms, berries, or stale biscuits causes interpersonal tension to mount. They soon discover "that a full stomach meant good spirits; an empty one, bickering and gloom" (287). Ron "sat and brooded over the low food supplies" (288), complaining that his mother could "make good food appear out of thin air" while he "prodded moodily at the lumps of charred, gray fish on his plate" (292), leading to the specious explanation that under the first of the Principal Exceptions to Gamp's Law of Elemental Transfiguration, "it's impossible to make good food out of nothing! You can Summon it if you know where it is, you can transform it, you can increase the quantity if you've already got some—" (293). Their lack of food and warmth is one of the key factors that precipitate Ron's dramatic abandonment, leaving Harry and Hermione emotionally bereft—a precipitous narrative nadir.[16]

Yet this shortage of food and heat is incredible. We could see this contradiction when they run into Ted Tonks and other outlaws making their meal by the same river: all Ted has to do is say *"Accio Salmon,"* and ta-dah: fish (*DH* 294). (Why are Ted et al. even here when magic can transport them continents away?) Furthermore, basic magical education includes training in turning objects into animals, which theoretically offers an endless meat supply (and contradicts the first Principal Exception). Even if we assume that the trio is squeamish about butchering a rabbit they just transfigured out of a hat or that their essential problem is that they just do not know how to cook, their food problem remains poorly outlined. Much is made of the one "unusually good meal" of spaghetti Bolognese and tinned pears (315), acquired when Hermione goes to a supermarket with the Invisibility Cloak. Why is this the only supermarket these adept Apparators go to during their months on the run, and why does she only buy enough for a single meal? They could have acquired a variety of preprepared foods, stowing them in the beaded bag Hermione has charmed to be of infinite capacity and zero weight. If one could "increase the quantity if you've already got some" (293), why is one of each item not sufficient forever? As for warmth, Hermione produces blue fires, but, for some reason, they are never enough for them to actually be warm.

This is not about wise technological restraint: it seems more likely that Rowling refuses to let her characters actually use the magic that she invented for them simply because she could not imagine a way to write a compelling story otherwise. When Ron rants about having "nothing to eat and freezing [his] backside off every night," Harry retorts that his "expectations" for the adventure were skewed if he had been expecting to "[stay] in five-star hotels" and find Horcruxes "every other day" (*DH* 306, 307). In fact, they could have significantly decreased their discomfort, but just as the ministry chooses to not give Arthur a window, the author refuses them food and heat—because indeed, it would not have lived up to our readerly expectations if they had stayed at a five-star hotel and found a Horcrux every other day.

A Work Ethic in the Context of Magic

What, after all, is a work ethic in the context of magic? Consider how we would regard someone waving their wand from an uncomfortable, straight-backed chair compared to someone waving their wand from a bed while watching TV. Under our current cultural narratives, the former would appear more hardworking than the latter even if both produced the same amount of product in the same amount of time. In these two scenarios, the former registers as more hardworking because they are suffering; the latter's lack of suffering is somehow less work-like. To Rowling, it seems that proper work has to involve some degree of suffering and the willingness to bear with such, even if that suffering were—as in this hypothetical—not inherently tied to the work, which in both cases is wand waving. To have cultural value, it seems that work must be undesirable and unpleasant—something one exerts oneself to do day after day by feats of mental and physical discipline. This is evidenced by her distinction between the deserving poor (the Weasleys, Remus) and the Gaunts, Mundunguses, and Aberforths of the wizarding world: the former "work hard," while the latter do not.

On the extreme end of the "undeserving" are the male Gaunts, who live in dire want. They have no qualms about using magic for even "frivolous" tasks; it is their misogyny that keeps them living in squalor. The Gaunts' revolting home is "more indescribably filthy than anywhere Harry had ever seen" (HBP 363). The windows are "thick with grime" (201), "the ceiling was thick with cobwebs, the floor coated in grime; moldy and rotting food lay upon the table amidst a mass of crusted pots" (363). Ironically, Marvolo's favorite insult for Muggles and Mudbloods is to describe them as "filthy" (205); his overfocus on blood "purity" is ridiculed by his failure to notice the real filth in his environs. Morfin is a "man in rags" with "hair so matted with dirt it could have been any color" (201), while Merope, Voldemort's mother-to-be, is just "a little cleaner than the two men" (205). They expect Merope, because female, to perform all the housework—and she cannot. Crippled by abuse, she struggles to even set a pot down correctly so that it tumbles to the floor, for which she is excoriated by her father for not using magic to do the work: "Grub on the floor like some filthy Muggle, what's your wand for, you useless sack of muck?" (205). They live in filth because the males will not and the female cannot use magic.[17]

Although certainly not intended as a model of wise magical restraint, Mundungus Fletcher also inexplicably abstains from using magic to reduce his material want. Rowling portrays him as a character who fails to value middle-class standards of hygiene and presentation because he is unwilling to work *properly*. Despite the many cleaning spells that exist, Mundungus is always "dirty" (*DH* 46), reeking of "stale sweat and tobacco smoke" and "a strong smell of mingled drink" (*DH* 220; *OP* 22), with "matted" and "straggly" hair (*DH* 220; *OP* 22), an unshaven face (*OP* 22), and "robes stained" (*DH* 220)—so unkempt as to be mistaken for a "pile of rags" at one point (*OP* 81). A wizard surely does not need to spend the night before the Quidditch World Cup under "a cloak propped on sticks" (*GF* 151). A small-time criminal who hawks Class C Non-Tradeable Substances and cauldrons that have fallen off the back of brooms (*OP* 171, 20), Mundungus is described by Molly as someone "[who's] never done an honest day's work in their lives" (*HBP* 85). White-collar labor within the institutionalized confines of a wage system (and an unfair one, considering the Weasleys' straits) positions her family as "honest" laborers. Mundungus is arguably quite industrious—he never lets a "good business opportunity" pass (*OP* 23)—but his kind of labor does not count as evidence of a good work ethic.

Consider lastly the more sympathetic Aberforth Dumbledore, owner of the Hog's Head—a tavern described as "one small, dingy, and very dirty room that smelled strongly of something that might have been goats" (*OP* 335). "The bay windows [are] so encrusted with grime that very little daylight [can] permeate the room," and the stone floor is buried "beneath what seemed to be the accumulated filth of centuries" (335). Given how easy magic could make cleaning, the only possible reason someone would operate a business in such filth must be by choice. While Aberforth does use a magical till (337), sparing himself the effort of manually opening the register, he fails to use magic for its many other obvious possibilities. Paradoxically, he is repeatedly described as engaging in manually wiping bar glasses but, unfortunately for the patrons of his establishment, "with a rag so filthy it looked as though it had never been washed" (338). Aberforth's contradictory relationship with cleaning echoes the texts' depiction of him as both negative (prone to tempestuous fisticuffs; unlearned and possibly illiterate; inferior to Albus) and positive (devoted to his sister; fights against Voldemort). There is some will, effort, and labor—but little of it seems to produce the socially acceptable result.

Poverty also exists in the wizarding world so that Rowling can manipulate readers' sympathies for and against certain characters based on her standard of who is "deserving" because they "work hard" enough. The Gaunts represent the polar end of a spectrum on which the Weasleys, Remus, Mundungus, and Aberforth are all placed; all are "dirty" and suspect, and the undeserving do not labor in ways that count.

The Aesthetics of Nonhuman Labor

Despite how important "hard work" apparently remains, not everyone in magical society shares its burdens equally. All manual, menial labor is optional, but in *Harry Potter*, certain bodies are not allowed to escape it. And because it is manual and menial, even as they perform the work that is deemed to count as hard and honest, these bodies are, to a certain degree, humiliated by their work.

To create the aesthetic of a low-tech world, Rowling's magical society exploits animals for physical labor. Farah Mendlesohn calls the series "a lament for Old England, for the values of the shires and for a 'greener' and simpler world" (166), a nostalgic preindustrial pastorality produced in large part by visible animal labor.[18] Although bewitching objects to work on their own is as easy as saying a magic word or two, Rowling peppers her magical society with animals because they lend their ennobling organicity to the labor. Compared to yoked oxen, a tractor lacks charm. The trains of the Underground or the conveyor belts of the postal service appear a soulless way to move people and mail. The Hogwarts carriages could surely be charmed to pull themselves, for example, but are instead pulled by winged skeletal horses. Although their labor is at first invisible, the thestrals' part in the annual ritual becomes hypervisible when much emphasis is placed on Harry finally being able to see (and ride) them in *Order of the Phoenix*.

Oakes particularly praises owl post as the "best example" of how Rowling's magical people limit their use of magic to what she considers to be a healthy, admirable degree (121): surely others must "yearn for the simplicity and directness of which Harry can be assured when he says, 'Hedwig, take this to Hagrid'" (122). Yet owl post is not actually more "simple" or "direct" than an email app, which delivers mail instantaneously. In reaching her romantic conclusions, Oakes also discounts the many textual examples of ways in which owls can be unreliable and inefficient mail carriers. You need to purchase or rent an owl, you might have one that is old and feeble and regularly "[collapses] on a delivery" (*CS* 30), that encounters foul weather and gets injured (*SS* 194), that bites (*PA* film), or that you have to cajole (*GF* 37), or you might have your mail "intercepted" (*OP* 278). In the Ministry of Magic, interoffice mail was initially delivered by owls, but they made such a "mess" with their droppings that they were replaced by charmed paper airplanes (*OP* 130). Nonhuman animal labor was the first choice when charmed objects would easily do; they were replaced with nonanimal solutions only when their organicity became inconvenient. Owl post is neither "simple" nor especially "direct"; it is aesthetically but not functionally superior.

What actually seems to motivate Oakes's position is the fact that Rowling's use of living animals would give a more pleasing user experience: "Even if it is human-to-owl face, it still provides witches and wizards with the links to living beings of which we are often deprived in our existence overflowing with email, pager, and voicemail messages" (122). Nonhuman labor appears less impersonal and more charming and rustic, harkening to a romanticized time when there was no alternative but to exploit animal labor. The potential for inefficiency aside, there is also the unacknowledged and extremely casual cruelty of magical animal exploitation, as owls are subjected to the elements and often carry letters or heavy packages tied to their legs or in their beaks, forbidding eating or drinking. Early in the series, we see how Hagrid, generally considered a champion of magical-animal welfare, uses owl mail: he "rolled up the note, gave it to the owl, which clamped it in its beak, went to the door, and threw the owl out into the storm. Then he came back and sat down as though this was as normal as talking on the telephone" (SS 52).[19] Throwing a living being out into the storm illustrates the ethical problems of using nonhuman animals as technologies, which Harry Potter entirely ignores: the animals that serve as technologies are treated worse than most of us treat our cell phones.[20] Poor old Errol, the Weasley family owl, nearly dies in several deliveries, and each collapse is treated as comical as the impoverished Weasleys attempt to squeeze the most value from their owl purchase. Harry Potter's magical society persists in sending physical mail by slow means, using up quills and parchment (both animal products) and ignoring the fact that the series has clearly efficient alternatives to using animals (Patronuses, Floo powder, Apparition).

Magical house-elves, too, are unnecessarily put to work, leading Sheltrown to ask, "Why does the wizarding community rely on the indentured servitude of house-elves rather than leveraging labor by magic?" (58).[21] As per my preceding discussion, it is largely because the existence of a nonhuman underclass serves Harry Potter's character and plot building. But within the logic of the world Rowling built, their function barely makes sense. It is unclear why "elf labor is needed at all in the basement [of Hogwarts], when we know that (for instance) dishes can wash themselves and put themselves away with a flick of the wand" (Dendle 167).

Though they are powerfully magical, house-elves are paradoxically forbidden to use magic to perform the work for which they have been bred and reared. The Malfoys seem to have used Dobby to shine shoes, but they inexplicably do not replace him after he is freed, suggesting that they did not need him to do much after all. (Is Narcissa washing her own dishes? Is Lucius drying?) Hepzibah Smith's old house-elf Hokey carries tea trays, and Winky appears to have been mostly used to serve as warden to her master's son, Barty Crouch Jr. At Hogwarts, where we see the happiest elves, about a hundred of them cook the meals, mop the floors, dust the shelves, warm the beds, and light the fires, apparently *manually*. It particularly defies sense that Hogwarts, a place so suffused with magic that it causes any Muggle technology to go "haywire" (*GF* 548), is inexplicably serviced by a staff that cannot use magic.[22]

Yet we, like the characters, see very little of their labor. Rowling raises the point—the invisibility of their labor is in part what enables their exploitation (*GF* 182)—then completely undercuts it by also rendering their labor nearly invisible. The little work we do see seems manual but not terribly arduous: scurrying house-elves carry things, peppering their service with much "beaming, bowing, and curtsying" (376). They seem to take advantage of only one magical technology, and it exists to enable their work's invisibility—the magic tables that deliver the food up to the tables in the Great Hall. Ironically, this convenient technology deprives them of the satisfaction they might derive from seeing the pleasure of diners or receiving compliments and gratitude. Hokey is also described physically carrying boxes in a way that, as is typical for house-elves, obscures her service: in the Pensieve, Harry "saw two leather boxes, one on top of the other, moving across the room as if of their own volition, though he knew the tiny elf was holding them over her head as she wended her way between tables, pouffes, and footstools" (*HBP* 435–36). Although allowed to use magic to lock away the boxes with "the usual enchantments" (438), it does not seem that Hokey would have been allowed to magic the boxes over—something that Hepzibah herself could have also easily done. At Professor Slughorn's Christmas party, house-elves carry trays of food by hand, "obscured by the heavy silver platters of food they were bearing, so that they looked like little roving tables" (315). The party is a *party* because certain special people are invited to enjoy this manual labor, performed just under the surface for their benefit.[23] By portraying house-elf work as largely a matter of item delivery, Rowling glorifies the idea of service—menial labor, cheerfully performed, by one subclass for a superior class.

Love's Menial Labors

According to Oakes, the way that *Harry Potter*'s housewives use magic to have dishes wash themselves rather than have them become "instantly clean" is another example of the author wisely modeling technological restraint (120)—which is an odd distinction. If the point of cleaning is to have clean things, what purpose does it serve for the dishes to be *seen* to wash themselves as opposed to becoming instantly clean? The answer is the spectacle.

Unlike house-elves, housewives are free to use as much magic as they want. Molly's array of cookbooks (*Charm Your Own Cheese*, *Enchantment in Baking*, and *One Minute Feasts—It's Magic!*) embraces magical expediencies (*CS* 34), and she can buy self-peeling sprouts and self-stirring cauldrons (*SS* 71), even if it is odd that the Weasleys would buy these upgrades when all it takes is a wand to power their mechanical mangle to "[turn] of its own accord" (*DH* 87). Yet despite all this potential automation, Molly is still always shown on her feet, physically laboring. Most of the books have at least one scene where Molly is cooking in a theatrical, complicated way, nearly always with the inclusion of her manually doing something other than waving her wand so that she performs her mothering in a way that registers as "hard work." Given the long history of erasing or undervaluing the housework that has been assigned to female bodies, it could be seen as feminist to make such a spectacle of her cooking. However, these performances of struggle are a transparently weak way of communicating the message that mothering is hard work, especially in the context of magic making all this exertion superfluous. The mother appears to be working hard largely for the sake of being *seen* to be working hard.

Let us consider some of this dinner theater in more detail. In *Chamber of Secrets*, an annoyed Molly is described as "clattering around, cooking breakfast a little haphazardly" (34): she manually throws sausages into the frying pan and manually serves them but "flicked her wand casually at the dishes in the sink, which began to clean themselves, clinking gently in the background" (34). The manual portions of the cooking are largely a way for her to vent her angry feelings by "clattering around" (34), making noise. She is annoyed because the boys stole the flying car to rescue Harry from the Dursleys, and angrily cooking a delicious meal is a passive-aggressive attempt to discipline her errant children: the message is *I am cooking for you even though you do not deserve it*. When she hears that the Dursleys had been "starving" him, she interrupts a series of magical steps to manually cut and butter bread for Harry, "with a slightly softened expression" (35). Her manual buttering of the bread is unnecessary both because of magic and Harry's own perfectly functional hands; the point is, of course, for Molly to exert herself so that the act fully registers as an act of motherly love. In manually buttering, she performs special labor just for him. Ultimately, it is not the work that matters but the willingness to exert and the performance of the exertion: to love is to be willing to do the manual work for another, and to be loved is to receive such menial service and *know* it.

Each time Harry and Molly reunite, she performs a variation of the same scene. In *Half-Blood Prince*, as soon as she sees him, Molly checks over how much he has grown and asks, of course, if he is hungry. She uses magic to "[rap] a large iron pot with her wand. It bounced onto the stove with a loud clang and began to bubble at once" (*HBP* 83). Then "she tapped the pot again; it rose into the air, flew toward Harry, and tipped over," at which critical moment Molly "slid a bowl neatly beneath it just in time to catch the stream of thick, steaming onion soup" (83). Linking a string of clauses by semicolons, the magical details extend the amount of text that would ordinarily be devoted to warming some soup, giving a mother's work positive attention. This time, she uses magic to slice the bread: "She waved her wand over her shoulder; a loaf of bread and a knife soared gracefully onto the table; as the loaf sliced itself and the soup dropped back onto the stove, Molly sat down opposite him" (83). As long as some small fraction of the cooking and serving is performed manually—it does not matter what—the entire magical orchestra is appropriately rendered a motherly act of laborious love.

For Molly to be presented as an ideal mother, she must be seen manually performing at least some of the work—and always already on the edge of overload. In *Goblet of Fire*, the twins misbehave yet again, and Molly once again cooks with annoyed pomp, "pointing her wand a little more vigorously than she had intended at a pile of potatoes in the sink, which shot out of their skins so fast that they ricocheted off the walls and ceilings," causing a bit of a mess (58). Speedily she proceeds to "[direct] her wand at a dustpan, which hopped off the sideboard and started skating across the floor, scooping up the potatoes" (58)—each sentence a chain of clauses that emphasizes every step of the work as an elaborate production. She then manually "slammed a large copper saucepan down on the kitchen table" (58)—again using the manual aspect to express her frustration—"and began to wave her wand around inside it. A creamy sauce poured from the wand tip as she stirred" (58). As the composition continues, she "poked" with her wand to light the stove, and "jabbed" her wand to open the cutlery drawer and direct knives to chop the rescued potatoes (58). She again resorts to using her own hands to "pull out still more saucepans"—just so she can be described as "putting down her wand" and mistakenly picking up her sons' fake wand (59), introducing yet more orchestrated chaos into the kitchen scene. Every dinner is always near ruin as if to insist that the work remains "hard" despite magic.

While "the mark of a good house-elf" is "that you don't know it's there" (GF 182), the opposite holds true for a housewife: she is marked as "good" by her hypervisible labor. Donning a "flowered apron with a wand sticking out of the pocket" (CS 33), Molly is proffered as a figure that relies quite a bit on magic but can still satisfy the traditional concept of a mother: one who dedicates herself to all other members of the household. Just as the trio must suffer discomfort while hunting Horcruxes, Molly cannot be in apparent leisure, sitting on an armchair eating snacks while the chores perform themselves. Even if the sprouts are peeling themselves, she must still be "[keeping] watch" over them (HBP 131). All the meals are home-cooked, just as every Christmas she makes "hand-knitted" sweaters and "homemade" treats (SS 200).[24] A small inclusion of manual labor—even opening a drawer by hand rather than wand—redeems the whole highly magical effort, rendering the mother's offering "handmade" or "homemade," with all the positive connotations that that entails: tangible evidence of a mother's willingness to devote her time and energy to tedious, repetitive labor for her family.

As Jeanne Hoeker LaHaie notes, the Weasley children are shown to be motivated to obey Molly not out of fear but because "they do not wish to make their mother unhappy, and they willingly do what she tells them to do in order to be restored to her good graces" (133). This guilt-fueled obedience is produced by their mother's hypervisible labor. Yet this gendered work is generally taken for granted and only occasionally appreciated, such as when, in the last book, "Harry watched as she waved her wand near the washing line, and the damp clothes rose into the air to hang themselves up, and suddenly he felt a great wave of remorse for the inconvenience and the pain he was giving her" (DH 110). She had lugged a "large basket of laundry in her arms ... pausing to lean against the henhouse. She looked exhausted" (109). In this scene, she carries the large and presumably heavy basket manually, and even though the clothes are hanging themselves up, Molly is still on her feet performing the chores, wiping the proverbial brow sweat so that the good protagonist can have a moment of guilty, character-building gratitude. The Weasley twins experience a similar pang when, having established a successful joke-shop business in *Half-Blood Prince*, they gift their mother a diamond-studded hat and "a spectacular golden necklace": "We find we appreciate you more and more, Mum, now that we're washing our own socks" (339). If mothering labor did not appear difficult, would such gratitude be produced?

The cultural value of labor is what motivates all this sweat and toil: the animals, house-elves, and mothers are not *allowed* to stop working manually or to overly indulge in the "easy out" provided by technology. This is not, as McKibben and others worry, because of the tragic loss of an individual sense of achievement amidst competition and not because of a fear of the atrophy of valuable skills; when it comes to tedious, anyone-can-do-it type of labor, the stakes differ. Ironically, because the work itself is devalued—unimpressively menial and quotidian—it gains great value on the performative level, its very undesirability and avoidability rendering its performance a noble sacrifice. This is especially the case when the work is performed for others' benefit. Sutton-Ramspeck notes that "there is more to cleaning in *Harry Potter* than obsessiveness, drudgery, and humiliation" because it "can be connected to love . . . and resistance" (72). In my reading, the cleaning communicates the love *because* it is—according to *Harry Potter*—humiliating.

Everyone recognizes that having to perform this kind of work is a punishment. School detentions, for example, often consist of doing menial work without magic. What are lines if not tedious manual labor? The boys also face punishments such as polishing the trophy-room silver with "elbow grease" and scrubbing bedpans in the hospital wing *"without magic!"* (*CS* 118; *PA* 173). This work is seen as the domain of the lower class—what Draco would call "servant stuff" (*SS* 250). Snape derides Sirius's contributions to the Order as being mere "cleaning" (*OP* 83), and he has Wormtail manually serve drinks and clean his house just to degrade him in front of Narcissa and Bellatrix—regarding which Wormtail complains, "I am not your servant!" (*HBP* 24). When Molly declares that the kids can help the Order by cleaning the headquarters, they grouse because it is work that they all recognize as demeaning. Ron grumbles that house chores make him "feel like a house-elf" (*OP* 159); he considers his mother's labor the lot of a nonhuman subclass born, bred, and enslaved for drudgery. The boys in particular understand that they are consigned to it because they are not yet of age, not yet men; unlike the girls, they expect to grow out of such work except to offer occasional assistance (such as the various examples of Arthur taking part in, for example, supervising the magical knives [82]). For the most part, in Rowling's worldview, the males will be the (grateful) recipients of the daily manual labor of others. As their gendered lot is to perform love through self-sacrificing, necessary, grand feats of heroism, they will be spared the responsibility of performing love through self-sacrificing, unnecessary, menial exertions.

To emphasize how much of Molly's household labor is unnecessary exertion, we can see that when male characters perform some of it—not as their usual job but to help out—they are never frazzled or challenged. In contrast to Molly's frenetic style, they rely much more on magic and do not seem particularly concerned about overuse. In *Goblet of Fire*, Bill and Charlie are tasked to set up the table and take the opportunity to turn work into play, "making two battered old tables fly high above the lawn, smashing into each other, each attempting to knock the other's out of the air" (60). A table leg is broken and instantly repaired in time to serve "dishes and dishes of Molly's excellent cooking" (60). Similarly, when Dumbledore offers to help Professor Slughorn clear up the huge mess he made of the Muggle house he occupies, it is both a display of magical efficiency and, as Dumbledore declares in the sixth movie, "fun." With "one identical sweeping motion" of their wands, "the furniture flew back to its original places; ornaments reformed in midair, feathers zoomed into their cushions; torn books repaired themselves as they landed upon their shelves; oil lanterns soared onto side tables and reignited; a vast collection of splintered silver picture frames flew glittering across the room and alighted whole and untarnished, upon a desk; rips, cracks, and holes healed everywhere, and the walls wiped themselves clean" (*HBP* 65). Although they are not, as in my earlier hypothetical, relaxing on cushions, the two men not only do not appear to exert themselves but actually enjoy cleaning up. For them, it is apparently not necessary to perform a fraction of it without magic nor to appear to nearly fail to coordinate all the moving parts.[25]

The reality is that in this world, all manual labor is unnecessary and could become a form of play, performed in the style of the male characters—instantly, easily, and without stress—but Rowling's magical society still has animals, house-elves, and mothers *choosing* to perform manual work and suffering for it for the affective spectacle. Despite her indefatigable efforts at cleaning up Grimmauld Place, even conscripting the kids to help, Molly never quite wins the "war on the house" (*OP* 117): it takes Sirius's effort, in the course of what sounds like less than a week's time, to transform the hellscape home into a place "barely recognizable" and ready for the holidays (501), suggesting that males would be able to best women even in these traditionally feminine areas should they be moved to bestir themselves.[26]

There is a noteworthy exception of a male character performing "unnecessary" manual labor without magic: Dobby's burial. After Dobby's tragic death, Harry shows that he has learned the lesson: that the performance of menial manual labor can be a gift of love. He wants to "do it properly" (*DH* 478)—that is, to dig the grave by hand.[27] This rare moment—wherein the text explicitly tells us that he could have used magic but *chooses* not to—also details his exertion to maximum effect and presents his choice as a sacrifice: "He dug with a kind of fury, relishing the manual work, glorying in the nonmagic of it, for every drop of his sweat and every blister felt like a gift to the elf who had saved their lives" (478). The repetitive, physical nature of the work is therapeutic, as it allows him to process "the things that had happened [and] heard . . . , and understanding blossomed in the darkness" (479). Despite how productive the experience is for him, however, he is so taken up with the idea that his labor is an unusual, uncalled-for, and excessive "gift" that he even (incorrectly) expects to have to defend his choice to others: "Harry had his retort ready for when they asked him why he had not simply created a perfect grave with his wand" (479). The line describing his preemptive shame exists more to exaggerate his sacrifice as there is no textual reason why he should have expected to be chastised or shamed for not using magic. (The only character to ever be chastised for not using magic in the series is Merope.) In fact, the others readily take up shovels of their own. Harry uses magic to inscribe the tombstone, but Rowling then takes pains to make it seem like it was practically, *affectively*, low-tech because Harry did it so poorly: "Slowly, under murmured instruction, deep cuts appeared upon the rock's surface. He knew that Hermione could have done it more neatly, and probably more quickly, but he wanted to mark the spot as he had wanted to dig the grave" (481). The text compares his inefficiency against Hermione's competence in an apparently unfavorable light—his spellwork is slower and messier—only to then celebrate his deficiencies as proof of his exertions for Dobby. This instance of magical use is painstakingly elaborated to lend solemnity to the occasion, producing the same impression of self-sacrificing labor as the texts do with every belabored example of Molly's cooking.

Yet the animals, house-elves, and housewives must do degrading manual work all the time, giving the "gift" of sweat and blisters day-to-day to keep others' lives replete with the homemade and handmade. Their willingness to labor without magic *as a regular practice* then confers onto privileged bodies the freedom to use magical technology without fearing overuse. Aside from the rare exception, privileged bodies only need to be *part* of a society that has some bodies doing things by hand. So long as some are working in a way that we have coded to count as "hard work," a society can allay their fears and continue to feel masters of, rather than mastered by, advanced technologies.

Conclusion

Rowling's characters inhabit a world that is more allegory than alternative and certainly no utopia. To the extent that her "good" characters model the traits and behaviors that some of us would like to see regained or preserved, it is not her version of magic that enables this. Yet many *Harry Potter* readers have insisted on distinguishing Rowling's magic from our technology, perhaps because of their own deep need to feel that something could exist that could stand against the technology that is, in our lives, all but impossible to give up.

The seven-part saga relies on the charm and appeal of wondrous magic to attract its audience only to conclude the story with the hero's surprisingly low-tech solution. In writing the climactic final face-off of the ill-fated pair, Rowling manages to produce the conditions that allow Harry to kill Voldemort using only his "signature move": Expelliarmus (*DH* 71). In this scene, Harry has good reason to believe that he is the true master of the Elder Wand, so by casting a disarming spell, Harry effectively makes Voldemort kill himself.[28] Voldemort, who "overconsumes the Horcruxes to the point of becoming posthuman" (Nguyen 210), is contrasted against the restrained hero, who resists the temptation of the Elder Wand and would not even wield Avada Kedavra against his worst enemy.

To set up for this scene, the beginning of *Deathly Hallows* has Remus chastise Harry for using Expelliarmus, dubbing it his "signature" spell for the first time in the series and implying that it is a weak choice, "close to suicidal!" (71).[29] But Expelliarmus is, arguably, one of the most powerful spells of all. To divest another from the one technology that they need to make their magic work well is to effectively reduce a magical person to someone who cannot even turn on the lights, much less fight back. Expelliarmus is an apt metaphor for *Harry Potter*'s attitude toward magical technology: the Disarming Charm makes *others* put down their wands while holding onto one's own. We should be wary of the pastoral idealization of the "hardships" and "toil" of a simpler life—the relishing of the handmade and homemade or the magical—and of assuming that such would serve as a bulwark against a technologically advanced life. I am not against technological restraint but wary of the moralistic and classist discourses underpinning many of these calls and of the ways in which certain bodies seem to be marked for certain kinds of manual labor over others. Despite his dramatic rejection of some powerful technologies, Harry is no champion of Luddites—nor does he plan to take up a life of daily menial manual exertion to live like an animal, house-elf, or housewife. The hero will not put down his own wand; he is merely ready to make others put down their wands.

CHAPTER 5

THE CHOSEN ONE

The Limits of Self-Determination in *Harry Potter*

> He watched the cat in his mirror. It was now reading the sign
> that said Privet Drive—no, *looking* at the sign; cats couldn't
> read maps *or* signs. . . . Was this normal cat behavior?
>
> —SORCERER'S STONE

> It is our choices, Harry, that show what we truly are, far more
> than our abilities.
>
> —CHAMBER OF SECRETS

In the opening pages of *Sorcerer's Stone*, Vernon Dursley—the self-proclaimed
authority on normativity—attempts to experience a "perfectly normal" morning but is interrupted by an uncanny encounter with a cat (4). "The first sign
of something peculiar," and our first hint that this novel will feature fantastical elements, is "a cat reading a map" (2)—the cat being the transfigured
Minerva McGonagall in disguise. Initially, Vernon "didn't realize what he
had seen," quickly performs a double take, and dismisses what he saw as a
"trick of the light" (2, 3). Looking again, he sees the cat now reading the street
sign—but "no," he corrects himself, the cat is merely "*looking* at the sign; cats
couldn't read maps *or* signs" (3). In this encounter, Vernon sees the cat reading

but does not "realize" it. We might say that because he refuses to recognize what he sees as a possibility, what he sees cannot become reality. He tries to shoo the cat away, to disappear what he refuses to realize, and is further discomfited when "it just gave him a stern look" (6). Attempting to process this experience, Vernon asks himself: "Was this normal cat behavior?" (6).

Vernon's obtuse refusal to abide by anything abnormal—from cats that read to "people who dress in funny clothes" to his nephew's magic (*SS* 3)—highlights how we read each other through cultural norms. Implicit in Vernon's question—*Is this normal?*—is the question of how other normal people, as he imagines them, would evaluate the situation. The query is not particularly reflective or introspective: it will take but a moment's assessment, experienced more as an intuitive feeling about his imagined community of fellow normals. We can also expect that for Vernon, the answer will be a clear-cut yes or no, allowing for no shades of gray. Under such a worldview, woe betide the abnormal—that which cannot be permitted to be treated as if it exists. Presenting Harry Potter as an abnormal boy who is pitifully oppressed by the aggressively conformist Dursleys, Rowling's messaging appears to beg for the acceptance of bodies and identities that defy mainstream norms. The series is replete with flagrantly boundary-blurring figures—legendary chimeras, animalized plants, plantified humans, animated objects, and shapeshifters—that are, at least to the degrees discussed in my previous chapter, accepted and valued by the series' heroes. A good person, we are told, looks beyond appearances and transcends societal prejudices to recognize who someone chooses to be.

In *Undoing Gender* (2004), Judith Butler queries the extent to which one's gender can truly be one's own. While gender is something that one *does*, it is experienced as something that one *is*—whether that is presumed to be the product of nature or nurture—and something one *has*, which could presumably be altered or lost (as implied by the term "emasculation"). The claims we make as a matter of course (to ourselves, to others) about what and therefore who we are give rise to the collective illusion that we each have the autonomy to name and define ourselves and thus to expect and even demand that others recognize us in the ways we wish. Yet "the terms that make up one's own gender" (Butler 1)—as well as, I would posit, any other aspect of one's self-identity—are "outside oneself, beyond oneself" (1), "dependent from the start on conditions that none of us author at will" and that have "no single author" (101, 1). Our ability to identify ourselves in any particular way (as a woman, as human, as tall, etc.) is contingent both on the appearance and constitution of one's body and on how that body is read by others. The way others read our bodies is, in turn, shaped and constrained by these preexisting terms and conditions. We attain a sense of "our" gender "to the extent that social norms exist that support and enable that act of claiming gender for oneself" (7). These shared norms are ever evolving as well: as we debate them and perform/misperform them, all of us participate continually in shaping and reshaping these norms. (Those with more cultural and/or institutional clout—say, someone like Rowling—have more impact.)

This is the "paradox of autonomy": that "we must be part of a larger social fabric of existence in order to create who we are" (Butler 100–101). We are necessarily dependent on existing norms to conceive and constitute ourselves, faced with the choice of either aspiring to be intelligible by attempting to meet those terms—to take refuge under these "sheltering norms" even as they evolve or fail to evolve (34)—or coping with the "estrangement" that follows from failing to be realized—alienation, exclusion, and mistreatment and perhaps even "threatened with unviability, with becoming undone altogether" (3). The more fundamental to self-conception the identifier in question is, the larger the stakes—one might be disadvantaged about not being recognized as tall in a society that favors the tall; one might be destroyed when not recognized as a "real" woman; one might be killed if not recognized as human. It might mean not being permitted "to breathe, to desire, to love, and to live" and, more extremely, "to court death" (8, 34). For Butler, the issue is to reconceive of justice as "also [concerning] consequential decisions about what a person is, and what social norms must be honored and expressed for 'personhood' to become allocated, how we do or do not recognize animate others as persons depending on whether or not we recognize a certain norm manifested in and by the body of that other" (58).

This chapter focuses on the way appearances shape and limit how any individual can conceive of their identity and to what extent that individual is able to control how their identity is read by others. The magical boundary blurring of *Harry Potter* offers an avenue for exploring the tension between an individual's self-image and appearance and their society's willingness to confirm or accept such autonomy. The chapter begins by discussing how Rowling glorifies the concept of self-determination—the right, if not the duty, to choose who one is—a liberal message then contradicted by how much of wizarding society systematically limits these choices without textual reproach. Indeed, Molly L. Burt reads Rowling's presentation of hybridity as "hypocritical" (220), arguing that in the series, all the hybrid characters suffer for their hybrid identities. While the diverse and fantastical spectrum of possibilities ostensibly celebrated in *Harry Potter* gestures toward inclusiveness, Rowling reinvests in rigid systems that classify bodies at birth based on factors beyond our individual control. From the limits of self-renaming to choice-eviscerating magical technologies to the suspicion attached to boundary-transgressing figures, the characters' lives are full of restrictions that severely constrain what and who they can be. In a context of near-limitless magical possibility, characters persistently refuse to even consider a wider range of options—possibilities that are effectively unrealizable. Ultimately, in this worldview, others remain the rightful arbiters of our identities.

The Pretense of Choice

According to the series' overt messaging, our choices are the most important determinant of who we are—a power of self-determination capable of defying nature, nurture, and even fate. To convey this message, the texts heavy-handedly deploy a "good" character to declare these views in quotable nuggets and many "bad" mouthpieces to violently espouse opposing ideas—that who we are is determined by our blood, body, or appearance.

If we focus only on what Albus Dumbledore says, the series appears to promote the idea that we can choose who we are. At the end of the second book—immediately after his face-to-face encounter with the man who had tried to kill him at age one—Harry has an identity crisis around the question of whether he is "good." This is one of many one-on-one conversations with Dumbledore, the sage father figure who will lead him, breadcrumb by breadcrumb, on the path to heroic manhood. Harry has just learned that, as a result of the fateful murder attempt, he has "a little bit" of Voldemort in him and is forced to reconsider the Sorting Hat's pronouncement that he should have been in Slytherin House (*CS* 333; *SS* 121). At this significant moment, Dumbledore reassures Harry that he has the power to choose who he is: "It is our choices, Harry, that show what we truly are, far more than our abilities" (*CS* 333). He points to Harry's choice of not joining Slytherin as proof of Harry's power to choose who he is despite external and internal pressures.

Dumbledore continues to be the voice for choice across the series, as at the end of *Goblet of Fire* when he reminds the students that they might soon have to "make a choice between what is right and what is easy" (724). In *Half-Blood Prince*, much is made of the contrast between critical choices made by Harry's and Voldemort's mothers: though both choose to die, Lily Evans is beatified for choosing to die to save her son, while Merope Gaunt is vilified for choosing to die and abandoning her son (262).[1] Dumbledore also devotes a weighty conversation to explain to Harry that "you are free to choose your way, quite free to turn your back" on the prophecy that appears to decree his destiny (512). In *Deathly Hallows*, after choosing to die in order to render Voldemort mortal, Harry sits at an imagined King's Cross for one last conversation, during which Dumbledore emphasizes that it is "up to you" whether to go back to finish the fight—and Harry is understandably surprised that, even at this juncture, "I've got a choice?" (722). This conversation enhances the portrayal of Harry's goodness, bravery, and self-sacrifice as he foregoes his comfort and safety for the sake of others.

To *Harry Potter* readers, the recurring motif of choice is comforting and inspiring. As Harry finds, it can feel like "all the difference in the world": "the difference between being dragged into the arena to face a battle to the death and walking into the arena with your head held high" (*HBP* 512). Feeling autonomy and free will even in the face of a dire magical prophecy empowers Harry to feel like someone with worth, someone who can hold their head with dignity. Having choice in what he does and therefore who he is is empowering—in Rowling's view, it is man making.

In contrast, *Harry Potter*'s consummate evil characters, the Naziesque Death Eaters (Ostry 93; Wente 92), insist that "blood purity" determines who one is and what one is worth. While it seems a contradiction that they worship as their leader someone they should consider impure—Voldemort's father was a Muggle—their willingness can, perhaps, be explained by the Death Eaters' strangely mathematical concept of "blood": they might think that Salazar Slytherin's powerful wizarding blood cancels out Tom Riddle Sr.'s Muggle blood.[2] To their minds, blood is conceivable in terms of fractions and wholes. Those of mixed parentage are described as being "half-and-half" or "half-blood" (*SS* 125; *DH* 257), as if two disparate blood types circulate in their veins in exactly equal amounts from each parent, acting on the body by turns. This (il)logic also presumes that magic is purely hereditary, which, if true, would be a convenient way of keeping power literally in the family. But it is not true: with none of the blood the blood-purists desperately fetishize, Muggle-borns somehow possess magic. The fact that magic can develop spontaneously in Muggles likely motivates the virulence of the anti-Muggle prejudice represented by the "Magic is Might" fountain (*DH* 242), depicting oppressed Muggles literally crushed underfoot.[3] This is surely part of why the Death Eaters amuse themselves with their garish aerial parade of the Roberts family at the Quidditch World Cup campsite (*GF* 120), as well as why "Hogwarts cofounder Salazar Slytherin felt strongly enough . . . to leave behind a basilisk concealed in Hogwarts to kill future students of Muggle parentage" (Wilson 295). To Death Eaters, individual choices are irrelevant: what one's body is, measurable in fractions, is completely conflated with who one is and what one is worth.

The series' next-tier "bad" characters—Rita Skeeter, Cornelius Fudge, and Dolores Umbridge—represent powerful wizarding institutions that espouse the same supremacist views about bodies and "blood." As an influential member of the press, Rita levies her power to call for the "stamping out" of vampires and foments anti-giant sentiment (*GF* 147). Dumbledore rightly accuses Fudge of "[placing] too much importance . . . on the so-called purity of blood!" and "[failing] to recognize that it matters not what someone is born, but what they grow to be!" (708). Though he would not likely be the one to pen the oppressive legislation, Fudge would certainly sign it; his regime has long discriminated against part humans and nonhumans, as discussed in the previous chapter. The sadistic Umbridge is more disturbing still: while she seems to abide half- and perhaps quarter-blood wizards, her animus against the Muggle-born is evident in her zeal to have them stripped of their wands and registered as criminals who stole magic from those she deems to be real wizards.[4] "Wands only choose witches or wizards," she declares to the Muggle-born Mary Cattermole—"You are not a witch" (*DH* 261). Charles D. Wilson conjectures that Umbridge accuses her of stealing a wand not because Umbridge believes it to be true but "to put the Muggle-borns in their place . . . , retroactively imposing a new legal reality on them" (295). Mary would likely conceive of her magical power as something contained in her body—something biological—yet the Muggle-born Registration Commission proves that even a biological "fact" is ultimately contingent on socio-juridical recognition. By legislative fiat, the wizarding powers of book seven systematically distinguish between those bodies that count as magical and those that cannot be real and thereby equal members of a wizard-led society. Like the series' worst characters, these establishment figures believe that individuals can be categorized by their bodies and treated accordingly, leaving little to individual choices and self-concepts.

The importance of intelligibility as magical is particularly vital in this society. Thus, any perceived threats to the hierarchy that privileges magical humans would fuel their drive to shore up the boundaries of their tightly defined circle of who can be included as equally deserving of rights. From Cattermole's garish trial to the beggared people who pitifully plead at Hermione-Bellatrix's feet (*DH* 525), the importance of being legible as a witch/wizard is painfully clear. Even the Muggle-loving Arthur Weasley finds himself saying "nobody *was* hurt" during the Quidditch World Cup Death Eater attack (*GF* 148), wherein a family of Muggles, including young children, were paraded midair, their bodies "contorted into grotesque shapes" (119), and the mother's underwear exposed. The only bodies whose pain truly counts are wizarding bodies.

But magical ability is not enough: magical humans are keenly aware that they are in the minority in a world where feeling, sentient, and powerful non-human creatures abound. The importance of also being legible as "human" is highlighted in the scene where Hermione witnesses how Winky is treated by ministry officials. Ironically, these officials consider themselves to be on the side of good (anti–Death Eater) as they aggressively question Winky regarding the Dark Mark. Repeatedly addressed as "elf" rather than by name, Winky is railroaded by the officials and by the master to whom she remains pathetically loyal (*GF* 136). It is evident that she is treated like this because she is a house-elf and that the wizards in the group share the advantage of operating as if the majority of their peers would agree with and approve of their presumption of species supremacy. Hermione processes what she finds upsetting about the situation with the limited language her society offers:

> "He didn't care how frightened she'd been, or how upset she was—it was like she wasn't even human!"
>
> "Well, she's not," said Ron.
>
> "That doesn't mean she hasn't got feelings, Ron." (139)

Hermione is forced to use an inapt expression to describe the wrong Winky suffers because human vocabulary provides no alternative. Responding to Ron's technically accurate correction, Hermione tacitly clarifies that by "human," she did not mean to refer to a scientific designation based on morphology or genetics. Rather, she uses the term as a shorthand for a being that is recognized as deserving of rights and protections. There is, neither in the Muggle world nor the magical one, no other term. Through this and other scenes, the texts ostensibly criticize those who hold Death Eater and ministry views.

Foolish, too, are those who judge others by how they look. For example, some figures are read as dangerous because of existing cultural norms—to their detriment. In the series' opening zoo scene, Dudley Dursley expects "the largest snake in the place" to behave a certain way and is ready to demand that behavior by tapping on the glass (SS 27). When the snake fails to behave as expected, Dudley dismisses it as boring and walks away. For the zoo animal whose room and board depend on being seen by human zoo-goers, this failure to look dangerous is possibly dangerous to the snake—its habitat is less likely to be invested in compared to more popular attractions, for example. However, for the liberated snake, being read as dangerous could be fatal, and indeed, when it escapes, the "bad" characters willfully fabricate lies about the snake that fit their expectations: "Dudley was telling them how it had nearly bitten off his leg, while Piers was swearing it had tried to squeeze him to death" (29). Harry issues the corrective that "as far as [he] had seen," the snake only "snapped playfully at their heels" (29), but as his opinion is worthless to the Dursleys, it is Dudley's and Piers's readings that are treated as real.

Similarly, we know that Uncle Vernon is wrong as usual when he judges Sirius Black by his picture on television. "No need to tell us *he's* no good," he snorts; all one needs to do is to "look at the state of him" to conclude he is a "filthy layabout," a "maniac," a "lunatic" (PA 17). Rubeus Hagrid's appearance has materially negative consequences, as he is endangered by the aggressive fear of others. Vernon, for one, immediately grabs his rifle (SS 47). In *Chamber of Secrets*, fear of Hagrid leads directly to his wrongful, torturous imprisonment, compounding the injustice he suffered at age thirteen when he was framed and expelled on the word of handsome, normal-sized Tom Riddle. While Hagrid "looked slightly alarming," this is purposefully contrived to give "a misleading impression" (GF 179), which becomes a sort of moral test that the "bad" characters fail, "for Harry, Ron, and Hermione knew Hagrid to possess a very kind nature" (179).[5] Fudge conjectures that Madame Maxine killed Barty Crouch solely because he suspects she is half giant, for which Harry calls him out (582). The texts deploy such misreadings as a recurring "gotcha" game, repeatedly revealing these first impressions as incorrect—a heavy-handed lesson about the wrongness of discriminating based on appearance.[6]

On one hand, a benign patriarch who continually emphasizes free will; on the other, a parade of deplorables. The series appears to say that neither one's parentage nor "blood" nor how their bodies present should be taken to indicate who someone really is (and thereby how much someone is worth). Many readers note the saliency of this message, such as Elaine Ostry: "The series enacts a great 'race war,' in which the heroes fight against those wizards who possess a vision of racial purity. Rowling intends to teach children that what matters is one's character, not color, pedigree, or wealth" (89–90). Focusing on Dumbledore's portrayal, Jenny McDougal declares that "above all, Rowling's series demonstrates that no one is born into one way of being, that we all have choices" (179). Based on the preceding, it would seem that Rowling is also sympathetic to the pain caused by others' refusals to validate our self-concepts and stalwartly against the restriction of autonomy when it comes to self-determination, as we are meant to conclude that Muggle-borns should be recognized as real witches and wizards and that we should look beyond menacing appearances to the kindness within.

How Much Choice, Really?

The series is quite realistic about the fact that our attempts at self-determination seem to depend completely on their (hu)man-produced context for intelligibility. Consider Harry Potter as wizard. Few *Harry Potter* readers would fail to remember the moment when Hagrid declares to the eleven-year-old protagonist, "Harry—yer a wizard" (*SS* 50). From the outset, the series argues that what one is can be revealed to us by another with superior knowledge about our bodies. Hagrid's certainty is based on knowing Harry's parentage: "With a mum an' dad like yours, what else would yeh be?" (51), he says, applying familiar blood logic. In the movie, Harry takes a little convincing, insisting at first that he's "just Harry"—that who he is is unchanged, regardless of how much wizarding blood might course through his veins. In the text, Harry is more ready to accept his new identity, quickly stammering to the Dursleys: "You *knew* I'm a—a wizard?" (53). Before the reveal, he had no cause to consider himself "abnormal," much less a wizard, even as "odd [things]" seemed to have happened around or to him (58). But the information about his parentage is taken to determine what he is, just as when we learn facts about our ancestry contained in our bodies (via DNA tests, for example), our self-concept is expected to change. Like Harry, we would likely feel we now know "who we are" and begin reinterpreting past experiences as if this new piece of information has unlocked truer interpretations. By the second book, Rowling opens by announcing to us, as a point of pride, that "Harry Potter *wasn't* a normal boy. As a matter of fact, he was as not normal as it is possible to be" (*CS* 3).

Hagrid's claim about what he is forces Harry to discard his previous self-concept and recategorize his identity as abnormal—but abnormal by virtue of being special, magical. This new self-concept is easy to embrace because it is an attractive one. Since the vile Dursleys stand for the "normal," being "abnormal" is both a compliment and an escape. The Dursleys are Roald Dahlesque caricatures of commonplace conservatives with narrow-minded views. "Having a wizard in the family was a matter of deepest shame" (*CS* 4); their stated mission is to "stamp it [abnormality] out of him" (*SS* 53). Now with the secret out, the Dursleys nevertheless insist that Harry never "MENTION HIS ABNORMALITY UNDER THIS ROOF" (*CS* 2). All his magic accessories are locked up, except those he hides under a loose floorboard in his room. Certain words ("magic," "Hogwarts," and "broomstick," for example) are taboo (*CS* 2; *PA* 20; *GF* 32). As "his one great link with the magical world whenever he had been forced to return to the Dursleys" (*DH* 67), Hedwig is also subjected to imprisonment and underfeeding. From "being treated like a dog that had rolled in something smelly" to being asked to hide in his room (*CS* 5), "making no noise and pretending I'm not there" during Vernon's business dinner (6), Harry is aggressively denied the opportunity to experience his new identity positively on Privet Drive. In their repressive behavior, we can recognize Vernon's response to *Sorcerer's Stone* cat-McGonagall: his desire to not realize that which he deems abnormal. The Dursleys are obviously wrong for refusing to recognize and validate Harry's "real" identity. Understandably, many readers interpret the sympathy the series produces for Harry's Privet Drive situation as inspiration to embrace their own kind of "abnormal" in the face of oppression—whether that be a matter of gender, sexuality, appearances, values, or interests.

To what extent can we say, then, that Harry *is* a wizard when he is on Privet Drive? The ability to choose who we are, to self-define, depends almost completely on others' willingness to recognize our self-definition—in other words, one's intelligibility in a particular context. It takes others to name for him his new identity and, even more importantly, to create a context in which that identity can thrive.[7] Without the alternative world populated by wizards and witches, Harry's "true" identity would have little to no expression. There would be no school to teach him how to practice magic, no shops at which to purchase essential items to live a magical lifestyle, no government to safeguard this alternative society's existence. No matter how much magical blood might course through his veins, he would only be a wizard according to himself, with no one to affirm his identity and no models for nor avenues to perform any aspects of wizarding identity. Ironically, the main way in which Harry *is* a wizard while on Privet Drive is in how much the Dursleys aggressively repress him for it. The opening of nearly every book resets Harry in Privet Drive, juxtaposing the "normal" Muggle world against the magical world so we can witness him crossing over to where he "really" belongs, again and again.

Another example comes in the fourth book when the Goblet of Fire pronounces Harry a Triwizard Champion, an honor for which "many would die" (*GF* 279). As soon as the goblet announces it, it is made fact—a contractual fiat, to which I will return—yet everyone seems to resist the assignation because they know him to be underage and Cedric Diggory has already been named the Hogwarts representative. "The next few days were some of Harry's worst at Hogwarts" as schoolmates that were usually friendly do not "[find] it in their hearts to support him as much as Cedric," the age-appropriate "champion" (296). Harry conjectures that the "dislike pouring in on him from all sides" is in part because he does not satisfy the appearance-based expectations of his fellow students. Tall and handsome, "Cedric looked the part of a champion so much more than he did" (296). The Slytherins go so far as to don large badges that say, "Support Cedric Diggory—the REAL Hogwarts Champion!" (297), refusing to recognize the reality of Harry's participation. Ironically, the identity of Hogwarts Champion had not been his choice but rather the goblet's, yet it is an identity he comes to accept and even embrace only to find that a large majority of his community does not (until he succeeds in the first task).

Moreover, the various magical technologies that organize their society—technologies that *Harry Potter* readers love—systematically strip people of autonomy, challenging Dumbledore's pretense of choice. None do so more than the technology that categorizes nearly every magical head reared in Britain: the Sorting Hat. As with the "good" characters who see past Sirius's and Hagrid's menacing looks, the Sorting Hat's motto is *"don't judge on what you see"* (*SS* 117). The hat sings of its own experience of being unfairly judged by its appearance—it is a hat!—instead of by its capacities (its magical "brains" [*GF* 177]) and seems to offer a fairer alternative: looking at what is inside. Indeed, it bears a weighty responsibility: to look inside children at the cusp of puberty and sort them all into four comically imprecise categories—the ambitious, the brave, the brainy, and the hardworking. Its ability depends on a claim of unerring omniscience:

> *There's nothing hidden in your head*
> *The Sorting Hat can't see*
> *So try me on and I will tell you*
> *Where you ought to be.* (*SS* 117)

At first glance, we would want to conclude that judging by what is inside is surely superior to judging by what is outside, but as the Death Eaters' blood logic shows, judging the within can also be profoundly problematic.

Despite its bossy declaration, the Sorting Hat yields to Harry's choice, which appears to confirm Dumbledore's pronouncement that people can and should be judged according to their choices rather than their "abilities" (*CS* 333). As discussed earlier, Harry's encounter with Voldemort-Quirrell prompts Harry to question whether he actually belongs in Slytherin—the House that he has been told "[turns] out. . . . Dark witches and wizards" like some sort of factory for evil (*GF* 178). As Dumbledore reveals, Harry does have "a little bit" of Voldemort in him (*CS* 333), and it is this piece of evil that the omniscient Sorting Hat sees when he looks inside eleven-year-old Harry. Like blood, this is described in literal terms: a quantifiable fraction of Voldemort's soul resides within Harry's body, alongside Harry's soul.[8] By choosing to not be in Slytherin, Harry has chosen to be good, despite being literally part evil.

The choice seems all the more dramatic because young Harry is presented with temptation. Slytherin would help him "on the way to greatness," which he soundly rejects: *"Not Slytherin, not Slytherin"* (*SS* 121). Dumbledore's pronouncements would appear to be confirmed—Harry's choices trump the predispositions and capacities stored in Harry's body—yet the reason Harry has this choice between good and evil is ultimately because of the composition of his body. His choice is still restricted by what the Sorting Hat sees inside. As Farah Mendlesohn puts it, "His 'choice' is actually between two heredities or destinies. It is not a free choice" (171). It is less clear that he would have been able to self-select into, say, Ravenclaw, being so decidedly unintellectual, or Hufflepuff, not being especially hardworking. Moreover, the choice is uniquely Harry's. In the fifth book, we are told that the Sorting Hat did waver in sorting Hermione, considering Ravenclaw before "it decided on Gryffindor in the end" (OP 399). This wavering seems very rare, and the language clearly suggests that the hat decided for her.[9]

As Nicholas Sheltrown argues, the Sorting Hat is an example of how, in their magical society, "technology is instrumental in revealing identity" (51)—an identity presumed to be always already set in stone, waiting to be uncovered. How the profoundly significant sorting ceremony works appears to be a surprise to all, perhaps even a secret purposefully withheld. In a Pensieve memory, we see two purebloods who appear in the dark about the ceremony: young Sirius asks James Potter, "Where are you heading, if you've got the choice?" (DH 671). The pureblood Ron, whose sizable family has gone to Hogwarts, is even tricked by his prankster brothers into expecting that sorting involves wrestling a troll (SS 118), suggesting no one in his all-wizard circle ever bothered to describe one of the most pivotal moments in their lives. Yet the Sorting Hat does more than declare who someone is—it indelibly shapes who they will become. We can see this in Goblet of Fire, where an otherwise inconsequential new student, "Baddock, Malcolm," is sorted into Slytherin. Harry "wondered whether Baddock knew that Slytherin House had turned out more Dark witches and wizards than any other" (GF 178). The Weasley twins "hissed" at Malcolm because the Sorting Hat's categorization immediately renders this eleven-year-old their enemy. Though Malcolm might not yet know it—at this point, he has been at Hogwarts for less than an hour—the enmity will soon be mutual: "Gryffindor and Slytherin students loathed each other on principle" (HBP 143).

Despite favoring choice, Dumbledore paradoxically continues to organize all students (and by extension, all English magical society) via the Sorting Hat, limiting their choices for life. The best he can say is that perhaps sorting happens "too soon" (DH 680). The Heads of Houses, who themselves were all presumably sorted in their youth, are in turn consigned to head those Houses without choice as to their students. In fact, the House system is the institutionalization of the Hogwarts Founders' choices. Godric Gryffindor, Salazar Slytherin, Rowena Ravenclaw, and Helga Hufflepuff "*valued different virtues / In the ones they had to teach*" (*GF* 177)—bravery, ambition, cleverness, and a willingness to work hard, respectively—and instituted the four Houses to satisfy Gryffindor's, Slytherin's, and Ravenclaw's biases for "their favorites." (Hufflepuff simply takes the remainder after the other three Founders made their selections.) To extend their will beyond their graves, they created the Sorting Hat to sort future generations in perpetuity.[10] The Sorting Hat is open about its history and purposes, in fact going out of its way to remind everyone every year, but no one—including Dumbledore—questions the system. Instead, the ceremony repeats annually with excitement and solemnity, with anxious first years lining up to be told who they are and will be.

The Goblet of Fire is another technology that purports to be "an impartial judge" for the choosing of Triwizard Champions (*GF* 188). Like the Sorting Hat, the goblet is an age-old tradition, presented in "a great wooden chest encrusted with jewels" that "excited interest" from all the students (254). The system is posited as absolutely fair—one writes their name and school on parchment, and the goblet omnisciently chooses the best candidates. Though it is known that the goblet can be tricked, insufficient safeguards are put in place to prevent this, and somehow its susceptibility does not detract from the supposition that it is fair. Apparently, Dumbledore's Age Line could have been thwarted by the simple expedient of having an older student cross the line for you. (And why not a parchment plane?) Definitely, the goblet was tricked by "an exceptionally strong Confundus Charm, [bamboozled] into forgetting that only three schools compete" (279). When the "impartial selector" is hoodwinked (255), Harry becomes the fourth champion in a tournament designed for three, and Hogwarts immediately has "two bites at ze [*sic*] apple" (278). A "binding, magical contract" now requires Harry to participate despite everyone's awareness that this is patently unfair to all the champions (256), that international relations will fray, and that this is very likely part of a ploy to endanger Harry's life.[11] Dumbledore, the voice for choice, declares that they "have no choice but to accept it" (280). It is made to appear that the goblet, rather than the humans who have all decided to use and obey the goblet, irrevocably restricts everyone's choices to the point that no one even considers ways to circumvent the "contract" (having Harry proceed as a champion in name only, for example).[12] The next time the Triwizard Tournament is held, the goblet will be ceremoniously trotted out again.

Every magical person's essential tool, the wand also systematically erases choice while creating the appearance of fairness and objectivity—another technology that "[illustrates] the pervasive force of determinism in a series that repeatedly insists upon the value and possibility of choice" (Byler 118). Ollivander has to correct his own language, beginning a sentence with "Your father . . . favored a mahogany wand," then revising to "I say your father favored it—it's really the wand that chooses the wizard, of course" (SS 82). His need to revise reflects his impulse to attribute greater agency to wizards than their heavily predetermined lives would seem to warrant. As with the other technologies, wands posit that each individual is comprised of certain elements that an omniscient magical eye can read: brave or cowardly, good or evil, brainy or dense, rigid or pliable, powerful or weak, good at Charms or Transfiguration, and so on. Lily Evans's willow wand is "swishy" and "nice . . . for charm work" (82), James Potter's mahogany wand is "pliable" with "a little more power" (82), Hagrid's oak wand is "rather bendy" (83), Fleur Delacour's rosewood wand is "inflexible" (GF 308), Viktor Krum's hornbeam wand is "rather thicker than one usually sees . . . quite rigid" (309), Bellatrix's wand is "unyielding" (DH 493), and Peter Pettigrew's new wand is "brittle" (494).[13] Effectively, everyone is also sorted by their wands: this is a "power not within wizard control that removes agency by, to some extent, determining a wand owner's future" (Pond 190). The fact that no one needs to change wands (unless they break or are lost) confirms that this society also believes that people are and should be fixed and unevolving. This technology not only reflects who their "masters" are at age eleven or twelve but continues to limit who their masters will be forever. The storyline of Voldemort and Harry's twin wand cores is also replete with determinism: Harry's phoenix wand—the "brother" of Voldemort's (SS 85)—likely chooses him because, like the Sorting Hat, it recognizes the bit of Voldemort inside.

While, in these subtle ways, Harry Potter depicts the extent to which all self-concepts depend on and are subject to reigning norms and technologies, it seems to also want to pretend that we can be masters of our own identities. Dumbledore's many pithy paeans to choice obscure how the power to self-determine any aspect of identity depends on others' willingness to make them real. The series makes much hay out of the concept of choosing who one is but ultimately glorifies a society that conceals the operation of systems that exist to radically constrain everyone's choices—and which ultimately reaffirm that who we are is fixed and essential.[14] People in positions of power, like Dumbledore, employ these norms and technologies that systematically restrict other people's choices of who they will grow up to become but manage to distance themselves from—even pay lip service against—the limiting of self-determination. No individuals in the system appear to be at fault for how people are treated differently, and the weight of tradition appears to compel continued compliance.

Transformative Aspirations Dashed

Jen Harrison argues that Rowling's depiction of "blurred boundaries . . . call into question the agency of the liberal humanist subject in controlling and maintaining a hierarchical system in the first place" (329). While I agree that, to some extent, any depiction of a category-defying figure can have some destabilizing effect in that it represents that which categorical labels refuse to represent, surely it matters if these figures are vilified or undercut by the author. Burt finds that all the hybrid characters experience significant prejudice and are all exploited by "socially superior characters"—particularly by Dumbledore, who deploys the hybrid characters of Severus Snape, Sirius, Lupin, Hagrid, and Harry to advance his Order of the Phoenix (232, 220). The "heroes [are misrepresented] as champions of such characters, when really Dumbledore and the Order are exploitative and single-minded in the same ways they accuse Voldemort's followers of being" (232).[15] A slightly more generous interpretation is that their provisional acceptance into the heroes' circle of protection is conditioned on loyalty performed and services rendered, echoing my argument about their attitudes toward nonhumans in chapter 3.

Wizarding society is relentlessly rigid about judging people by how well they fulfill *what* they are, insisting on reading people by the discourses of their particular categorical classifications—a viewpoint that is presented with approval. The female- and male-bodied characters are expected, by and large, to meet certain thresholds of femininity and masculinity, respectively. Through the narrator's—and often Harry's—eyes, all bodies are measured against the categories they are deemed to belong to, then assessed for how they fall short of the idealized representations of that category. Never mind hybridity: such rigid attitudes immediately constrain deviance from categorical norms.

For example, several female characters are textually abused for the ways they fail at femininity, their "abnormal" bodies the subject of relentless ridicule.

Aunt Marge, Harry's most abusive relative, is described as a heavyset, mustached woman with little neck (*PA* 22). The half giant Madame Maxine is introduced by "a shoe the size of a child's sled" (*GF* 243). Even though they are about the same size, Maxine's size strikes Harry as "even more unnaturally large" than Hagrid's, likely because she is female (243). The texts present her with backhanded compliments, describing her, for example, as a surprisingly graceful dancer "for a woman so large" (420). She appears desperate to offset her "handsome" face, "deep voice," and "thick fingers" by always dressing in satin, a delicate-appearing, feminine fabric (243, 244). When she comes forward to greet Dumbledore, the narrator further marks the wrongness of her size by describing how she extends her hand for a kiss, and "Dumbledore, though tall himself, had barely to bend to kiss it" (244); her size disrupts the highly gendered performance in which the male body is supposed to be taller and then bow deeply to reach the female hand. With her "heavy-jawed face" and "thick fingers" that hold Harry's arm "in a surprisingly strong grip," Rita Skeeter is off-putting (303). There is something about her meticulously feminine adornments (the "elaborate and curiously rigid curls" and red fingernail polish on her "large, mannish hands") that "contrasted oddly" with her unfeminine bodily features (303, 307). These descriptions are tied with another gender transgression: her unscrupulous ambition is coded as an excessive sexual appetite by allusions to a hunting animal (her polished, two-inch nails are described as "scarlet-taloned fingers" [303]) and to fellatio ("She put the tip of the green quill into her mouth, sucked it for a moment with apparent relish" [304]). The quill represents a phallus she should not possess: "He had a funny feeling Rita Skeeter's Quick-Quotes Quill might just explode with excitement" (310). One of the most odious characters, Umbridge wears enough pink, floral, and frill to decorate a Victorian parlor, but her middle-aged female body is continually contrasted against her attempts to appear like a girl. Presenting like "a large, pale toad" with "a broad, flabby face, as little neck as Uncle Vernon, and a very wide, slack mouth" (*OP* 146), she nevertheless attempts to emulate that particular feminine aesthetic and is mercilessly mocked for it. In all three cases, the female characters make great effort to be seen as attractively feminine women, making sartorial and behavioral choices toward that end only to be skewered by the texts for having bodies that fail.

Male characters who are effeminate in clothing, appearance, or behavior are also a laughing matter, though with less textual disgust. Igor Karkaroff's "fruity, unctuous" voice and "goatee (finishing in a small curl) [that] did not entirely hide his rather weak chin" immediately mark him as untrustworthy (*GF* 247). Ron's *Goblet of Fire* secondhand dress robes "look more like a dress" and invite derision (411); the old wizard at the Quidditch World Cup who wears a "long flowery nightgown" incites Hermione's uncontrollable giggling (83); and the boggart-Snape's cross-dressing is *riddikulus* (*PA* 139). For a male to appear like a girl is debasing—for instance, Ron considers it a snappy insult to dub Victor "Vicky" (*GF* 421). Like the female bodies that stray into masculinity, male bodies are told to stay in the gender lane into which they were born and ridiculed for their transgressions.

Wizarding society is also presented as rightly suspicious of boundary-blurring figures. Centaurs immediately inspire the question, "Was it a man, or a horse?" (*SS* 252). In the implied logic of the series, which considers mythological creatures as if they are and have always been real, centaurs would have existed for millennia, but Harry can only consider them in binary terms that suggest something is abnormal about a species that appears as both. The *Monster Book of Monsters* is monstrous because it is a book that behaves as if it has snapping jaws and "scuttled sideways . . . like some weird crab" (*PA* 12, 13); Harry's first response is to strap it down with his belt. The animalized Whomping Willow, likened to a "charging bull" and a python (*CS* 75), is similarly monstrous, depicted as attacking Harry and Ron rather than defending itself. "Spear-carrying merpeople who'd looked more than capable of murder" are deployed as antagonists to frighten the young champions (*GF* 503). (Unsurprisingly, Umbridge proposed to have merpeople "rounded up and tagged" to mark them as fully animal [*OP* 302].) A sphinx (half woman, half lion) is imported as a dangerous Triwizard Tournament obstacle (*GF* 629), and the thought of chimaeras "appalled" them (*OP* 442). The basilisk in the Chamber of Secrets is a "monster" that "even other monsters [don't] want to name," a "*snake . . . born from a chicken's egg, hatched beneath a toad*" (*CS* 281, 290)—these hybrid origins rendering it more monstrous. With Buckbeak's rescue, *Harry Potter* overtly argues for tolerance toward the half-eagle, half-horse creature but only after marking its hippogriff body as potentially dangerous and requiring special handling (*PA* 114). Shapeshifters suffer from heightened suspicion from the boggarts who seem to exist to scare people to the "part-human" werewolves who have been subject to a special code of conduct since 1637 (*PA* 133; *SS* 263).

Wizarding society classifies Mandrakes as plants—they are the subject of Herbology class, not Care of Magical Creatures—despite all the ways they are morphologically, psychologically, and behaviorally similar to humans. Above the earth, their tufts of leaves denote a plant. But when yanked out, "instead of roots, a small, muddy, and extremely ugly baby popped out of the earth" (*CS* 93). The text thus refers to the Mandrake as, unequivocally, a "baby," with "sharp little fists" and teeth that they "gnashed" (93, 94). This first Mandrake is also referred to as "he," suggesting visible human male genitalia. While his skin is "pale green" and "mottled," the baby "was clearly bawling at the top of his lungs" (93), implying that the internal composition of the Mandrake baby is also humanlike. Compared to the Venomous Tentacula that is "teething" and gets a "sharp slap" like a badly behaved dog (93), the Mandrakes are also treated much like human babies—cared for and reared, protected from the cold with human clothing—as they proceed across human-developmental stages all the way through adolescent acne and "a loud and raucous party" (234, 251). As the basilisk begins to petrify more and more victims, the welfare of the Mandrakes becomes commensurately more important—not for themselves but for those their stewed bodies will save. Margaret J. Oakes describes them as "one of the funniest subplots in the series" (126), without reference to how they are painstakingly raised from babies to adulthood for the purposes of being consumed. As I argue elsewhere, the many ways in which Mandrakes are like humans inspire the impulse to deny these affinities, particularly because of the degree to which they depend on the Mandrake as an ingredient in their potions and remedies (Chez, "Mandrake's Lethal Cry"). When "fully mature"—ready to "move into each other's pots"—their lives are abruptly ended when they are "[cut] . . . up and [stewed]" (*CS* 234), treated like any other edible plant.

Given this treatment of boundary-blurring figures who are born that way, it is no surprise that Rowling presents all those who *choose* to straddle categories with suspicion. The breeding of experimental creatures is banned, for example, and we get two examples of illicit crossbreeds, both of which are dangerous: the fire-breathing chicken mentioned in passing in *Order of the Phoenix* and the blast-ended skrewts (*OP* 129; *GF* 196). The repulsive new breed—created by Hagrid's illicit breeding of manticores and fire crabs— appear as "deformed, shell-less lobsters, horribly pale and slimy-looking, with legs sticking out in very odd places and no visible heads" (*GF* 196). Lacking even visible mouths, the skrewts' bodies defy existing classification systems even in a magical world. Yet Rowling still sorts them according to the gender binary in a patently sexist fashion; the males, Hagrid surmises, are armed with stingers, while "the females've got sorta sucker things on their bellies. . . . I think they might be ter suck blood" (197).

When characters do attempt to manipulate "facts" about themselves to change how they are seen, the texts refuse them this power. Consider one deceptively simple request: changing one's proper name. Naming is a highly public battleground for self-identification, highlighting the tension between one's choices and the society in which one must necessarily operate. Much like other norms that delimit our freedom to be read in certain ways (and thereby read ourselves), naming is an identity marker that is, nearly universally, given to us by people who preexisted us. In most cultures it is typically a parental prerogative, expressing their wishes for who their child will grow to be, including assigning a gender and other cultural connotations. People tend to develop their sense of who they are and attach it to the name used to address them since birth, but as someone grows up and comes to learn the cultural meanings attached to their name, some may not feel that their given name reflects them (or who they want to be). When someone tries to change their given name, the degree to which they meet with resistance speaks volumes about cultural attitudes regarding the nature of identity and the permissibility of self-determination.

Naming, not naming, and misnaming are a recurring challenge that particularly plagues the series' main villain. Voldemort is the name Tom Riddle chooses for himself at a young age to erase the affiliation with his namesake, the Muggle parent who abandoned his pregnant mother: "I, keep the name of a foul, common Muggle, who abandoned me . . . ?" (CS 314). Paradoxically, he "[fashions] . . . a new name" that remains an anagram of his birth name ("Tom Marvolo Riddle" becomes "I am Lord Voldemort"), which symbolically keeps him rooted to the Tom he is trying to deny. Yet this new name is also "a name I knew wizards everywhere would one day fear to speak" (314). By renaming himself and then making that name unspeakable, Voldemort attempts to become unnamable: to escape the constraints of being in any way named by others—a move he explicitly associates with power. In this, he is quite successful: almost everybody shudders, winces, gasps, or drops things at the mention of the name Voldemort (referring to him as You-Know-Who or He-Who-Must-Not-Be-Named) and even his followers avoid it (calling him the Dark Lord).

It becomes an empowering act on Dumbledore's, Harry's, and a handful of Order members' parts to fearlessly call him Voldemort. In book two,

Dumbledore approves of Harry's unusual comfort with saying "Voldemort," insisting that we must "always use the proper names for things" (*SS* 298)— suggesting that he believes that the name Voldemort chose for himself *is* the proper one. Dumbledore appears to respect his choice to rename himself but rejects Voldemort's bid to become wholly unnamable. Those who refuse to abide by Voldemort's taboo are presented as unusually brave as they deny him the power to entirely control whether he is named. In contrast, others' refusals to abide saying or, in some cases, even hearing the chosen name mark their weakness of character, such as with McGonagall (11), Slughorn (*HBP* 72), Ron (*DH* 273), and Hermione (who rises in esteem in Harry's eyes when she becomes able to withstand saying the name [*OP* 328]).[16]

Yet Dumbledore readily contradicts himself, as we learn in book six that he has wielded Voldemort's birth name like a weapon. In a Pensieve memory, we see that, early on in Voldemort's villainous career, Dumbledore attempts to put him in his place by using his given name rather than his "proper," self-chosen name. When Voldemort corrects him, Dumbledore refuses to comply: "I know what you are known as," he says, "but to me, I'm afraid, you will always be Tom Riddle" (*HBP* 442). In either case, Dumbledore simply chooses to use the name that he believes would most disrespect or wound Voldemort at the time. In this scene, we are encouraged to admire how, in intentionally refusing to use Riddle's chosen name, Dumbledore executes one of his characteristically subtle power moves. The text explicitly articulates that "Dumbledore's refusal to use Voldemort's chosen name was a refusal to allow Voldemort to dictate the terms of the meeting" (442), to deny him the power of choosing a new name to represent his new identity and free himself from a link to the father that abandoned him. As Tolonda Henderson argues, "Calling someone by their deadname is incredibly disrespectful and harmful," yet the moment is presented "as a brilliant strategy" on the part of Dumbledore, the character that represents "all that is good" (165). By essentially deadnaming him, Dumbledore humiliates the young Voldemort by reminding him of his Muggle parentage, his abandonment, and his profound vulnerability as a child.

Even if the misnaming did not operate as a way to dredge up trauma and fling it in their face, failing to get someone's name "right" is understood to be a deep harm, an obliteration of their personhood. When the journalist Rita gets Arthur Weasley's name wrong ("Arnold") in an article, it empowers Draco to further mock him and his family: "Imagine them not even getting his name right, Weasley. It's almost as though he's a complete nonentity, isn't it?" (*GF* 203). When Voldemort dies, the text also deadnames him in a sentence designed to thoroughly disempower him: "Voldemort fell backwards, arms splayed. . . . Tom Riddle hit the floor with a mundane finality, his body feeble and shrunken. . . . Voldemort was dead" (*DH* 744). "Mundane" and "feeble," the once powerfully feared Voldemort is stripped down to his "real" identity. Dumbledore's power plays show that what is at heart with naming is a negotiation of power. As a cultural axiom, people are not supposed to have the power to name themselves; that power is supposed to always lie with others. The deadnaming moment is, according to *Harry Potter*, a victory for the "good" guys.[17]

Although we are given the pleasure of reading trans characters, Rowling's society does not particularly condone being trans for fun. There are precious few portrayals in the series of an innocuous interest in exploring the world with a different body. In his very first Polyjuice experience, Harry spends a few seconds reflecting on how navigating the world with a different body feels. "So this was what it felt like, being Goyle," he thinks (*CS* 217). By habit, he reaches up to "brush his hair out of his eyes" but "met only the short growth of wiry bristles, low on his forehead," and soon realizes he has perfect vision (217). That is all: they rush off to infiltrate the Slytherin Common Room. When, in *Deathly Hallows*, he becomes Albert Runcorn, "he was more than six feet tall and, from what he could tell from his well-muscled arms, powerfully built," so much so that Ron—who is usually taller than Harry—remarks, "Blimey, that's scary" to the Harry that "now towered over him" (240). So much for self-reflection; it's on to adventure. Earlier in the last book, six people polyjuice into him, with various reactions: Fleur feels ashamed of being "'ideous" (51), Ron takes the opportunity to check out Harry's chest for tattoos, and Hermione finally realizes that his vision "really is awful" (52). And off they go. Inhabiting a different body should be wondrous, but the texts seem to not want us to wonder.

Characters that choose to transgress identity boundaries are presumed suspicious and—according to the series—for good reason. Everyone who polyjuices to take on the appearance of another person does so to disguise their "true" identities and deceive others, whether it be "good" characters (duping Draco in *Chamber of Secrets*; concealing Harry among other Harrys, attending a wedding, breaking into Gringotts Bank, and visiting Godric's Hollow in *Deathly Hallows*) or "bad" characters (Barty Crouch Jr.'s year in the guise of Mad-Eye Moody to entrap Harry in *Goblet of Fire*; Crabbe and Goyle as first-year girls in *Half-Blood Prince*). Every polyjuicer is understood to be engaging in a form of identity theft.

Moreover, it is also evident that the series is deeply interested in the possibilities of corporeal self-transformation but dramatically resistant to disrupting the rigid boundaries of natal categories. For one, Rowling designates Polyjuice Potion as being strictly for human-to-human transformations. Hermione's failure to distinguish cat fur from human hair becomes a comical excuse for her exclusion during the Slytherin espionage mission. As predicted by a girl who died in part because she was a victim of bullying, everyone's impulse would be to ridicule her animalization: "You'll be teased something *dreadful*," Moaning Myrtle gleefully says; "Wait till everyone finds out you've got a *tail*!" (*CS* 226). Her status is treated as a disfiguring illness, consigning her to a hospital bed not for treatment but to remain out of sight. The text invites readers to laugh along as Nurse Pomfrey shields Hermione from oglers with curtains "to spare her the shame of being seen with a furry face" (227). It is implied that every second spent in this hybrid body is negative. There is no sense of interest, wonder, or fun at the possibility of temporarily experiencing the world with a part-feline body. What can she now hear, see, smell, taste, and feel? The Weasley twins' Canary Creams are another example of humans morphing into animal bodies, and while these are definitely for fun, they are never used consensually. No one chooses to experience temporary "canariness"; all who consume them are the victims of pranks (*GF* 367, 403).

While Animagi are considered fully human and this magic is legal, their choice to develop the ability to transform into animals renders them subject to surveillance and control.[18] They are required to register with the ministry, recording their "markings, so you can't abuse it" (*GF* 487)—evidence of their suspicion that the ability to transform one's body into animal form would be nefariously used to disguise one's "true" identity. Given the example of Umbridge's sadistic Muggle-born Registration Commission, this Animagi registry cannot be presumed to be innocent bureaucracy. While Remus mentions that "one reason the Ministry keeps a close watch on those attempting to do it" is because "the Animagus transformation can go horribly wrong" (*PA* 354)—that is, out of concern for the transforming magician's safety and welfare—the primary reason is actually the safety of others.

Across the series, all Animagi are indeed shown to weaponize transformative magic to disguise their identity and enable illicit behavior. James Potter,

Sirius Black, and Peter Pettigrew are presented as merely mischievous, even precocious, for having taught themselves such advanced magic at that age. Their purpose even appears laudable: they give the lonely Remus Lupin some much-needed friendship and validation. (Sirius's power also enables him to survive and escape Azkaban.) As Hermione points out, however, their behavior verged on the criminally negligent. Remus acknowledges that "there were near misses, many of them" (*PA* 355)—that is, many times that he might have infected others with the incurable condition that he himself hates. Peter's ability to transform into a rat allows him to fake his own death, frame Sirius, and conceal himself as the Weasley's pet for twelve years. In *Goblet of Fire*, Rita becomes a beetle to enable her vile brand of muckraking journalism. Even McGonagall's introduction as a cat in *Sorcerer's Stone* is another instance of transfiguration for the purposes of espionage; she would not have been able to sit on a fence on Privet Drive all day in human form.

In the series, to be animalized is almost universally negative. At the age of eleven, the bullying Dudley is afflicted with a pig's tail by the rather irresponsible Hagrid, who adds a fatphobic insult to the injury: "Meant to turn him into a pig, but I suppose he was so much like a pig anyway there wasn't much left ter do" (*SS* 59). Worse still, Hagrid punishes the son for his father's rudeness; at this point, Hagrid knows nothing about the boy that would warrant leaving him "howling in pain" (59). We are told as a comical aside that Dudley must undergo surgery to remove the tail after bearing with it for a month (90). Dudley's trauma also becomes a humorous callback in *Goblet of Fire* right before the Weasley twins engorge his tongue into something likened to a python (40, 50). His animalizations are meant to be understood as poetic justice.

In *Goblet of Fire*, Crouch-Moody transfigures Draco Malfoy into a white ferret as punishment for attempting to hex Harry when his back is turned. The ferret's experience is described in what should be sympathetic terms, but everything about the cartoonish moment invites the reader to indulge in sadistic satisfaction. We can laugh at the ferret-Draco "shivering on the stone-flagged floor" (*GF* 204), giving a "terrified squeak" (205), being magically tossed "ten feet into the air" so that he falls "with a smack to the floor, and then bounced upward once more. . . . Its legs and tail flailing helplessly" over and over until finally saved by Professor McGonagall (205). Even if Hermione has some qualms about the possibility that Malfoy could have been "really hurt," all our heroes laugh; Ron declares this "the best moment of my life!" (207). When Hagrid humiliates Draco further by publicly reminding him that he "made a good ferret" (234), the text notes that Harry found this "particularly satisfying" but hastens to excuse the hero's sadism by reminding the reader that Draco had attempted to get Hagrid fired the year before (235). In other words, Draco deserves it.

Consider how vastly uncomical and inappropriate the scene would have been had this been a "real" ferret or if it had been Draco in his human body. Had it been a ferret being tortured thus, it would have been highly inappropriate to show the heroes laughing at what would have registered as animal abuse even in a society in which nonhumans can be generally poorly treated. Had it been Draco in his human body, it is impossible to imagine that the fake Moody would have been allowed to stay on as a professor without challenging our understanding of Hogwarts or Dumbledore. The moviemakers likely perceived that portraying this scene faithfully would not have gone over well with audiences. Instead, the ferret is gently tumbled up and down a couple of feet and never touches the ground. He is also made to travel down Vincent Crabbe's pants, adding an element of homosexual panic to the scene. Draco's temporary nonhuman body legitimizes torture and humiliation that appears to be happening to neither a ferret nor a human and therefore not a body that counts at all. In the film, Crouch-Moody foregoes this species ambiguity, preferring instead to legitimize his actions by explaining that "technically, it's a ferret." Not surprisingly, when Dudley next aggravates him, Harry itches to "jinx Dudley so thoroughly he'd have to crawl home like an insect, struck dumb, sprouting feelers" (*OP* 15).[19]

No one chooses to polyjuice into a person of another sex and gender unless pressed by necessity, suggesting that transgender bodies are undesirable. There are two occasions of transgender polyjuicing, proffered for comedy. One is in *Deathly Hallows* when Hermione and Fleur transform into Harrys, and the latter complains that she is now "'ideous"—that is, stripped of her prized femininity (51). In *Half-Blood Prince*, Vincent Crabbe and Gregory Goyle are ridiculed for polyjuicing into female students. Ron "guffawed," somewhat incredulous: "He's got Crabbe and Goyle transforming into girls? . . . No wonder they don't look too happy these days" (*HBP* 455). His attitude suggests that it is impossible for a male-bodied person to be "happy" with or to choose even a temporary female body; they have to be forced into it and are thereby debased. Harry refers to one of them as "she" before correcting himself to use the pronoun befitting their "real" identity: "she—what am I talking about?—*he* dropped the scales" (454–55). While the text posits that Crabbe and Goyle would likely be relieved to still be referred to with masculine pronouns (that is, that they would appreciate still being recognized by their "real," natal gender), Harry could be said to be misgendering them to further emphasize their debasement.

Harry is implicitly praised by the text for menacing the polyjuiced Goyle, sneaking up while invisible to whisper, "Hello . . . you're very pretty, aren't you?" (*HBP* 464). It is treated as a great joke and even a success on the side of good—in the series' general embrace of the idea that the bullies of bullies are good—as Harry laughs while Goyle "gave a high-pitched scream of terror, threw the scales up into the air, and sprinted away" (464). Yet the comment "You're very pretty, aren't you?" is correctly understood by Goyle as a sexualized threat against the female bodied. Nothing good follows such a greeting, whereby a female-bodied person is made to feel her sexual vulnerability; she understands in a flash that her body is seen as an open invitation for sexual advances. Temporarily having a female body has rendered Goyle vulnerable to an extent that the young Slytherin has not previously experienced. Despite her disconcerting investment in at least some rape-legitimizing discourses, as discussed in chapter 1, we really could not imagine Rowling describing our hero menacing a "real" eleven-year-old girl in this way. The fact that this is presented as a joke also suggests that Rowling believes misogynist aggression is more acceptable if, to her mind, the female bodied is not "really" female—and when the underlying joke is homophobic. Her belief in the fixedness of a sex/gender identity—no matter how radically a body may be transformed—grounds the humor of this episode.[20]

The series' big bad, of course, does more than change his name: Voldemort is a man who *chooses* to remake almost every aspect of who he is. As Voldemort, he develops a signature "high, cold" voice (*DH* 174, 339, 500), as well as a body that is increasingly readable as androgynous or feminized. Bojana S. Vujin and Viktorija E. Krombholc discuss Voldemort's various parallels to the monstrous feminine from his "peculiar desexualised masculinity" to his "unnaturally pale, tall, and thin" form and "long, pale fingers" to his voice, along with his association to the Medusa, to argue that he is an example of feminine-coded villainy (31–32). The more pieces of his soul he slices off through murder, the more his appearance transgresses species lines as well: "His face shone through the gloom, hairless, snakelike, with slits for nostrils and gleaming red eyes whose pupils were vertical" (*DH* 3). Henderson rightly notes that Voldemort is "the only character to welcome long-term changes to his appearance," and it can be no coincidence that transgender, trans species Voldemort happens to be "the embodiment of pure evil" (167). Through Pensieve memories across *Half-Blood Prince*, we learn that, in youth, he was a "very good-looking orphan" (360), consistently described by Dumbledore or the narrator as "handsome" at every appearance as if to emphasize how tragic it is that he chooses to sacrifice such good looks in his sick pursuit of power (269, 364, 432, 434). His transformation into his new name is distinctly tied to his physical transformation: it is when Harry first marks that his appearance has changed that Harry stops calling him Tom Riddle. Dramatically, and for the first time, he is not memorialized in the Pensieve as "handsome": "Harry let out a hastily stifled gasp. Voldemort had entered the room. His features were not those Harry had seen emerge from the great stone cauldron almost two years ago: They were not as snake-like, the eyes were not yet scarlet, the face not yet masklike, and yet he was no longer handsome Tom Riddle" (441).

Voldemort's embrace of morphological, ontological deviance—presented as shocking and wrong—appears to be symptomatic of whatever pathologies motivate his evilness and further evidence that *Harry Potter* thinks that choosing to transform *what* you were born as is wrong. The overarching messages of insistent natalism contradict the playfulness with which Rowling presents identity transformation: most of the characters who engage in transformations are temporarily engaging in mischief, skullduggery, or downright evil.

The Retrenchment of Natal Identities

There are two pale exceptions to Rowling's natalism in the series. As a Metamorphmagus, Nymphadora Tonks has been received as an inspirational character. A "forceful, opinionated, and independent woman" (Gallardo-C. and Smith, "Happily Ever After" 93), she can "change [her] appearance at will" (*OP* 52), and she engages in corporeal transformations just for fun—the only character to do so.[21] She playfully changes her hair to "bubble-gum pink" to look less "peaky" (52)—a color choice that was less mainstream at the time *Harry Potter* was published. She defies ageist conventions by choosing to disguise herself as a "tall, tweedy woman with iron-gray hair" (524). She also transgresses species lines: while Hermione's felinity was shameful and virtually every single instance where the texts say that a human looks like an animal is derogatory—for example, bat-like Snape, toad-like Umbridge, whale-like Dudley, pug-like Pansy Parkinson, snake-like Voldemort—Tonks transforms her nose to a "beaklike protuberance like Snapes's, [shrinks it] to something resembling a button mushroom, and then sprouts a great deal of hair from each nostril" (85), then takes on a pig snout that makes her look like a "female Dudley" (85). Even if these are short-lived experiments under-taken only to inspire laughs over the supper table, she is taking on a risk. As our wizarding-norms announcer puts it, she could have at least been "okay-looking when she isn't doing stupid things to her hair and her nose" (*HBP* 94). To Ron, it is unfathomable, unrealizable, that his cool, good-looking brother Bill would choose Tonks; indeed, Rowling pairs Tonks with Remus, a significantly older man who, as a werewolf, lives in the margins of society.

Notably, Tonks never uses her power to look more like Fleur, the series' highest beauty ideal and Bill's choice for a wife. Tonks's restraint can be con-trasted against Hermione's much-criticized investment in beautifying prep for the Yule Ball, which Heilman and Donaldson equate to plastic surgery (151). While perhaps this is an unfair characterization—dental work, better posture, a hair-smoothing serum, and a smile are not the same degree of appearance manipulation as liposuction, breast implants, or a facelift—Hermione does spend three hours to make corporeal changes to more closely conform to dominant beauty standards, which is in the spirit of most cosmetic surgery. It is a success in those terms: everyone is impressed at her transformation. These relatively small tweaks cause her to not "look like Hermione at all" (*GF* 414), which can be interpreted as a young woman sacrificing her identity—albeit for a night—to look pretty.[22] In contrast to this and to every Hogwarts girl's apparent obsession with wrangling their appearance to conform to these norms,[23] Tonks is a rare example in the series of someone willing to trans-form their appearance to *lower* themselves in attractiveness. In the context of every other character's profound lack of curiosity for different ways of being, Tonks also stands out: her power appears easy and free—and, as far as we know, limitless—and exercised in significant part for the sheer pleasure of experiencing a different body, with little regard for popular opinion.

Given that limitless potential, it is telling that Tonks does limit herself to supper-table animal snouts and colorful hair. As with almost all the polyjuic-ers, Tonks never crosses gender lines, even if, as Mundungus's experience disguising himself as a veiled witch in *Order of the Phoenix* shows, such a disguise would be more effective.[24] Was she not the least bit curious about what it would be like to relieve herself while standing up? Did she never wonder what it would be like to have the gender and body of someone like Albert Runcorn, a body that allows Harry to wield instant and effective authority over others? All her transformations are temporary, the bubblegum-pink hair being the only relatively consistent feature that she adopts, reaffirming the series' overall stance that we should follow the dictates of our natal biology. Moreover, the trajectory of Tonks's character arc across the series hardly inspires. Yes, she is an Auror, which we are told is the coolest possible career option—"They're, like, the elite. . . . You've got to be really good" (*OP* 228)—but she is given no heroic moments and cannot walk from point A to point B without tripping over something. Remus, who introduces her with the name he knows she hates, Nymphadora (49), initially accepts her correction to Tonks, but after their marriage, he goes on to call her Dora (*DH* 514). The spunky Auror devolves into a lovesick wraith, stripped of her metamorphing power and resurfacing at the end of the series only to praise Ron, worry Remus, give birth, worry about Remus, and die.

Another pale exception to Rowling's natalism is the car that becomes sentient and liberates itself. The flying Ford Anglia begins as a Muggle car that has been expanded in interior capacity, charmed to fly, and can become invisible. These changes do not at first appear to constitutionally change what the car *is*. On the overly taxing flight from London to Hogwarts, however, the text begins to describe the car in more animalized terms. It begins to "whine," and Ron surmises it is "probably just tired" (*CS* 72), blurring the line between object and living being. Its windshield wipers wave "feebly, as though in protest" (73), which motivates Ron to speak reassuring words "more to the car than to Harry" (73); the car's feelings become more important because of how much they depend on the car's cooperation to survive. Despite Ron's attempts to speak "cajolingly" to the car (73), it begins to "shudder"; its engine "groaned" (73), then "died completely" (73). When the engine restarts, the car whisks them away from the violent Whomping Willow. Ron's attempts to praise it for its quick action ("Well done, car—") prove insufficient to placate the increasingly autonomous being: "The car . . . had reached the end of its tether" (75). The language represents the car as a leashed pet animal that escapes from its human masters, ejecting them and their belongings to "[rumble] off into the darkness, its rear lights blazing angrily" (76).

Disappearing for many chapters, "apparently it had taken to trundling around the forest on its own" (*CS* 274) but reappears at a critical moment to rescue the boys from ravenous acromantulas, "headlights glaring, its horn screeching" (279). Now fully independent—"Ron didn't touch the accelerator but the car didn't need him" (279)—its enduring loyalty earns it "a grateful pat" (280). Echoing the motif of suspicion against transformations, Fang, the natal dog, "didn't seem at all keen on it" (274). While the Ford Anglia is just another one of Rowling's comical anthropomorphizations, what is significant is that our heroes come to recognize and afford it respect, which is more than they do the teacups with legs or the baby Mandrakes. Admittedly, the car earns this meager recognition by risking itself for its masters, but the change in attitude began earlier when they acknowledge that they rely on the car's good humor to ride. This aligns it with Buckbeak, compared to which the car both gives and achieves more: it does not have to continue to serve as a vehicle for humans. The Ford Anglia manages to do what no other magical object in the series does: for its abilities and devotion, it gains recognition from Ron and Harry as a sentient, independent being with feelings that does not have to continue in service. The victory is partial, however: the car ultimately must live outside of society, the majority of which will refuse to recognize it as a life deserving respect and autonomy.

Is Cedric Diggory's rock-Labrador real in the same way that the text refers to Hagrid producing "a real, live" owl from his overcoat in *Sorcerer's Stone* (52)? When Neville accidentally transplants his ears onto a cactus (*GF* 237), does the cactus change ontological status? Does Professor Slughorn become an "it" when he takes the form of an armchair (*HBP* 64)? Is Harry a trans merperson while under the influence of gillyweed (*GF* 494)? Rowling's answers to these questions are consistently no: virtually all characters get treated according to how they were categorized at birth. Even though Sirius's feelings became "less human, less complex" in the form of a dog, with "animal emotions" enough to confuse dementors (*PA* 371), the cat Crookshanks can recognize that he "[is] no dog" and that Scabbers is not a real rat (364). Even though, for much of twelve years, Sirius was a dog, to the point that his laugh sounds like barking, and Peter was a rat, such that "skin looked almost grubby, almost like Scabbers's fur, and something of the rat lingered around his pointed nose and his very small, watery eyes" (366), this long-term corporeal blurring does not affect their categorization as the humans they were born as. Scabbers's "true identity" (377), the text insists, remains human. Perhaps the reason that Transfiguration is "some of the most complex and dangerous magic" taught at Hogwarts is because of its category-blurring potential (SS 134).

Categories in wizarding society should be impossible to pin down, and attempting to hew a hierarchy based on ontology would seem most futile indeed—but that does not stop them from trying. Given how "the line between human and animal, or indeed between animate and inanimate, is fluid throughout the series" (Dendle 163), the wonder of it is that Rowling's magical society still insists on rigidly categorizing and sorting at all. In Rowling's wizarding world, the potential to transform how one is read by others is theoretically limitless, but in her characters' realities, the limits are firm. "Too often the Harry Potter series' endorsement of choice leads to choosing more of the same" (Byler 137), as a vast range of transformative choices are cast as either beyond the pale or completely omitted. In theoretically enabling choices that are then excluded as inappropriate or unimaginable, Rowling effectively declares those choices unrealizable.

Conclusion

Despite giving her characters the limitless magical potential to transform their identities, Rowling punishes attempts at self-refashioning and casts suspicion over any being that dares to be hybrid or trans. Transformations are taken to be costumes and disguises and not different expressions of oneself. The two limited exceptions, Tonks and the Ford Anglia, are marginal and marginalized. While playing with magical transformation, Rowling ultimately does not want people to change their bodies and confuse the question of "what" they are—which limits their choices of "who" they are because they are not intelligible in any other way than how they were born. The idea that any individual has or even *ought* to have total autonomy in how they are seen by others is—of course—as fantastical as a world with magic, as all of our norms and meanings are and should be at least to some degree social. Aspects of identity are and should be social negotiations—but these conversations have long excluded certain voices from participating as equal voices. Ultimately, only Harry and, to some degree, Sirius and Hagrid are granted the privilege of feeling aggrieved when their community refuses to read them as they would wish.

Somehow, we ignore the rigidity of Rowling's turn-of-the-twenty-first-century vision. While Rowling encourages readers to consider *Harry Potter* a liberal series promoting nonconformity and self-determination, Dumbledore's grand declarations regarding the power of our choices to determine who we are ultimately seem to apply only to the question of being "good" or "evil"—not to any other aspect of identity. His paeans to choice pay weak lip service and when put together with the fun, fantastical hybrids of Rowling's imagination, effectively convince many readers that the series promotes much more choice in our identities than it actually does.

ROWLING ALSO STINKS

Fandom and the Problematic Living Author

While writing this book, I often felt uncomfortable referring to "the reader" as if there is just the one I could imagine having the responses I would expect them to have. Perhaps this is a discomfort that I ought to have felt more often in my scholarship, but this time, I was especially conscious of it, knowing how vehemently divergent responses to *Harry Potter*, and their author, have been. In this closing essay, it feels important to speak only for myself and from my own experience—to situate myself more explicitly as a reader and speak from my own positionality as someone who has lived as cisgender all my life, who has identified as a feminist since learning the word in high school, who felt the magic of reading and rereading the original series countless times, who has felt disgusted by Rowling's antitrans activism, and who is far from an expert in trans lives and experiences.

From the beginning, I was never interested in J. K. Rowling's biography; I didn't even know her first name was Joanna until about fifteen years after *Sorcerer's Stone*. I had little enthusiasm for Rowling's expansions and revisions to the Potterverse, partly because I prefer narrative closure over endless serialization. Despite my preferences, the *Harry Potter* franchise—and her influence as a public figure—kept growing. Postpublication nuggets of information—Rowling wrote the novel while on the dole! Dumbledore was gay all along!—seeped into my awareness without my seeking them out.

In the spring of 2020, I was coping with New York City's COVID-19 lockdown by playing *Animal Crossing*, at one point refashioning my island to include Hogwarts, Diagon Alley, and the Ministry of Magic and developing custom designs to share with fellow players online. By June, various *Animal Crossing Harry Potter* online groups began fracturing as some of us turned our islands into areas of protest and others complained that we were overreacting. Questions about J. K. Rowling's attitudes toward trans people had been making headlines before, but for me, it took her June 2020 essay to confirm suspicions.

The Rowling of "J. K. Rowling Writes about Her Reasons for Speaking Out on Sex and Gender Issues" appears to be more interested in shoring up her public perception than in reflecting on the critique she had received. Any good writer—and Rowling is a good writer—can wield language to attempt to influence readers' reception of a text, and to me, the essay sounded insincere. The carefully crafted piece begins by casting the early transgressions for which she was being virally castigated as "accidental." Positioning herself as an innocent victim of persecution, Rowling describes the "occasion" of "absent-mindedly" liking Maya Forstater's tweet and of following Magdalen Berns in 2019 as a means to the end of contacting her for research purposes.[1] Writing in June 2020, Rowling could claim that these two "dots were joined"—rashly, unfairly—"in the heads of twitter trans activists."[2] While I agree with Valentijn De Hingh that Rowling's tone aims to be "respectful," even "strikingly empathetic" to trans people, at least in comparison to worser others and to some of her later tweets,[3] nevertheless, Rowling's 2020 essay is "full of unverifiable statistics and transphobic dog whistles" (Adegbeye), which were upsetting to read.[4]

The various responses of many Potter fans—ranging from impassioned defenses to boycotts to book burning (Nolan)—have largely played out online, where the discourse is often fast, loose, and ill-fated. Rowling's sense of being persecuted is in part understandable: the virality of the discourse must be blindingly unsettling even as she insists, with casual aplomb, "I must have been on my fourth or fifth cancellation by then" ("J. K. Rowling Writes"). The vitriol must have felt particularly unfair because, I believe, she did not, at least before 2020, feel animus toward trans people. I also do not want to discount the relevance of Rowling's own experience with domestic abuse and sexual assault, which she shares in this essay.

Like De Hingh, I have more sympathy for someone speaking from a place of trauma,[5] but the question of animus is trickier. To many, active animus is the litmus test for "real" discrimination—that is, a hatred that fuels a desire to abuse or exterminate another on the basis of a demographic-identity category.[6] This is similar to how some people vehemently reject being called "racist": in their heart of hearts, they do not feel what they would call "hate" against people of color. They might fear people of color or fear what they believe they know about the cultures of people of color; they might feel sympathetic but disbelieve claims that either historical or systemic racism was as severe as has been said or their impact so difficult to overcome; they might feel the apathy of someone who has the privilege of having no truck with the experiences of people of color. All these statements, I think, might apply to how Rowling felt about trans people in 2020. She almost certainly felt fear,[7] a phobia that was not allayed by her conceptual understanding that "the majority of trans-identified people . . . pose zero threat to others," but I do feel confident in conjecturing that Rowling was not lying when she insisted that she "[wants] trans women to be safe" and that "trans people need and deserve protection" ("J. K. Rowling Writes"). While I certainly do not consider trauma, phobia, or a lack of animus to be valid justifications for Rowling's attempts to maintain the status quo of a biology-based gender binary, I would have thought worse of her if I believed she did categorically hate trans people, as many do.

There is, to my mind, also a difference between someone who holds an active animus and someone who is unable to recognize that there are many whom their circle of care does not include and what these limitations say about their politics and ethics—though Rowling is perhaps overestimating the meaningfulness of that difference. It is the difference between people like the Death Eaters, Dolores Umbridge, or Rita Skeeter, who would seek to abuse and exterminate, and people like Horace Slughorn, Cornelius Fudge, and indeed every character but Hermione Granger, whose priorities are also primarily wizards like themselves. The latter group does not in any way "hate" or even "dislike" house-elves, for example, but there is no doubt that house-elves are not their priority when everyone ignores or mocks Hermione's S.P.E.W. campaign or when Slughorn casually uses house-elves to test his alcohol for poison. In *Half-Blood Prince*, Slughorn insists to Harry that he bears no animus toward Muggle-borns: "You mustn't think I'm prejudiced! . . . No, no, no! Haven't I just said your mother was one of my all-time favorite students? And there was Dirk Cresswell in the year after her too—" (71). The irony is rife; both these Muggle-borns face discrimination and are killed. Like Slughorn, Rowling can insist that she is not prejudiced ("I know and love trans people," she tweeted on June 6, 2020 [@jk_rowling, "Sex"]) even as she actively uses her powerful platform to amplify positions that delegitimize and worsen the lives of the trans people she claims to know and love. (And while I sincerely doubt she "hates" animals, what is their fate in her series? Like too many of us, including myself, she proves that it doesn't take animus to cause or participate in incredible pain and suffering.)

But Rowling has been more than just apathetic to the plight of trans people. While there may not have been animus in 2020, the essay betrays some unfounded skepticism about whether every person identifying as trans should really "count" as trans. For example, she imagines droves of predatorial men who would pretend to be gender dysmorphic in order to commit sexual assault and, on that basis, suspects all trans-identified persons. She also questions why it seems that so many more women, particularly young women, apparently want to be men, suggesting that she believes that a majority of trans identification comes from a suspect place.[8] Projecting her own memories of feeling "ambivalence" around growing up female with a father who wanted a son, in the 2020 essay, she frets that vulnerable young women might be seeking to escape misogyny by becoming men—perhaps a bit rich from an author who used initials to degenderize her name for publication and still publishes under a masculine pseudonym.

Rowling fails to recognize that amplifying certain ideas—which, especially when stripped of nuance, are nefariously used to exclude and oppress a very vulnerable group—can cause harm no matter how much she may like or sympathize with at least some trans people.[9] For her to understand that she can be fairly called antitrans, she would first have to concede that fearing a category of people en masse is a manifestation of a troubling ism, that she is underestimating historical and present systemic and individual harm, and that, being who she is, she necessarily is insulated from these harms that she underestimates. But more than any fear or animus, I believe Rowling has been motivated by the sense that protecting natal females is at odds with protecting trans people, and if she must choose, she knows which it will be. She may want trans people to be "safe" but not if it might cost natal females who stay in their lane anything. This is why she worries about "[throwing] open the doors of bathrooms and changing rooms"—because allowing legitimate trans users to avail themselves of these essential facilities would also "open the door to any and all men," including the ill-intentioned. Readers note that she peppers her recent novels with sinister men wearing clothing designed for women as a form of disguise (Kirkpatrick), which, as I argue in chapter five, is in line with her presentation of sex and gender in *Harry Potter*. Her fear that some might take advantage of the opportunity is not, of course, wholly unfounded, but is the only answer simply to go on as we are? Exclusion is, at best, an excessively restrictive solution to a legitimate concern and, at worst, an excuse to categorically disbar a vulnerable group. Perhaps Rowling could devote some of her vast resources or even just a fraction of her wit to develop solutions for some of the difficult issues at hand. Indeed, when there are only male and female bathrooms, locker rooms, and prisons, where would Rowling propose trans people go? Instead, she has chosen to remain ignorant about the effects of some of her statements because it enables her to remain myopically focused on the priorities she has chosen. As OluTimehin Adegbeye argues, "People like Rowling . . . [are] *loud and wrong on purpose*. . . . Because the ignorance *is the point*." And unfortunately, Rowling's ongoing activism against the recognition and expansion of protections and rights for trans people shows that her position has only become angrier and more turgid.

At heart for many of us is the larger question of what to do about texts that, perhaps, when consumed as children, still carry positive emotional content because of individual relationships formed with the texts. Because of the overtly liberal, progressive messaging of the texts, it takes some adjustment to accept that "the very narrative that was viewed to be inclusive of every child came from the mind and imagination of someone who is trans-exclusionary and (at the time of this writing) has not been open to changing her views" (Dahlen and Thomas 11). We have had to give up "Dumbledore's Army!" as a liberal rallying cry; we feel unable to participate in fan communities with the same ease; we can no longer comfortably analogize real life to *Harry Potter* situations without feeling an urge to add qualifying statements about Rowling's politics. I feel so much sympathy for the trans, nonbinary, genderqueer fans who had invested enough of their identity to feel a significant loss upon learning that, as Mallory Yu puts it, "the woman who created a wizarding world that meant everything to me doesn't care to include me or my community." Dana Aliya Levinson shares how Rowling's books "literally helped keep me alive." Aja Romano feels a sense of betrayal, having "entrusted so much of myself to the author" and learning "she had been plotting on some tiny level to erase me" ("Harry Potter"). De Hingh describes feeling "as though a cosy blanket was ripped from my naked body." To Gabrielle Bellot, "it [feels] like a slap in the face." Jackson Bird experiences it "like a punch in the gut."

Fans have had to come to terms with how Rowling's current words affect their perception and continued consumption of her previous ones. I was twenty to Harry's eleven—a significant age gap. Moreover, I had known all along that Rowling had not meant to fully include me; as with much of what was available for me to consume at the time, people of color in her books were just a literary garnish. I have also never had the personality to be a die-hard fan or to form parasocial relationships—all of which spared me from feeling anything like heartbreak or betrayal. Nevertheless, the context in which I understood her writing has been irrevocably changed. I had observed many of the issues I have written about in these chapters before 2020, but the sense of turnoff I felt on reading this essay alongside her snarky tweets significantly affected how I felt about her books and other products. "That's how the stain works," Claire Dederer explains in *Monsters: A Fan's Dilemma* (2023): "The biography colors the song. . . . It touches everything. Our understanding of the work has taken on a new color, whether we like it or not. . . . It works its way forward and backward in time. The principle of retroactivity means that if you've done something sufficiently asshole-like, it follows that you were an asshole all along" (44–45). For me, I saw that I had been giving the texts far too much benefit of the doubt—or did it just feel that way because my own politics and perception of her have changed? Just as Rowling's trans-exclusionary politics have retroactively tainted *Harry Potter* for me, my current politics—which demand so much more than the politics of my twenties—also influenced my rereading.

Scholars working on *Harry Potter* already feel like we must issue so much apologia for our work. Unfortunately, Rowling's terrible politics also feel like an opportunity for an "I told you so" from those who have always dismissed scholarship that is about children's, popular, or fantasy literature. And now, thanks to the author, we bear an added burden. Like many, I have soured on buying any merchandise, not wanting to enrich her or this strain of her activism any further, but I feel no qualms about continuing to read Rowling's work as a scholar. I agree wholeheartedly with Lana A. Whited that "the separation of writer from writings is a good, even necessary, development if the Rowling scholarship that is already well established is to mature and diversify" (10). It surely remains valid to read the texts without regard for, or indeed contrary to, Rowling's original intent—and to spin reams of binary-exploding, genderqueer fan fiction. Given Rowling's current political engagements, however, I believe we no longer have the freedom to do so without acknowledging her politics and positioning ourselves in relation to them. As Stitch rightly puts it, "Being aware of what you're consuming and from whom shouldn't be too much to ask." Moreover, silence on the issue might cause us to be (inaccurately, if that's the case) presumed to be supportive of her trans-exclusionary politics.

Yes, *Harry Potter* "helped teach a generation the power of not just tolerance, but fierce acceptance and unconditional love" (J. Bird), that "bravery can come in many forms, . . . people can surprise you and it's okay to lean on your friends when you need support" (Stevens), "that love is stronger (and more mysterious) than any magic, that strength comes not just from inside yourself but from the people beside you, that evil isn't limited to genocide but also to prejudice and oppression" (Yu). Nevertheless, Hermione and the other empowered female characters are sidelined and held down by a glass ceiling in a society where the female characters are otherwise depicted as appearance obsessed, boy crazy, and potentially dangerous in their femininity. Nurturing women are presented as valuable because of their self-effacement yet paradoxically as antagonists to male independence. Male homosocial relationships are promoted as the right priority over relationships with mothers, female teachers, female friends, or female romantic partners. The construct of Harry as the hero is in significant part produced by a tenuous façade of humility that survives only with the right entourage. Dramatic humane acts are celebrated as spontaneous, case-by-case exceptions that are possible only when an anthropocentric end is thereby achieved. Magical technology is central to the success of the series even as it lectures us about our technological dependencies and then lionizes (yet devalues) the manual labor of animals, mothers, and a laboring underclass. Characters who attempt to go beyond fairly conservative, binary ways of being are textually chastised. As my chapters show, the series can effectively empower people to think of themselves as good, even heroic, despite their beliefs that women are not the best leaders, that the exploitation of Others for their labor is justified, that people should not get to choose to remake or even rename themselves, and that indeed a lack of animus for an Othered group is enough.

I think many fans struggle with the thornier question of whether it is okay to *enjoy* the series at all. It can be difficult to publicly avow even still liking *Harry Potter*, as if admitting so is tantamount to betraying trans people or supporting the series' limited liberalism. I do not think that anyone who can still enjoy the texts or films is, by that very enjoyment, trans exclusionary or a "bad" liberal. I can forgive myself for having, as a younger reader immersed in that cultural context, enjoyed the ride despite its many bumps: the sexism and heterosexism undercutting the feminism, the anthropocentric representations of nonhuman Others, the plot holes, the cruel humor, and all the rest. I can also forgive myself if, in the present day, I reread the texts and relive memories of who I was at that time, in that period, with degrees of nostalgia because that is more about me and my past—*Harry Potter* was part of my life experiences. For me, much of the magic of the series *is* gone, but this is not some sort of proof of the strength of my convictions or allyship. How much a piece of art feels "tainted" is, to *some* extent, a measure of one's politics, but that's not the only factor—and especially for a piece of art that is as long and multivocal (read "contradictory") as *Harry Potter* is. It is full of issues, which I have labored to lay out in this book, but I still feel wondrous interest in the notion of a cookie that might temporarily turn me into a canary and chuckle inwardly when I hear Jim Dale take on the indignant voice of an anonymous student complaining about Professor Snape's assignment: "*Two rolls of parchment!*" (*PA* 185). The joys of rereading *Harry Potter* will never be unalloyed, but it does not follow that there may be no joys.

Readers have always hewed their own interpretations well beyond the limits Rowling set forth—we just may not have noticed how far we had left her behind. Perhaps the lasting magic of the series is how we have picked and chosen what and how we read and to critique and surpass any author's proffered limits, and we can continue to do so. For my part, I thank *Harry Potter*, despite its limitations, for offering a space of resonance—and tension—that helped me become more broad-minded than its author.

NOTES

Introduction

1. For the most famous examples, see Bloom; Byatt. See also Stephens.

2. There is an association between higher education and liberal views, so this surveyed group was already more likely to be liberal. See Kurtzleben.

3. Diana C. Mutz finds that Harry Potter consumption was linked to anti-Trumpism. See also Sundmark.

4. See Allcorn and Ogletree. Race, of course, also operates in patriarchal societies, but I do not emphasize those intersections in this book. See Dahlen and Thomas for an excellent collection of essays that addresses these issues.

5. Alas, because of Rowling's whitewashing of all nonwhite characters (Dahlen and Schell 87), the texts seem to say that these negative stereotypes are true of most female-bodied people regardless of race or ethnicity.

Chapter 1: Nicer Patriarchies: *Harry Potter*'s Raised Glass Ceiling

1. On Dumbledore's relationship to toxic masculinity, see, for contrast, Sugrue.

2. In one of her most memorable postpublication amendments, Rowling outed Albus Dumbledore as gay in 2007 (Grossman), even though nothing in the original series clearly denotes this.

3. Annette Wannamaker wisely counsels against thinking of readers, even the young, as "blank [slates] onto which culture is written" (19), and I take her point. However, while some young readers can do this critical work, readers' abilities ought not be a blanket excuse for what an author promotes. Just as we would criticize the way the Dursleys raised Harry even if he appears to have turned out remarkably well, we should criticize texts that promote harmful messages to young people even if some of them prove capable of ignoring or challenging those messages.

4. The very pretty Cho Chang also has this loyalty-diverting effect on Harry without the use of potions. In *Goblet of Fire*, Harry sees Cho applauding a new Ravenclaw first year and

"for a fleeting second, [he] had a strange desire to join the Ravenclaw table too" (178). See more discussion of Cho in chapter 2.

5. All emphases original unless otherwise noted.

6. An instance of the series' heteronormativity is that no females appear affected and have no need to cover their eyes and ears.

7. Patriarchy, after all, is more than a system placing males above females; it is also about ranking some males above other males. See chapter 2.

8. Notably, when the "acclaimed Chairwizard of the International Association of Quidditch," Hassan Mostafa, also falls under the veelas' entrancement, his reaction is to attempt to eject the Bulgarian team's mascots (*GF* 105–6, 110). This resonates with misogynist arguments that women do not belong in workplaces with men and/or need to follow certain dress codes because their sexuality is "distracting."

9. Blaming Fleur to protect Ron's sense of self is an example of Harry's devotion to his homosocial bond: "Homosociality strongly promotes male-male peer group loyalty, which in turn enables the denigration and subordination of women to be so prevalent" (Vogels 226–27). See chapter 2.

10. The Weasley brothers' attempts to shame her for dating are explained away as protective impulses, even if, in Ron's case, it is also fueled in part by his own sexual insecurities. Control, of course, is one way to attempt to protect someone else, but it comes at the price of denying that other person the right to autonomy in a way that the aspiring protector themselves would likely reject if it were to happen to them.

11. Harry reacts poorly to girls who break with these norms: "Two more girls asked him, a second year and (to his horror) a fifth year who looked as though she might knock him out if he refused" (*GF* 389). Although "quite good-looking," she is significantly taller than Harry, which compounds her transgression (389).

12. The effect of Ginny's kiss is later described as similar to a veela's: "blissful oblivion, better than firewhisky" (*DH* 116).

13. Harry has a similar reaction to Hepzibah Smith, the morbidly obese elderly woman who flirts with the young, handsome Tom Riddle in *Half-Blood Prince*; he seems repulsed by the contrast of her unattractive body and her attempt to use her "feminine" charms.

14. In her June 2020 essay, Rowling shares that she survived a sexual assault in her twenties ("J. K. Rowling Writes").

15. I would not agree McGonagall is depicted as "more responsible than any other adult for Harry's transition from impetuous child to discerning adult" (Glassman 153). Surely, it would be Dumbledore.

16. See chapter 3 for discussion of other ways in which the texts produce the idea that mothers are to be valued to the extent that they perform unnecessary labor.

17. In the Battle of Hogwarts, Molly Weasley cries to Bellatrix Lestrange, "You—will—never—touch—our—children—again!" (*DH* 736). Sarah Margaret Kniesler and Margaret S. Mauk interpret the "our" to mean everyone's children (Kniesler, "Unbreakable Vow" 279; Mauk 123), which seems unlikely given that Mrs. Weasley says this in response to Bellatrix's very personal and specific taunt "What will happen to *your* children when I've killed you? . . . When Mummy's gone the same way as Freddie?" (*DH* 736, emphasis added).

18. My next chapter goes into a deeper analysis of Ginny's relevance as his love interest; here, I focus on how her abilities are presented as secondary to his.

19. Quidditch is largely a male-dominated sport; most players at Hogwarts and the World Cup are male. When the Gryffindor Captain Oliver Wood first addresses his team in

Sorcerer's Stone, he begins with "Okay, men" (*SS* 185). Angelina Johnson has to correct him to include "women," and Lee Jordan proceeds to devote a portion of his game commentary to how she is "rather attractive" (185, 186). Ludo Bagman makes a similar self-correction when greeting the Triwizard Champions: "'Gentlemen . . . lady,' he added" (*GF* 274). The female players are afterthoughts, reflecting the fact that Quidditch is seen as primarily a male sport. See also Chandler and Nauright.

20. The other female Seeker we read of, Cho Chang, is also described as an able flyer but inferior to Harry in a humiliating way: "She'd decided to mark him rather than search for the Snitch herself"—a choice for which she would "have to take the consequences" (*PA* 261).

21. Farah Mendlesohn also notes that given her brains, Hermione is in the wrong House: "Her very presence in Gryffindor is a fix to ensure Harry has his courtiers" (172).

22. Similarly, the boys think that it is "very good for her" that she loses at chess, "the only thing Hermione ever lost at" (*SS* 217).

23. Even after years of friendship, Harry has a strong impulse to hide his poor homework grade from her (*OP* 309). When he messes up slightly in his Charms O.W.L. (Ordinary Wizarding Levels) examination, "he was glad Hermione had not been in the Hall at the time and neglected to mention it to her afterward," but "he could tell Ron," who did worse (713).

24. Snape is not altogether incorrect in describing Harry as thinking himself above the rules ("Famous Harry Potter is a law unto himself. Let the ordinary people worry about his safety!" [*PA* 284]). Harry's attitude toward rule breaking is encapsulated in this throwaway line: "Harry didn't care, he was one-up on Malfoy, and that was worth five points from Gryffindor any day" (*CS* 239). While the group pays for his *individual* rise in power relative to a rival, Rowling also posits throughout the series that his individual rise to power against Malfoy should be considered a Gryffindor victory—a *group* win.

25. In the cinematic *Sorcerer's Stone*, it is Hermione's idea to sneak into the Restricted Section of the library, and Ron claims the credit for her rule-breaking bravery, saying ironically, "I think we've had a bad influence on her."

26. As the series progresses, Hermione certainly breaks more rules but only if she recognizes an important cause; otherwise, she remains the voice that attempts to counsel against rule breaking for the boys' pettier reasons (and is typically ignored). It is notable, and disappointing, that her ethical fortitude is not celebrated by the texts as much as Harry's. The *Half-Blood Prince* chapter entitled "Hermione's Helping Hand" even depicts Hermione breaking not just a rule but an ethical principle: because of her increasing attraction to Ron, she confunds his competition for the position of Keeper (227). This is in line with the series' portrayal of female characters losing their heads when in love—Fleur, as earlier mentioned, and Nymphadora Tonks, who loses some of her power in *Order of the Phoenix*.

27. Lily Evans, Harry's mother, is also described as especially talented in Charms and Potions and did receive some special attention from Professor Slughorn. However, her talents seem emphasized mostly so that Harry could be thought to have inherited them. (He did not.)

28. While it is presented as significant that she scored "three hundred and twenty percent" in her third-year Muggle Studies exam, this detail merely sets the stage for her to discontinue the pursuit of twelve O.W.L.s because she "can't stand another year like this one" (*PA* 430).

29. It is a satisfying callback—albeit very little and very late—when Ron appears to have a similar hysterical moment in *Deathly Hallows* and forgets that he can use magic to prod the Whomping Willow into stillness (651).

30. This kind of characterization resonates with how, in the United States, many who are uncomfortable with a female president like to imagine her sitting in front of a big red button marked "NUCLEAR" and being insufficiently sober minded to make the critical call.

31. A few popular American shows also leaned into this revision of the separate spheres, portraying a female lead that is book-smart to the point of rigidity and hyperrationality, needing the counterbalance of a dumber male lead that operates on instinct and courage: *The X-Files* (1993–2018), *Bones* (2003–2017), and *Castle* (2009–2016).

32. Hidalgo's essay argues that Hermione is a "replacement" for Lily, without a trace of critique about the positioning of a female peer in such a role. In fact, Hidalgo appears to regret that "Hermione's maternal role is trickier in the films because while we can choose to imagine a seemingly older Hermione in the books, in the movie we see that she is clearly Harry's age" (84). One might consider instead that watching the movies makes one realize how much the texts normalize girls' performance of mothering work—that is, if undercutting oneself should even be considered a mother's work—for their male peers. For her part, Hidalgo argues that Hermione's maternal work for Harry is not sexist because Hermione does not "give up anything to do so" (82); she still manages her own pursuits. This is comparable to arguing that the persistence of a gendered second shift, wherein employed women still perform more of the household and caregiving tasks compared to their also-employed husbands, is not problematic so long as the women are still able to do their paid work.

Weiss also compliments Hermione for mothering Harry, even while acknowledging she is a "child" herself, before reducing her to a mere *part* of him: "Hermione functions as Harry's conscience; she is his more mature, responsible side, and the part of him that possesses self-control" (23). Weiss goes on to say, "In return, Harry helps Hermione harness her intellectual prowess into successful quests and augments her ability to enjoy life outside her academic pursuits" (23). Apparently, Hermione helps Harry, and in return, Harry gives her the opportunity to help him and teaches her to lighten up.

33. The text is curiously silent as to how Hermione fares in resisting the Imperius Curse. Given that it "takes real strength of character" (*GF* 213), I suspect that the text remains silent because Rowling wanted to maintain Harry's specialness but did not want to say that character is something that Hermione lacks.

34. Yes, in *Cursed Child*, we learn that Hermione rises through the ranks and becomes Minister of Magic (31)—the position that the series' great patriarch, Albus Dumbledore, thrice rejected as a position more befit for people like Cornelius Fudge.

35. Harry is described as acting by "instinct" sixteen times across the series, including some key moments, such as grabbing Professor Quirrell's face in *Sorcerer's Stone* and clutching his wand firmly when Voldemort triggers Priori Incantatem in *Goblet of Fire*. He acts "without thinking" ten times across the series, and it always turns out well. As Remus says, Harry is correct to "follow his instincts, which are good and nearly always right" (*DH* 441).

36. The first to call popular attention to this phenomenon was perhaps Jared Sandberg in "The Art of Showing Pure Incompetence at an Unwanted Task." Sandberg writes about employees—who all happened to be male—who admitted to feigning incompetence exclusively regarding tasks they did not want to do. This weaponized incompetence "almost always works to deflect work one doesn't want to do—without ever having to admit it." Sandberg writes about the strategy being primarily used at workplaces, although he mentions the possibility of its implementation at home. Since then, the strategy has been often discussed in popular media as a way for men in heterosexual relationships to avoid housework and childcare.

37. The potions puzzle is cut out of the movie entirely so that Hermione is sidelined only to nurse the fallen Ron.

38. In the movie, there is an added scene where, now unpetrified, Hermione rushes to the boys and congratulates them for "solving" the case, to which Harry appears very gracious in giving his helpmate credit: "We couldn't have done it without you."

39. Elaine Ostry also blames genre but without using that as an excuse for the problems of the genre (98).

Chapter 2: Bros before Chos: Masculinities and Male Homosociality in *Harry Potter*

1. Terri Doughty's response echoes the "masculinity-in-crisis" narrative—a narrative with "a long history" and that "has been revealed to be predicated on a mourning of the passing of male privileges, over and above celebrating—or even understanding—girls' progress": "That men continue to disproportionately hold positions of power and unequal shares of material wealth, but simultaneously are more likely to academically underachieve and more likely to be unemployed, throws up a key insight: if indeed there is any kind of crisis, it is not of all men and of masculinity in total" (Ravn and Roberts 185).

2. Coming from a wizarding family, Ron does know a bit more about the new world Harry is thrust into at age eleven, but that advantage does not seem to be worth very much. Ron did not even know about the Sorting Hat system, and his greater knowledge consists mostly of a tendency to parrot wizarding prejudices about nonhumans.

3. The happy product of an abusive upbringing, Harry appears to have benefited from Dumbledore's choice to leave the orphaned infant with the Dursleys to prevent the possibility that he would be raised to be arrogant and entitled in the wizarding world. We are eventually told that living with the Dursleys was necessary for his protection, but it sure seems like Dumbledore chooses to let Harry suffer abuse for the purpose of keeping him humble. (Our omniscient Dumbledore could have significantly reduced Harry's suffering by sending a few secret letters to Petunia. Why wait eleven years to get him out of his cupboard?)

4. Professor Slughorn's dinner parties are presented as sordid, elitist networking, but it is noteworthy that he is alone in making efforts to forge positive connections across House lines, even Gryffindor and Slytherin.

5. It is equally senseless that Ron is named Prefect. By the novel's end, Dumbledore reaffirms Harry's superiority by admitting that he had meant to give Harry the badge but gave it to Ron only to spare Harry the trouble (*OP* 844). To right this apparent wrong, the start of *Half-Blood Prince* has Harry being named Quidditch Captain, which "gives you equal status with prefects" (107). Ron's lower position is immediately reemphasized as he awkwardly says, "This is so cool, you're my Captain—if you let me back on the team, I suppose, ha ha" (107).

6. In *Half-Blood Prince*, Harry cluelessly remarks that he does not understand why so many people have applied to join the Quidditch team under his captaincy. Hermione duly performs the propping up but is somewhat "impatient" (*HBP* 219). I believe that these small moments of impatience from Hermione are Rowling's attempts to have it both ways: distinguishing her heroine from a girly type of girl even as Hermione participates in the same work of reflecting a male back twice his size.

7. Notably, when Harry witnesses, in Snape's traumatic memory, that his father enjoyed Peter's adulation as he played with the Snitch, Harry "wondered why James didn't tell Wormtail

to get a grip on himself" (OP 645), suggesting that he believes the onus ought not lie entirely on the person showing off to simply stop. Wormtail is another example of an inferiorly regarded male who reacts poorly, murderously, to living in the shadow of superiorly regarded males.

8. Conveniently, the text does not remind the reader of how much Crouch-Moody cheats to help enable Harry's Triwizard success. In addition to contriving his inclusion, Crouch-Moody provides all the essential information for the first two tasks and, in the labyrinth, clears his obstacles, stuns Fleur, and imperiuses Viktor. One of the judges, Ludo Bagman, is also unduly invested in Harry's win but for his own reasons.

9. Later, at their first D.A. meeting, Terry Boot is also impressed by Hermione's ability to perform a Protean Charm, a N.E.W.T.-level spell (OP 399), but Hermione's achievement receives a fraction of the compliments.

10. Even Ron knows to perform this humility. When he is named Prefect over Harry, he is at pains to "defiantly" proclaim that "I'm not enjoying it, I'm not Percy" (OP 184), in spite of ample evidence to the contrary. Hermione, too, learns to not appear "arrogant" about her superior cleverness and knowledge, but unlike Harry, neither Hermione nor Ron do so with an entourage that praises them or gives them more authority.

11. Significantly, as part of his growth in Deathly Hallows, Ron is depicted as rising to the level of deserving praise and responding with humility. Having managed to make his way into the Chamber of Secrets to get basilisk fangs, he has taken the lead and made an independent contribution to the main quest. For the first time, Hermione effusively praises him in tones and terms usually reserved in the series for Harry ("It was Ron, all Ron's idea! . . . Wasn't it absolutely brilliant? . . . He was amazing!"); for the first time, Ron does not bask in the attention (DH 623). Alas, he is still presented slightly less well than Harry, as he then says, "It was nothing," but still "looked delighted with himself" (623).

12. Although both Ron and Hermione are described as Harry's best friend, Hermione maintains a much higher degree of independence, choosing more difficult subjects and spending significant time away pursuing her own interests.

13. In the films, it would have been impossible to omit Harry's reaction to Ron's meanness in the same way that the texts do. To maintain the sense that Harry neither approves (because he is of superior character) nor disapproves (because he is loyal), Harry often appears to be not quite listening, laughing along good-naturedly in the background or looking away with a distracted expression.

14. Throughout Ron and Hermione's rift in Half-Blood Prince, Harry attempts to remain as neutral as possible. "Determined as he was to remain friends with both Ron and Hermione," he never calls out Ron's cruelty, instead "spending a lot of time with his mouth shut tight" (HBP 304).

15. Although owl mail is being intercepted at this time, Harry's concern about whether his dad was a bully would be of little consequence to anyone who might read such a letter.

16. Organizations that claim to be fraternal often depend on this kind of loyalty to function—as well as to enable gross injustice and protect the organization and its members from exposure and prosecution.

17. On another occasion, Ron counsels Harry not to return to the Mirror of Erised, and Harry calls him out for "[sounding] like Hermione" (SS 212).

18. This involves a resumption of their usual dynamic, with Ron trying to "[keep] the bitterness in his voice to bare minimum" as he remarks that girls would surely be clamoring to be Harry's date to the ball (GF 389).

19. Rowling's less toxic masculinity remains emotionally inexpressive: "He didn't tell Ron this, of course, but his heart felt lighter than air" (GF 360, emphasis added).

20. Perhaps because it would have been insupportable for Rowling to send a girl on a quest to save a boy, Fleur is relegated to saving her little sister (and failing to do so).

21. Yes, Dumbledore is belatedly outed as gay, but across the series, male bodies are expected to appear and behave and desire in heterosexual ways. The Weasley twins joke about inserting "a long and lethal-looking metal instrument" in their obnoxious classmate's ear or in "any part of your body, really, we're not fussy where we stick this" (*OP* 343), and their threat is presented as a welcome defense of Harry. Bill Weasley jokes about an unfortunate wizard who "had a Probity Probe stuck up his . . ." (*HBP* 108). Perhaps reflecting Rowling's changing politics after the series' end, in *Harry Potter and the Cursed Child* (2016)—authored by Jack Thorne and based on a story with collaboration by Rowling and John Tiffany—Harry's and Draco's sons fall in love.

22. As for the more "androgynous" character of Hermione, she is also unappealing to Harry, who feels himself perpetually in competition with her cleverness, as discussed in the previous chapter. Similarly, he is repulsed by the fifth-year girl who brazenly asks him to the Yule Ball, because she is much taller: "Imagine what I'd look like trying to dance with her" (*GF* 389).

23. See chapter 1 for more discussion of how *Harry Potter* promotes rape culture.

24. It is very suggestive that Hermione's attempt to humanize Cho is mistranslated by Harry's subconscious as a threatened castration. Later in the book, Harry has another castration nightmare where a mermaid steals his Firebolt and uses it against him, "[poking] him painfully in the side with the end of the broomstick, laughing at him" (*GF* 489).

25. See Stefan Robinson et al. for illuminating interviews of young men in the United Kingdom for whom intense "bromances" (intimate and positive homosocial relationships) are more fulfilling than heterosexual relationships, which they see as demanding inauthentic performances to "please" girls. As one participant explains, "A girlfriend will judge you and a bromance will never judge you" (Robinson et al. 860).

26. Considering he has left Draco in a pool of blood, Harry's lack of compunction is disturbing. His first impulse is to hide the Half-Blood Prince's book (*HBP* 525), and when handed down his detentions—to perform "useless, boring work" for a part of his Saturdays for the rest of the term, which is almost over—he disagrees that it is fair punishment and complains that he is missing the last Quidditch match of the season (528).

27. The movie, in contrast, includes several new scenes to make their romantic relationship appear more substantive and less abrupt.

28. In *Deathly Hallows*, when Ron uncharacteristically takes Hermione's side in her proposal to seek answers from Xenophilius Lovegood, Harry—"half amused, half annoyed"—calls him out for betraying him only to "get back in her good books" but lets it pass unpunished (396). At this point, both boys appear more willing to make limited concessions to their bond in order to help each other accommodate romantic heterosexual relationships.

Chapter 3: Moral Mediocrity: The Minimal Standards of *Harry Potter*'s Anthropocentric Humaneness

1. A short chapter published in 2022, written in 2018 and based on a 2017 presentation at Chestnut Hill College's Harry Potter conference, begins some of the arguments I expand on here. See Chez, "Sorry, Not Sorry."

2. It also appears that dementors are in some way forced to work as prison torturer-guards, as the *Daily Prophet* refers to the end of their service as a "revolt" in *Order of Phoenix*

(845). See Bealer for a discussion of how wizarding society weaponizes dementors to satisfy both practical and disciplinary purposes.

3. When Professor Snape tests Neville's Shrinking Solution on Trevor, a toad, it is considered not okay because Trevor is a pet (*PA* 128).

4. In *Sorcerer's Stone*, we hear of owls needing to "be nursed back to health by Hagrid" (194); the Weasley's "elderly and feeble" owl, Errol, routinely "[keels] right over and [lays] motionless" from his latest delivery (*GF* 28; *PA* 7). See chapter 4 for further discussion of nonhuman labor.

5. See chapter 1 for discussion of veela and rape culture.

6. Cats, however, are one of the series' exceptions. The "batty old cat-obsessed neighbor" (*OP* 20), Mrs. Figg, bores the ten-year-old Harry with photos of her excessive cats, which coupled with a cabbage smell is enough for him to "hate" going to her house (*SS* 22)—a fairly serious insult considering he is not allowed to go virtually anywhere else at this point. The school janitor, Argus Filch, has an unnatural connection to his cat, Mrs. Norris, who acts as "a sort of deputy in his endless battle against students" (*CS* 124), leading many students to harbor, as their "dearest ambition," the desire to "give Mrs. Norris a good kick" (*SS* 133), including Ron, who urges Harry to let him do so while under the Invisibility Cloak and suggests they use her to practice stunning on (*SS* 274; *GF* 574). Dolores Umbridge is obsessed with cat-themed décor, to Harry's disgust. Crookshanks, I am convinced, exists as a robust and positive minor character solely because Rowling wanted to play with the dog-cat-rat motif.

7. Percy Weasley notes that "stamping out vampires," who are also considered part human, is "*specifically*" forbidden by the ministry's Guidelines for the Treatment of Non-Wizard Part-Humans (*GF* 147), implying that perhaps some rampant vampire murder necessitated this protective legislation.

8. Hermione defends Hagrid from Umbridge by saying, "She's trying to make out Hagrid's some kind of dim-witted troll, just because he had a giantess for a mother" (*OP* 450), positing that Umbridge has made a classification mistake rather than a discriminatory one. Madame Maxime, we are left to assume, takes after her magical-human parent when it comes to magical talent and intellectual capacities. In *Order of the Phoenix*, however, Hagrid makes a reference to her being "fiery" and "rarin' ter attack," attributing her temper to "the French in her" (432).

9. Inexplicably, the acromantula Hagrid raises speaks perfect English (*CS* 277).

10. Although I focus on goblins, house-elves, etc. as nonhuman beings, they are also read as metaphors for human populations. The representation of goblins in the texts and films clearly echoes anti-Semitic tropes. See Carey; Lopes; Di Placido.

11. The centuries-old tension seems to arise from the fact that goblins only approve of leasing items for the life of the lessee, which conflicts with wizarding society's desire to build intergenerational wealth with goblin treasure. Goblins "connect ownership to a thing's maker, not to the person who purchased it," but "this definition of ownership is not legitimate to Wizards" (Chica 81). Much conflict could have been avoided if only wizards and witches would respect goblins' contractual terms and negotiate prices for a lifetime lease. Instead, the tension is framed as a goblin failure to understand that their treasures *must* be sold.

12. On the same page, we read that Bill Weasley "had preferred his meat bloody ever since he had been attacked by Greyback" (*DH* 510), so Griphook's dinner is not the only dinner bleeding on the table.

13. As the ruby-adorned sword chooses to appear in Neville Longbottom's hands during a critical moment at the Battle of Hogwarts, the text ultimately confirms that it is *Gryffindor's* sword, further casting Griphook's reappropriation as wrong.

14. Scully astutely notes that Harry immediately suspects that Firenze's hoofprint bruise comes from Bane—that he readily assumes violence from the separatist (116)—and that this is even more problematic because Firenze, with his "white-blond hair," "palomino body," and "astonishingly blue eyes" (SS 256), is "practically Aryan" (Scully 116), while Bane is "black-haired and -bodied and wilder-looking" (SS 253).

15. Similarly, Hermione seems untroubled by Crookshanks chasing gnomes at the Burrow. The gnome is described as "giggling madly as Crookshanks inserted a paw into the boot, trying to reach it" (GF 60). The mad giggle renders this as a game, excusing Hermione—and the reader—from feeling compassion for the gnome.

16. In Professor Gilderoy Lockhart's dueling club, Harry uses this power to communicate with snakes to command a snake to stop menacing another student: "Miraculously—inexplicably—the snake slumped to the floor, docile as a thick, black garden hose" (CS 194). Similarly, Tom Riddle controls the basilisk through Parseltongue. It is telling that the ability to communicate with a nonhuman animal is not considered an avenue for reciprocal interspecies understanding; rather, Rowling conflates the ability to speak to snakes with the ability to control them. The fact that people who can understand Parseltongue somehow lose the ability to *hear* it is an illogical premise that enables heightened drama in *Chamber of Secrets* and *Deathly Hallows*.

17. In the film, Harry leads the dragon toward a stone bridge, causing the dragon to crash into it and fall into an abyss with a lingering moan. The fate of the dragon is irrelevant: the stadium waits with bated breath for Harry's safe return and explodes into glorious cheering as he—and only he—emerges, with the dragon heroically vanquished.

18. This echoes my analysis of the mollycoddling mother figures in chapter 1.

19. Jackie C. Horne cuttingly describes the house-elves as being "allowed, in the best Rudyard Kipling/Gunga Din fashion, to die in order to save their human masters" ("Answering the Race Question" 96).

20. After the rescue, Buckbeak simply becomes Sirius's property, part of the estate to be inherited by Harry and through him passed back to Hagrid (HBP 53). While his life is indeed saved, he remains captive so that he may continue proving "useful." Presumably, he would prefer freedom because he has to be tethered in the cave with Sirius and shut up in Mrs. Black's bedroom (GF 521; OP 158). But to mitigate what might otherwise present as captivity or slavery, the texts are silent about his feelings. In contrast to Hedwig, who is described as suffering whenever she is denied the freedom to fly and hunt, Rowling largely depicts Buckbeak as rather like a giant chicken, pecking the ground for food, forestalling any readerly concern for his lack of freedom.

21. This is compared to many more frivolous reasons for which Harry risks detention.

22. In the movie, Hedwig is not caged; she is more of a Dobby figure that actively participates in the battle trying to protect Harry. Immediately after flying at Severus Snape's face, she appears to fly right into a curse aimed at Harry. A video compilation put out by MuggleNet in 2018 celebrates how "20 years ago today Hedwig died saving Harry Potter."

23. In contrast to Dobby's funeral, Hedwig does not get a burial. The circumstances—a high-speed chase—forbid it. However, Harry unceremoniously burns her body: he uses a spell to blow up the sidecar in which her caged body is, using her corpse as cannon fodder to attack a nearby Death Eater (instead of, more logically, directing a spell at the Death Eater) (DH 59).

24. Also noteworthy are Aunt Marge, the bulldog breeder who "couldn't bear to leave her precious dogs" (PA 18), and the zany Xenophilius Lovegood, who is pleased that his daughter has been bitten by a garden gnome (DH 140).

25. Hagrid can view even potentially dangerous creatures as deserving of care in part thanks to his own "monstrosity": being half giant, he is unusually big, strong, and hardy. He simply does not have to be afraid. Just as Harry becomes able to think of dragons as "*all right, really*" after his victory over the Hungarian Horntail (*GF* 367), Hagrid is able to see any monstrous creature as merely "*interestin'*" because he feels confidently safe around them (*PA* 218).

26. Effectively weaponized on the "good" side, Grawp is partially redeemed during the Battle of Hogwarts as he fights under Hagrid's direction (*DH* 619), closing the series with Rowling's ultimate take: even a very dumb and violent species can have its (human) uses. I agree wholeheartedly with Scully's interpretation of the Battle of Hogwarts as incongruously tacked on: "The finale of the series wants, *needs*, to have magical beings come together. The Battle of Hogwarts becomes an integrationist fantasy of magical cooperation" (116). "In fact," as Juliana Valadão Lopes notes, "with the exception of Hermione, all of the characters who are wizards fight for the *permanence*" of the unequal status quo (185). Again, the Death Eaters lower the bar: "Dobby remembers how it was when He-Who-Must-Not-Be-Named was at the height of his powers, sir! We house-elves were treated like vermin. . . . [L]ife has improved for my kind since you triumphed. . . . [I]t was a new dawn, sir" (*CS* 178).

27. The many other moments in which Hagrid fails to be kind to nonhumans (some discussed in this chapter) are also presented as contradictions that are the result of an illogical position motivated by pure emotion.

28. However, by *Deathly Hallows*, Hermione has no problem accepting the reformed Kreacher's food and service (228), confirming the series' loudest message: that slavery is okay as long as the slaves are treated kindly.

29. Harry is not objecting to slave ownership per se; he is objecting to the ownership of Kreacher specifically, who he blames for Sirius's death (*HBP* 52).

30. See chapter 2 for more on Ron as sidekick in the context of male homosociality.

31. In *Order of the Phoenix*, Dumbledore notably makes the case for why Kreacher should be "treated with kindness and respect," as "a being with feelings as acute as a human's" (832), but says nothing about slavery.

32. Justice can contribute to happiness: fair treatment, the equal access to resources and opportunities, and the reassurance of having such can make me feel valued by my society and materially improve my quality of life, which can contribute to my happiness. However, justice is just one of many possible factors that may make anyone happy and, by itself, may not be sufficient to bring it about. Conversely, a sense of happiness can contribute to a sense that justice exists, so that someone who has not received an equal share on paper may still feel sufficiently paid in happiness. As house-elves are bred and reared to be "happy" in serving their masters, injustice literally is the source of their happiness. We are told that this is why nearly all the house-elves do not want to be free. We can point to their breeding and rearing—brainwashing, as Hermione says—but still butt up against the question of their present and real agency; to forcibly free them would, paradoxically, be a different form of injustice (denying them the agency to choose happiness over justice). This paradox is particularly aggravated by the history of "white saviors" doing exactly this—imposing inflexible ideas of what justice must look like to "save" others, whose "brainwashing" is taken to justify further encroachments on their agency and autonomy.

33. In *Deathly Hallows*, Ron is also rewarded with Hermione's first kiss when he thinks to rescue, rather than conscript, the Hogwarts house-elves to battle (*DH* 625). This is a rare moment where Rowling allows Harry to appear less humane (he is the one to voice the

possibility of deploying the slaves to fight) in order to elevate Ron. Ron's concern is obviously an improvement to his previous callousness, but, again, the bar seems rather low; the text grants him a significant reward for no longer seeing house-elves as *expendable* chattel. Moreover, "the kiss distracts Ron, Hermione, Harry, and even the reader from the house-elves, and no one ever acts on the idea to evacuate the elves" (Scully 103), who soon show up to fight "in a ludicrously and pathetically manual fashion" (Byler 136). While, at the end, "teachers and pupils, ghosts and parents, centaurs and house-elves" sat "all . . . jumbled together" at the house tables, and even Grawp gets fed through the window, the text is conveniently silent about who prepares the postvictory feast on which they dine (*DH* 745).

34. We eventually find that reassurance dashed. Kreacher's ultimate act of resistance against Sirius has very real consequences as the house-elf proves instrumental in the Death Eater ploy that leads to his master's death. The text makes it difficult for the reader to support his bid to free himself from a master he loathes—Sirius was "good," and he was Harry's hope for escaping the Dursleys—but simultaneously amplifies Dumbledore and Hermione's opinion that Kreacher's cooperation with the Lestrange sisters is understandable and excusable. In this rare moment, nonhuman resistance—even when it causes the death of a "good" character—is given surprising license. Had the series featured more moments like this, I would be less skeptical of Rowling's treatment of Hermione and S.P.E.W.

35. Rowling also includes jarring levity in mentioning that Hagrid's flobberworms have died from "too much lettuce" in the middle of his telling them, through tears, that Buckbeak, the hippogriff, has been sentenced to death (*PA* 220).

Chapter 4: Why Work? Magic, Technology, and the Value of Manual Labor in *Harry Potter*

1. As per Maryann Nguyen, Dumbledore is "surrounded by posthuman technology . . . yet he shows incredible self-restraint . . . and consciously makes the decision not to slip into over-consuming these technologies" (210).

2. To Rowling, it seems, only a caricature-level degree of consumerism deserves scorn. Would avid consumers of *Harry Potter*–licensed products—most of which are collectibles that cannot be said to serve any practical purpose—be within the bounds of what Rowling would deem acceptable consumerism?

3. See Bromberg-Martin et al.

4. Nguyen identifies Voldemort as driven by an "inferiority complex" that drives him to attain "prestige, power and a sense of belonging" through technological overconsumption (214). Kari Newell offers a playful analysis of Voldemort's psychosocial issues as a "nursing care plan" (213).

5. Snape is the only other wizard who manages to learn this "trick" from "his master," and the text animalizes and objectifies him ("a huge, batlike shape flying") instead of complimenting his achievement (*DH* 599).

6. Sheltrown rightly foregrounds how essential wands are not only as the technology that enables all other technology but also as "technical instruments of identity development, as well as passports to a qualified status in a wizarding society" (50). Cut off from magical training and a fully functional wand, Hagrid's situation would seem to be fairly untenable, but he still gloats as he walks on a Muggle "broken-down escalator" that he does not know "how the Muggles manage without magic" (*SS* 67).

7. Another inconsistency is that if children raised in the magical world are forbidden from using magic outside of school until age seventeen, how do they turn on the lights at home? Though the Trace cannot be enforced in children in magical families, we see no examples of any wizarding family allowing underage children to practice their magic over the holidays, suggesting that their society sees value in forcing young people to live out part of their year without directly performing magic. (Nothing forbids them from using charmed objects, however. Consider that driving the flying Ford Anglia does not trigger the Trace in *Chamber of Secrets*.) For example, Molly sets Harry and Ron to peel a "mountain" of sprouts by hand, and Ron pleads with his older brothers—who recently outgrew the Trace—to "free" them from the tedious work with magic (*HBP* 327). Ever the imps, the twins pretend to be seriously concerned about the younger boys missing out on this "very character-building stuff" designed to "[make] you appreciate how difficult it is for Muggles and Squibs" (328). However, there is little in the series to suggest that magical society is particularly concerned with cultivating sympathy or charity for Muggles, who are left to manage their problems on their own, or Squibs, who face significant prejudice and disadvantage if they choose to remain in wizarding society.

8. The detail about the Kwikspell correspondence sheds some light on magical people who cannot keep up with even beginner's magic. They may be people who have "*no memory for incantations*" or fail to grasp how to hold their wands (*CS* 127).

9. In previous generations, there were more innovators, virtually all male: Nicolas Flamel, Dumbledore, Gellert Grindelwald, Snape, and Luna Lovegood's parents (even if Xenophilius does not appear to be a *good* inventor). Also, Harry's father and his male friends invented the Marauder's Map.

10. Harry's poverty in the Muggle world is also awkwardly contrived as he would know from events in *Chamber of Secrets* that he could exchange his wizard coins for Muggle money at Gringotts. He could have at least obtained a radio, for example, to listen to the news in *Order of Phoenix*, purchased food to hide under the floorboards, and upgraded his clothing to things that would fit. Had he done so, however, he would not have cut quite so sympathetic a figure; his woeful summers are a key part of his character portrayal.

11. The Weasleys spend nearly all their *Daily Prophet* Grand Prize Galleon Draw winnings—seven hundred Galleons—on a single trip to Egypt (*PA* 9). The Weasley parents also travel to Romania in *Sorcerer's Stone* and Egypt in *Chamber of Secrets*. Perhaps they are merely poor at financial planning.

12. Although the Floo Network seems widely used, no one else appears at Diagon Alley or elsewhere dusted over in soot—just another telling inconsistency in Rowling's deployment of dirt to mark "poor" bodies. When they arrive, Molly digs out a little brush to sweep off their soot, another item that was likely purchased, instead of using a cleaning spell (*CS* 56).

13. The Weasleys secured prime tickets only because Arthur abused his authority, helping Ludo Bagman's brother escape legal consequences for an enchanted Muggle artifact (*GF* 61).

14. The mysterious ubiquity of minor discomforts is not limited to the poor. Hogwarts's stately impressiveness is a given, but the castle is also unexpectedly lacking in creature comforts. Certain areas, such as the Gryffindor Common Room and the Great Hall, are kept warm with "roaring fires," but "the drafty corridors . . . become icy" (*SS* 194). To emphasize the misery of Potions classes for Harry, the dungeons are bitterly cold—despite all their individual cauldrons aflame—such that "their breath rose in a mist before them" (194). Similarly, it is not clear why St. Mungo's Hospital needs to rely on Knuts from a charity fountain.

15. In the movies, the tents are significantly different: bright, colorful, and spacious enough for five in *Goblet of Fire* and dark, cramped, and dingy in *Deathly Hallows*—another example of exaggerated austerity for the Horcrux hunt.

16. As Sheltrown points out, many of the characters' apparently insurmountable problems also "could have been more readily remedied with basic Muggle technologies" (57). Only at one point do they seem to consider using a contemporary Muggle technology to solve their problems: when they quickly deem procuring an Aqua-Lung impracticable for the second Triwizard task (*GF* 482).

17. Harry exclaims in disbelief that a witch could be in such "desperate need of gold": "But she could do magic! . . . She could have got food and everything for herself by magic, couldn't she?" (*HBP* 262). Dumbledore conjectures that she might have lost some of her powers due to "despair" but that ultimately "Merope refused to raise her wand even to save her own life," which also floors Harry, himself the son of a mother who performed the "ultimate sacrifice" for him (262). Arguably, Merope models resistance to magical overuse—in fact, any magical use—but when the venerable Dumbledore explains that Merope chose to not use magic to keep herself alive, this choice is presented as proof of a deep character flaw. From Merope's case, we can see that the series does not mean to promote a no-technology position: all the "good" characters agree that a good mother would have used magic to acquire whatever she needed to live for the sake of her son.

18. Although steam powered, the *Hogwarts Express*, too, is all about nostalgic aesthetics. This is unquestionably technology—and was once the epitome of cutting edge—but gets a pass because it is now old-timey and quaint. The train also does not appear to be magically hastened, enabling Harry Potter to enjoy a long, eventful ride to school in nearly every installment. As Vernon Dursley sarcastically quips, there *should* be a sense of disappointment at this mode of conveyance—*Did* the magic carpets all "get punctures" (*SS* 89)? (Much later, we learn flying carpets are proscribed.) *Harry Potter*'s aesthetics—the cauldrons, mangles, robes, and broomsticks—effectively disguise magic's similarity to technology, repackaging all that same potentially body-and-soul-ruining convenience into a more palatable alternative. These medieval aesthetics elicits the sense that wizarding folk lead "simpler"—and therefore more satisfying—lives.

19. See chapter 4 for more on owls. Ron sends his owl the same way: "He threw Pigwidgeon out the window. Pigwidgeon plummeted twelve feet before managing to pull himself back up again; the letter attached to his leg was much longer and heavier than usual" (*GF* 364).

20. Oakes also praises the goblins' (ab)use of the dragon for security, noting that "while I assume that dragons need to be fed occasionally, the safety of the bank's vaults does not depend upon electricity that could fail, security codes that could be broken, or even locks that could be picked" (122)—sparing not a word of sympathy.

21. Slavery is the more accurate term than "indentured servitude" for their condition. See chapter 4 for more analysis of the house-elves.

22. The sole human caretaker, Filch, is a Squib. When Harry downplays his "crime" of tracking in mud, the flu-afflicted Filch shouts, "It's only a bit of mud to you, boy, but to me it's an extra hour of scrubbing!" (*CS* 126). This valid point is cruelly undercut by the description of the dripping mucus from his "bulbous nose" as he shouts it.

23. In the movie, students take the place of the elf servers. Neville Longbottom makes it sound like this is the only way a magically untalented student, like him, can attend the exclusive soirée.

24. It is unclear what it takes for something to be called "hand knitted" in the wizarding world. The second film shows needles charmed to work on their own.

25. In *Order of the Phoenix*, Dumbledore asks Professor McGonagall to conjure extra chairs for his office (469), even though he could have done so instantaneously himself. This is not magical restraint; this is a man displacing the need to perform the menial magic onto his female deputy—a maternal figure, as per chapter 1.

26. This resonates with the texts' portrayal of Harry as not being bothered to apply himself to schoolwork; it is quietly implied that should he put in the effort, perhaps Hermione's academic lead would not be so dramatic. See chapter 1.

27. In chapter 3, I discuss this from the perspective of how nonhumans are treated; here, I focus only on the novel's emphasis on the nonmagical, manual nature of the work.

28. It is a common trope of the hero movie genre to contrive such endings: the "good" character never seeks to kill, but somehow circumstances conveniently force him to kill in self-defense, or his enemy's death happens without him directly pulling the trigger.

29. I find this a poorly executed contrivance. While Harry does use that spell against Voldemort in *Goblet of Fire*, it was purportedly because Voldemort declared this a "duel," and Expelliarmus was the only spell he had learned at the dueling club two years earlier (660). And while he did teach that spell to Dumbledore's Army in *Order of the Phoenix*, he did not use it during the Death Eater battle in the Department of Mysteries. In the entirety of *Half-Blood Prince*, he did not use the spell once, neither when he was striking down Draco (Levicorpus, Sectumsempra) nor attacking Death Eaters after they killed Dumbledore (Petrificus Totalus, Impedimenta, Stupefy, Crucio, Incarcerous, Sectumsempra, Levicorpus). No wonder we need Remus to announce it as his "signature."

Chapter 5: The Chosen One: The Limits of Self-Determination in *Harry Potter*

1. Not enough readers mark the disturbing moment in Severus Snape's "worst memory" when, upended by Levicorpus, his "graying underpants" exposed (*OP* 647), he is thoroughly humiliated. The scene means to present brave, young Lily as his sole defender, in contrast to everyone who is cheering and laughing at his abjection, but the text curiously implies that Lily's heart is not quite so pure: her "expression had twitched for an instant as though she were going to smile" (648). I find her response to be troubling—a shocking streak of sadism wholly inconsistent with her characterization. Perhaps this crack in her goody-two-shoes persona is Rowling's attempt to explain why she ends up with the arrogant, bullying James Potter or to add dimension to her otherwise overly saccharine depiction.

2. When Draco Malfoy first introduces the notion, there is also some contradiction: he explains that "the other sort" should not be allowed into Hogwarts because "they're just not the same, they've never been brought up to know our ways" (*SS* 78). This is a different type of argument—cultural prejudice—that is linked to a biological one.

3. While Death Eaters might claim to believe that "magic is might" (*DH* 242), ironically, Dumbledore is the one who more truly espouses this belief, as he believes that anyone with magical talent should be allowed admission to Hogwarts. If Death Eaters truly believed magic is might, then all magical beings—regardless of parentage or species—would deserve recognition at the top of the hierarchy.

4. Squibs muddle the question of wizarding "blood" as well: they are, by definition, the blood descendants of pure-blood magical parents but apparently lack "magical blood." Maureen Saraco reads Squibs through the lens of disability theory in "Squibs, Disability and Having a Place at Hogwarts School of Witchcraft and Wizardry." Karen A. Brown offers an interesting reading of Umbridge as a near Squib, conjecturing that insecurity drives her cruelty (76).

5. In nearly every scene that includes Hagrid, his abnormal appearance is referred to gratuitously, irrelevantly, or as comic relief, such as when he becomes stuck in a doorway while George Weasley lies bleeding on the couch (*DH* 69). By inviting readers to both laugh at and sympathize with some of her characters, Rowling can serve taboo cake and let readers eat it too.

6. Menacing appearances are not misleading when it comes to most, however. As Lauren R. Camacci notes, "Rowling is not kind to her baddies" (192): she is often "mean *and* moralizing. They [her characterizations] are an attempt to get you to dislike the character immediately, or not to trust them, and the eviler, the worse and more consistent the descriptor" (193).

7. See Sridevi Rao and Preethi Gorecki's discussion of whether Dobby does, indeed, become a free elf when his society severely restricts the possibility of such an existence.

8. In *Deathly Hallows*, this evil piece of soul is described during the King's Cross Station scene as "a small, naked child, curled on the ground, its skin raw and rough, flayed-looking" (706).

9. Raymond I. Schuck remarks that "in no other case does the Sorting Hat appear to deliberate" (19), but in *Sorcerer's Stone*, Harry notes that "sometimes . . . the hat shouted out the House at once, but at others it took a little while to decide" (120). This is not only in the case of Neville, who Schuck analyzes as either too "scatter-brained" to be accurately read or, as we later learn, could have been in Harry's place (19): Seamus Finnigan "sat on the stool for almost a whole minute" (*SS* 120). The language suggests that Hermione did not express her choice, which we know is Gryffindor, but surely the *omniscient* hat would know her preference (106). In the epilogue to *Deathly Hallows*, Harry tells his younger son Albus that he will have a choice of House. "The Sorting Hat takes your choice into account," he confidently declares, because "it did for me" (*DH* 758)—a prediction that should be incorrect. In *Harry Potter and the Cursed Child*, Albus is sorted into Slytherin, and we are never told if he attempted to assert a choice—only that he is left "*thoroughly discombobulated*" by the announcement (21).

10. Readers and fans, too, have clamored to take the online Pottermore Sorting Hat Quiz, which can still be found online.

11. It is a galling question why the Goblet of Fire can omnisciently assess all submitted names yet be unable to discern that one of those names does not attend the school under which it was listed. And had Harry overslept for the second task, as he was close to doing, would the goblet have struck him down?

12. The movie wisely omits this declaration of not having any choice. Instead, the imperi-used Barty Crouch insists on following the tournament rules, and Dumbledore goes along for a different problematic reason: to use Harry as bait to draw out the schemer.

13. The fact that Neville uses his dad's old wand until after *Order of the Phoenix* is a metaphor for his grandmother's insistence that he replace his father; Neville is denied the opportunity to be chosen by a wand that befits him. Ron begins his Hogwarts career with Charlie's old wand as a symbol of his poverty and the fact that he lives in the shadow of his brothers.

Given the rules of wandlore, however, it is odd that Charlie would have sought to replace the wand that chose him.

14. Notably, the phrase "no choice"—as in, the characters have "no choice" but to behave this or that way—is used almost forty times across the series, frequently with Harry, including the moment he "pushed . . . away" his moral discomfort with tricking Griphook to secure his assistance: "What choice did they have?" (*DH* 508).

15. I agree with Lily Anne Welty Tamai and Paul Spickard's reading of Harry as "an example of hybrid vigor"—the problematic colonial idea that multiracial people can "embody . . . the best of both worlds" (146). Certainly he, too, is exploited by Dumbledore for his hybridity—for the "greater good."

16. It is perhaps mildly sadistic of Dumbledore and Harry to persist in saying Voldemort's name despite how clearly unsettling this is for everyone else.

17. Harry seems to have adopted this weapon as well, as he derides Dudley's self-refashioning as Big D (a fair name, by all accounts), teasingly insisting, "You'll always be Ickle Diddykins to me" (one of Aunt Petunia's pet names for Dudley) (*OP* 13). Perhaps this is just another moment out of the many examples in the series when a strategy or move that would otherwise be deemed "bad" becomes conveniently legitimate when done for "good" ends, such as when Dumbledore breaks the law in administering Veritaserum to Barty Crouch Jr. in *Goblet of Fire* and Harry becomes surprisingly comfortable using two of the three Unforgivable Curses in *Deathly Hallows*.

18. Eric Saidel argues that when he is in human form, Sirius is a man, but "when he looks like a dog, he's neither. Padfoot-Sirius [is] a unique kind of being—a man-dog—that combines both features of humans and dogs" (33).

19. The same suspension of ethics that happens with ferret-Draco occurs with Rita Skeeter, who, in *Goblet of Fire*, is trapped by Hermione in a glass jar and blackmailed while in beetle form. Had she been in human form, her captivity would have cast Hermione in a completely different light. See chapter 3 for more on nonhuman captivity.

20. After learning that Crabbe and Goyle polyjuiced into girls, Harry does become more open to the possibility that another male might better conceal their identity that way, as when he corrects Hermione's supposition that "it must have been a girl or a woman" who attacked Katie Bell in the ladies' room (*HBP* 517).

21. When he first learns of this, Harry is intrigued by the possibility that he might be able to learn how to hide his most distinguishing feature, his lightning scar (*OP* 52). That way, he could hide a central aspect of his identity.

22. The next morning, Hermione "confessed" to Harry that the smooth, sleek hair was the product of "liberal amounts" of magic potion (*GF* 433); the word choice suggests that there is something excessive and shameful in her manipulation of her appearance. The text then distinguishes her from the girly girls by having her "matter-of-factly" declare that it is still not worthwhile to do every day (433).

23. See chapter 1.

24. Despite Rowling's tongue-in-cheek allusion to a phallus ("the tip of her nose . . . caused the veil to protrude slightly"), at this point, Harry can only suspect the "witch" of being Umbridge in disguise, unable to imagine anything but a female body under a witch's clothing (*OP* 336). The reminder of his phallus might have been Rowling's way to mark the feminized body as still "truly" male. Just as Ron expresses disbelief that Crabbe and Goyle are polyjuicing into girls, Harry is "stunned" to learn that the veiled witch was Mundungus (370).

Epilogue: Rowling Also Stinks: Fandom and the Problematic Living Author

1. The Forstater saga is lengthy. As a starting point, see Ivy. Magdalen Berns was a lesbian feminist activist who campaigned against Scotland's Gender Recognition Reform Bill of 2022, which would have made it less onerous to change one's legal gender (Carr).

2. Rowling flatteringly describes her supporters as "a cross-section of kind, empathetic and intelligent people" ("J. K. Rowling Writes")—and wouldn't that be the group one would wish to be aligned with?

3. Rowling's online declarations since belie these claims of accident and coincidence. See Romano, "Is J. K. Rowling Transphobic?"; Gardner; Uspenskiy.

4. The essay provides no citations for some claims that should be objectively provable, and Zinnia Jones's three-part analysis with sources "We the Mudbloods: J. K. Rowling and the Trans-Exterminationists" goes some way toward exposing that.

5. Let's not forget, moreover, that trans people are statistically more likely to suffer physical and sexual abuse (Stotzer 1362; Cook-Daniels and Munson 142; Dinno 1441; Moeder; "Responding to Transgender Victims").

6. In US constitutional law, proving animus against a particular group on the part of legislatures is a bar that many plaintiffs must reach. See Pollvogt; Araiza.

7. In an interview on the subject, Judith Butler incisively breaks down how Rowling effectively seeks to define a person by their penis and "assumes that the penis is the threat, or any person who has a penis who identifies as a woman is engaging in a base, deceitful, and harmful form of disguise" (qtd. in Ferber).

8. As per Sarah Wheaton, "Heightening the tension is an explosion of referrals for gender-dysphoria services for children and young people in the U.K., which have gone from 50 in 2009 to 2,500 annually by 2020. . . . For trans-rights activists, those numbers reveal undercapacity in British health care. . . . Rowling and other so-called gender-critical feminists (the more neutral term) see things differently. For them, the spike in reported gender dysphoria is evidence of persistent misogyny and homophobia."

9. Rowling also tweeted, "The idea that women like me, who've been empathetic to trans people for decades . . . 'hate' trans people because they think sex is real and has lived consequences is a nonsense" (@jk_rowling, "Idea").

WORKS CITED

Adegbeye, OluTimehin. "Ignorance Is Power Too: Why J. K. Rowling Deliberately Repeats Untruths about Trans People." *Correspondent*, 7 Aug. 2002, thecorrespondent.com/631 /ignorance-is-power-too-why-jk-rowling-deliberately-repeats-untruths-about-trans-people.

Alexander, Julie. "The Filmic Heroine." *Hermione Granger Saves the World: Essays on the Feminist Heroine of Hogwarts*, edited by Christopher E. Bell, McFarland, 2012, pp. 16–33.

Allcorn, Ashley, and Shirley M. Ogletree. "Linked Oppression: Connecting Animal and Gender Attitudes." *Feminism and Psychology*, vol. 28, no. 4, Mar. 2018, pp. 457–69, doi .org/10.1177/0959353518759562.

Appelbaum, Peter. "Harry Potter's World: Magic, Technoculture, and Becoming Human." *Harry Potter's World: Multidisciplinary Critical Perspectives*, edited by Elizabeth E. Heilman, RoutledgeFalmer, 2003, pp. 24–52.

Araiza, William D. "Animus and Its Discontents." *Florida Law Review*, vol. 71, no. 1, 2019, pp. 155–216, scholarship.law.ufl.edu/flr/vol71/iss1/4.

Armstrong, Rachel. "Sexual Geometry of the Golden Trio: Hermione's Subversion of Traditional Female Subject Positions." *A Wizard of Their Age: Critical Essays from the Harry Potter Generation*, edited by Cecilia Konchar Farr, State U of New York P, 2015, pp. 235–50.

Arxer, Steven L. "Hybrid Masculine Power: Reconceptualizing the Relationship between Homosociality and Hegemonic Masculinity." *Humanity and Society*, vol. 35, no. 4, Nov. 2011, pp. 390–422.

Bausman, Cassandra. "'Elder' and Wiser: The Filmic *Harry Potter* and the Rejection of Power." *Transforming Harry: The Adaptation of Harry Potter in the Transmedia Age*, edited by John Alberti and P. Andrew Miller, Wayne State UP, 2018, pp. 38–70.

Bealer, Tracy. "Consider the Dementor: Discipline, Punishment, and Magical Citizenship in Harry Potter." *Dialogue*, vol. 6, no. 3, 2019, pp. 36–47.

Bell, Christopher E. "Introduction." *Hermione Granger Saves the World: Essays on the Feminist Heroine of Hogwarts*, edited by Bell, McFarland, 2012, pp. 1–13.

Bellot, Gabrielle. "How JK Rowling Betrayed the World She Created." *Literary Hub*, 10 Jun. 2020, lithub.com/how-jk-rowling-betrayed-the-world-she-created/.

Berndt, Katrin. "Hermione Granger, or, a Vindication of the Rights of Girl." *Heroism in the Harry Potter Series*, edited by Berndt and Lena Steveker, Routledge, 2016, pp. 159–76.

Bird, Jackson. "'Harry Potter' Helped Me Come Out as Trans, But J. K. Rowling Disappointed Me." *New York Times*, 21 Dec. 2019, nytimes.com/2019/12/21/opinion/jk-rowling-twitter-trans.html.

Bird, Sharon R. "Welcome to the Men's Club: Homosociality and the Maintenance of Hegemonic Masculinity." *Gender and Society*, vol. 10, no. 2, Apr. 1996, pp. 120–32. *JSTOR*, jstor.org/stable/i209825.

Bloom, Harold. "Can 35 Million Book Buyers Be Wrong? Yes." *Wall Street Journal*, 11 Jul. 2000, wsj.com/articles/SB963270836801555352.

Bromberg-Martin, Ethan S., Masayuki Matsumoto, and Okihide Hikosaka. "Dopamine in Motivational Control: Rewarding, Aversive, and Alerting." *Neuron*, vol. 68, no. 5, Dec. 2010, pp. 518–34, doi.org/10.1016/j.neuron.2010.11.022.

Brown, Karen A. *Prejudice in Harry Potter's World: A Social Critique of the Series, Using Allport's "The Nature of Prejudice."* Virtualbookwork.com, 2008.

Burns, Katelyn. "J.K. Rowling's Transphobia Is a Product of British Culture." *Vox*, 19 Dec. 2019, vox.com/identities/2019/12/19/21029874/jk-rowling-transgender-tweet-terf.

Burt, Molly L. "'Perfectly Normal, Thank You Very Much': Exploitation of Hybridity in the Borderlands of Harry Potter." *The Ivory Tower, Harry Potter, and Beyond: More Essays on the Works of J. K. Rowling*, edited by Lana A. Whited, U of Missouri P, 2023, pp. 219–35.

Butler, Judith. *Undoing Gender*. Routledge, 2004.

Byatt, A. S. "Harry Potter and the Childish Adult." *New York Times*, 7 Jul. 2003, nytimes.com/2003/07/07/opinion/harry-potter-and-the-childish-adult.html.

Byler, Lauren. "Makeovers, Individualism, and Vanishing Community in the Harry Potter Series." *Children's Literature*, vol. 44, 2016, pp. 115–46.

Camacci, Lauren R. "The Face of Evil: Physiognomy in Potter." *Open at the Close: Literary Essays on Harry Potter*, edited by Cecilia Konchar Farr, UP of Mississippi, 2022, pp. 188–200.

Carey, Brycchan. "Hermione and the House-Elves: The Literary and Historical Contexts of J. K. Rowling's Antislavery Campaign." *Reading Harry Potter: Critical Essays*, edited by Giselle Liza Anatol, Praeger, 2003, pp. 103–15.

Carr, Stewart. "The Lesbian Who Launched 1,000 Feminists: Story of Same Sex Rights Campaigner Whose Work Inspired J.K. Rowling's Activism." *Daily Mail*, 21 Jan. 2023, dailymail.co.uk/news/article-11568569/Tragic-story-feminist-campaigner-work-inspired-JK-Rowlings-activism.html.

Chandler, Timothy J. L., and John Nauright. *Making Men: Rugby and Masculine Identity*. Routledge, 1996.

Cherland, Meredith. "Harry Potter and the Discourse of Gender." *Journal of Adolescent and Adult Literacy*, vol. 52, no. 4, Dec. 2008/Jan. 2009, pp. 273–82. *JSTOR*, jstor.org/stable/40058129.

Chevalier, Noel. "The Liberty Tree and the Whomping Willow: Political Justice, Magical Science, and Harry Potter." *Lion and the Unicorn*, vol. 29, no. 3, Sept. 2005, pp. 397–415. *Project Muse*, doi.org/10.1353/uni.2005.0041.

Chez, Keridiana. "The Mandrake's Lethal Cry: Homuncular Plants in J. K. Rowling's *Harry Potter and the Chamber of Secrets*." *Plant Horror: Approaches to the Monstrous Vegetal in Fiction and Film*, edited by Dawn Keetley and Angela Tenga, Palgrave Macmillan, 2016, pp. 73–90.

Chez, Keridiana. "Sorry, Not Sorry: The Limits of Empathy for Nonhuman Creatures." *Open at the Close: Literary Essays on Harry Potter,* edited by Cecilia Konchar Farr, UP of Mississippi, 2022, pp. 166–77.

Chica, Christina M. "The Magical (Racial) Contract: Understanding the Wizarding World of Harry Potter through Whiteness." *Harry Potter and the Other: Race, Justice, and Difference in the Wizarding World,* edited by Sarah Park Dalen and Ebony Elizabeth Thomas, UP of Mississippi, 2022, pp. 71–85.

Clifton, Lindsay. "Work in a Magical World: Revisiting the Stratification of Castes in Harry Potter." *Legilimens! Perspectives in Harry Potter Studies,* edited by Christopher Bell, Cambridge Scholars, 2013, pp. 67–74.

Cook-Daniels, Loree, and Michael Munson. "Sexual Violence, Elder Abuse, and Sexuality of Transgender Adults, Age 50+: Results of Three Surveys." *Journal of GLBT Family Studies,* vol. 6, no. 2, Apr. 2010, pp. 142–77, doi.org/10.1080/15504281003705238.

Cordova, Melanie J. "'Because I'm a *Girl,* I Suppose!' Gender Lines and Narrative Perspective in *Harry Potter.*" *Mythlore,* vol. 33, no. 2, spring/summer 2015, pp. 21–35.

Cothran, Casey A. "Lessons in Transfiguration: Allegories of Male Identity in Rowling's *Harry Potter* Series." *Scholarly Studies in Harry Potter: Applying Academic Methods to a Popular Text,* edited by Cynthia Whitney Hallett, Edwin Mellen P, 2005, pp. 123–34.

Cotter, David A., et al. "The Glass Ceiling Effect." *Social Forces,* vol. 80, no. 2, Dec. 2001, pp. 655–81, doi.org/10.1353/sof.2001.0091.

Dahlen, Sarah Park, and Kallie Schell. "'Cho Chang Is Trending': What It Means to Be Asian in the Wizarding World." *Harry Potter and the Other: Race, Justice, and Difference in the Wizarding World,* edited by Dahlen and Ebony Elizabeth Thomas, UP of Mississippi, 2022, pp. 86–104.

Dahlen, Sarah Park, and Ebony Elizabeth Thomas. "Introduction." *Harry Potter and the Other: Race, Justice, and Difference in the Wizarding World,* edited by Dahlen and Thomas, UP of Mississippi, 2022, pp. 1–13.

Deckha, Maneesha. "The Salience of Species Difference for Feminist Theory." *Hastings Women's Law Journal,* vol. 17, no. 1, winter 2006, animallaw.info/article/salience -species-difference-feminist-theory.

Dederer, Claire. *Monsters: A Fan's Dilemma.* Alfred A. Knopf, 2023.

De Hingh, Valentijn. "I'm Trans and I Understand JK Rowling's Concerns about the Position of Women: But Transphobia Is Not the Answer." *The Correspondent,* 18 Sept. 2020, thecorrespondent.com/702/im-trans-and-i-understand-jk-rowlings-concerns- about-the-position-of-women-but-transphobia-is-not-the-answer.

Dendle, Peter. "Monsters, Creatures, and Pets at Hogwarts: Animal Stewardship in the World of Harry Potter." *Critical Perspectives on Harry Potter,* edited by Elizabeth E. Heilman, Routledge, 2009, pp. 163–76.

Dinno, Alexis. "Homicide Rates of Transgender Individuals in the United States: 2010– 2014." *American Journal of Public Health,* vol. 107, no. 9, Sept. 2017, pp. 1441–47, doi.org /10.2105/AJPH.2017.303878.

Di Placido, Dani. "The 'Harry Potter' Anti-Semitism Controversy, Explained." *Forbes,* 5 Jan. 2022, forbes.com/sites/danidiplacido/2022/01/05/the-harry-potter-anti-semitism -controversy-explained/?sh=713545f66776.

Doughty, Amie A. "Just a Fairy, His Wits, and Maybe a Touch of Magic: Magic, Technology, and Self-Reliance in Contemporary Fantasy Fiction." *Children's Literature and Culture,* edited by Harry Eiss, Cambridge Scholars, 2007, pp. 53–76.

Doughty, Terri. "Locating Harry Potter in the 'Boy's Book' Market." *The Ivory Tower and Harry Potter: Perspectives on a Literary Phenomenon*, edited by Lana A. Whited, U of Missouri P, 2002, pp. 243–87.

Dresang, Eliza T. "Hermione Granger and the Heritage of Gender." *The Ivory Tower and Harry Potter: Perspectives on a Literary Phenomenon*, edited by Lana A. Whited, U of Missouri P, 2002, pp. 211–42.

Duggan, Jennifer. "Transformative Readings: Harry Potter Fan Fiction, Trans/Queer Reader Response, and J.K. Rowling." *Children's Literature in Education*, vol. 53, 2022, pp. 147–68, doi.org/10.1007/s10583-021-09446-9.

"Female." *Merriam-Webster*, 2024, https://www.merriam-webster.com/dictionary/female.

Ferber, Alona. "Judith Butler on the Culture Wars, JK Rowling and Living in 'Anti-Intellectual Times.'" *New Statesman*, 22 Sept. 2020, newstatesman.com/long-reads /2020/09/judith-butler-culture-wars-jk-rowling-living-anti-intellectual-times.

Flood, Michael. "Men, Sex, and Homosociality: How Bonds between Men Shape Their Sexual Relations with Women." *Men and Masculinities*, vol. 10, no. 3, Apr. 2008, pp. 339–59. *Sage*, doi.org/10.1177/1097184X06287761.

Foster, Tara. "'Books! And Cleverness!' Hermione's Wits." *Hermione Granger Saves the World: Essays on the Feminist Heroine of Hogwarts*, edited by Christopher E. Bell, McFarland, 2012, pp. 105–24.

Gallardo-C., Ximena, and C. Jason Smith. "Cinderfella: J.K. Rowling's Wily Web of Gender." *Reading Harry Potter: Critical Essays*, edited by Giselle Liza Anatol, Praeger, 2003, pp. 191–205.

Gallardo-C., Ximena, and C. Jason Smith. "Happily Ever After: Harry Potter and the Quest for the Domestic." *Reading Harry Potter Again: New Critical Essays*, edited by Giselle Liza Anatol, Praeger, 2009, pp. 91–108.

Gardner, Abby. "A Complete Breakdown of the J. K. Rowling Transgender-Comments Controversy." *Glamour*, 25 Apr. 2023, glamour.com/story/a-complete-breakdown-of-the -jk-rowling-transgender-comments-controversy.

Gercama, Atje. "'I'm Hoping to Do Some Good in the World': Hermione Granger and Feminist Ethics." *Hermione Granger Saves the World: Essays on the Feminist Heroine of Hogwarts*, edited by Christopher E. Bell, McFarland, 2012, pp. 34–51.

Gierzynski, Anthony, with Kathryn Eddy. *Harry Potter and the Millennials: Research Methods and the Politics of the Muggle Generation*. Johns Hopkins UP, 2013.

Glassman, Kate. "'Always Dependently, Solidly Present': The Preeminence of Minerva McGonagall." *Open at the Close: Literary Essays on Harry Potter*, edited by Cecilia Konchar Farr, UP of Mississippi, 2022, pp. 135–53.

Grossman, Lev. "Dumbledore = Gay." *Time*, 22 Oct. 2007, techland.time.com/2007/10/22 /dumbledore_gay/.

Hammarén, Nils, and Thomas Johansson. "Homosociality: In between Power and Intimacy." *Sage Open*, vol. 4, no. 1, Jan./Mar. 2014, pp. 1–11, doi.org/10.1177/2158244013518057.

Harding, Kate. *Asking for It: The Alarming Rise of Rape Culture and What We Can Do About It*. Hachette, 2015.

Harrison, Jen. "Posthuman Power: The Magic of Hybridity in the Harry Potter Series." *Children's Literature Association Quarterly*, vol. 43, no. 3, fall 2018, pp. 325–43. *Project Muse*, doi.org/10.1353/chq.2018.0037.

Harry Potter and the Chamber of Secrets. Directed by Chris Columbus, performances by Daniel Radcliffe, Rupert Grint, Emma Watson, Richard Harris, Alan Rickman, Maggie Smith, Fiona Shaw, Kenneth Branagh, and Robbie Coltrane, Warner Brothers, 2002.

Harry Potter and the Deathly Hallows—Part 1. Directed by David Yates, performances by Daniel Radcliffe, Rupert Grint, Emma Watson, Michael Gambon, Alan Rickman, Maggie Smith, Fiona Shaw, Ralph Fiennes, and Robbie Coltrane, Warner Brothers, 2010.

Harry Potter and the Deathly Hallows—Part 2. Directed by David Yates, performances by Daniel Radcliffe, Rupert Grint, Emma Watson, Michael Gambon, Alan Rickman, Maggie Smith, Fiona Shaw, Ralph Fiennes, and Robbie Coltrane, Warner Brothers, 2011.

Harry Potter and the Goblet of Fire. Directed by Mike Newell, performances by Daniel Radcliffe, Rupert Grint, Emma Watson, Michael Gambon, Alan Rickman, Maggie Smith, Fiona Shaw, Brendan Gleeson, and Robbie Coltrane, Warner Brothers, 2005.

Harry Potter and the Half-Blood Prince. Directed by David Yates, performances by Daniel Radcliffe, Rupert Grint, Emma Watson, Michael Gambon, Alan Rickman, Maggie Smith, Fiona Shaw, and Robbie Coltrane, Warner Brothers, 2009.

Harry Potter and the Order of the Phoenix. Directed by David Yates, performances by Daniel Radcliffe, Rupert Grint, Emma Watson, Michael Gambon, Alan Rickman, Maggie Smith, Fiona Shaw, Imelda Staunton, and Robbie Coltrane, Warner Brothers, 2007.

Harry Potter and the Prisoner of Azkaban. Directed by Alfonso Cuarón, performances by Daniel Radcliffe, Rupert Grint, Emma Watson, Michael Gambon, Alan Rickman, Maggie Smith, Fiona Shaw, David Thewlis, and Robbie Coltrane, Warner Brothers, 2004.

Harry Potter and the Sorcerer's Stone. Directed by Chris Columbus, performances by Daniel Radcliffe, Rupert Grint, Emma Watson, Richard Harris, Alan Rickman, Maggie Smith, Fiona Shaw, Ian Hart, and Robbie Coltrane, Warner Brothers, 2001.

Hayles, Dianne. "Nonhuman Animals, Inclusion, and Belonging in *Harry Potter and the Philosopher's Stone.*" *Knowing Their Place: Identity and Space in Children's Literature,* edited by Terri Doughty and Dawn Thompson, Cambridge Scholars, 2011, pp. 187–99.

Heilman, Elizabeth E., and Trevor Donaldson. "From Sexist to (Sort-of) Feminist: Representations of Gender in the Harry Potter Series." *Critical Perspectives on Harry Potter,* edited by Heilman, Routledge, 2009, pp. 139–61.

Henderson, Tolonda. "Chosen Names, Changed Appearances, and Unchallenged Binaries: Trans-Exclusionary Themes in Harry Potter." *Harry Potter and the Other: Race, Justice, and Difference in the Wizarding World,* edited by Sarah Park Dahlen and Ebony Elizabeth Thomas, UP of Mississippi, 2022, pp. 164–77.

Hidalgo, Alexandra. "Unstoppable Force: Maternal Power and Feminism." *Hermione Granger Saves the World: Essays on the Feminist Heroine of Hogwarts,* edited by Christopher E. Bell, McFarland, 2012, pp. 66–86.

Horne, Jackie C. "Harry and the Other: Answering the Race Question in J. K. Rowling's Harry Potter." *Lion and the Unicorn,* vol. 34, no. 1, Jan. 2010, pp. 76–104. *Project Muse,* muse.jhu.edu/article/377032.

Horne, Jackie C. "Harry and the Other: Multicultural and Social Justice Anti-Racism." *Harry Potter and the Other: Race, Justice, and Difference in the Wizarding World,* edited by Sarah Park Dahlen and Ebony Elizabeth Thomas, UP of Mississippi, 2022, pp. 17–50.

Hunter, Joel. "Technological Anarchism: The Meaning of Magic in Harry Potter." *Harry Potter for Nerds: Essays for Fans, Academics, and Lit Geeks,* edited by Travis Prinzi, Unlocking P, 2011, pp. 105–34.

Ivy, Veronica. "J. K. Rowling's Maya Forstater Tweets Support Hostile Work Environments, Not Free Speech." *NBC,* 20 Dec. 2019, nbcnews.com/think/opinion/j-k-rowling-s-maya -forstater-tweets-support-hostile-work-ncna1105201.

Jones, Zinnia. "We the Mudbloods: J. K. Rowling and the Trans-Exterminationists." *Gender Analysis*, 30 Jun. 2020, genderanalysis.net/2020/06/we-the-mudbloods-j-k-rowling-and -the-trans-exterminationists-book-1/.

Kellner, Rivka Temima. "J. K. Rowling's Ambivalence towards Feminism: House Elves— Women in Disguise—in the *Harry Potter* Books." *Midwest Quarterly*, vol. 51, no. 4, Jun. 2010, pp. 367–84.

Kemmerer, Lisa. "Introduction." *Sister Species: Women, Animals, and Social Justice*, edited by Kemmerer, U of Illinois P, 2011, pp. 1–44.

Kirkpatrick, Emily. "J. K. Rowling Proves Her Commitment to Transphobia in Her New Novel." *Vanity Fair*, 14 Sept. 2020, vanityfair.com/style/2020/09/jk-rowling-transphobia -new-novel-troubled-blood-controversy.

Kniesler, Sarah Margaret. "Alohomora! Unlocking Hermione's Feminism." *Hermione Granger Saves the World: Essays on the Feminist Heroine of Hogwarts*, edited by Christopher E. Bell, McFarland, 2012, pp. 87–103.

Kniesler, Sarah Margaret. "The Unbreakable Vow: Maternal Impulses and Narcissa Malfoy's Transformation from Villain to Hero in J. K. Rowling's *Harry Potter* Series." *A Quest of Her Own: Essays on the Female Hero in Modern Fantasy*, edited by Lori M. Campbell, McFarland, 2014, pp. 267–81.

Kurtzleben, Danielle. "Why Are Highly Educated Americans Getting More Liberal?" *NPR*, 30 Apr. 2016, npr.org/2016/04/30/475794063/why-are-highly-educated-americans -getting-more-liberal.

LaHaie, Jeanne Hoeker. "Mums Are Good: Harry Potter and Traditional Depictions of Women." *Critical Insights: The Harry Potter Series*, edited by Lana A. Whited and M. Katherine Grimes, Salem P, 2015, pp. 123–45.

Levin, Bess. "Putin: I Now Consider JK Rowling My Sister from Another Mister." *Vanity Fair*, 25 Mar. 2022, vanityfair.com/news/2022/03/ ladimir-putin-jk-rowling-russia-cancel-culture.

Levinson, Dana Aliya. "I'm a Trans Harry Potter Fan, and There Are a Few Things I Want J. K. Rowling to Know." *Huffington Post*, 11 Jun. 2020, huffpost.com/entry/jk-rowling -transgender-harry-potter-fan_n_5ee17ed4c5b6c727a2a491c5.

Lewis, Danny. "Reading Harry Potter Might Make You a Better Person." *Smithsonian Magazine*, 7 May 2015, smithsonianmag.com/smart-news/reading-harry-potter-might -make-you-better-person-180955196/.

Lopes, Juliana Valadão. "'All Was Well'? The Sociopolitical Struggles of House-Elves, Goblins, and Centaurs." *Open at the Close: Literary Essays on Harry Potter*, edited by Cecilia Konchar Farr, UP of Mississippi, 2022, pp. 178–87.

Mauk, Margaret S. "'Your Mother Died to Save You': The Influence of Mothers in Constructing Moral Frameworks for Violence in *Harry Potter*." *Mythlore*, vol. 36, no. 1, fall/winter 2017, pp. 123–40. *Proquest*, proquest.com/docview/1977272796.

Mayes-Elma, Ruthann. *Females and Harry Potter: Not All That Empowering*. Rowman, 2006.

McDougal, Jenny. "Doubting Dumbledore." *A Wizard of Their Age: Critical Essays from the Harry Potter Generation*, edited by Cecilia Konchar Farr, State U of New York P, 2015, pp. 159–79.

McKibben, Bill. *Enough: Staying Human in an Engineered Age*. Henry Holt, 2003.

Mendlesohn, Farah. "Crowning the King: Harry Potter and the Construction of Authority." *The Ivory Tower and Harry Potter: Perspectives on a Literary Phenomenon*, edited by Lana A. Whited, U of Missouri P, 2002, pp. 159–81.

Moeder, Nicole. "Number of Trans Homicides Doubled Over 4 Years, with Gun Killings Fueling Increase: Advocates." *ABC News*, 12 Oct. 2022, abcnews.go.com/US /homicide-rate-trans-people-doubled-gun-killings-fueling/story?id=91348274.

MuggleNet. "20 Years Ago Today Hedwig Died Saving Harry Potter." *YouTube*, 27 Jul. 2017, youtube.com/watch?v=ilme-L4IVfA.

Mutz, Diana C. "Harry Potter and the Deathly Donald." *PS: Political Science and Politics*, vol. 49, no. 4, 2016, pp. 722–29, doi.org/10.1017/S1049096516001633.

Newell, Kari. "A Nursing Care Plan for Tom Riddle." *A Wizard of Their Age: Critical Essays from the Harry Potter Generation*, edited by Cecilia Konchar Farr, State U of New York P, 2015, pp. 213–21.

Nguyen, Maryann. "Flirting with Posthuman Technologies in Harry Potter: Over-Consumption of a Good Thing—Technology as Magic." *Cultural Politics in Harry Potter: Life, Death, and the Politics of Fear*, edited by Rubén Jarazo-Álvarez and Pilar Alderete-Diez, Routledge, 2020, pp. 205–19.

Nolan, Emma. "J. K. Rowling Book Burning Videos Are Spreading Like Wildfire across Tiktok." *Newsweek*, 16 Sept. 2020, newsweek.com/jk-rowling-books-burned-tiktok -transgender-issues-1532330.

Oakes, Margaret J. "Flying Cars, Floo Powder, and Flaming Torches: The Hi-Tech, Low-Tech World of Wizardry." *Reading Harry Potter: Critical Essays*, edited by Giselle Liza Anatol, Prager, 2003, pp. 117–28.

Olver, Catherine. "Eye Wonder? Reflecting Harry in Animal Eyes." *The Ivory Tower, Harry Potter, and Beyond: More Essays on the Works of J. K. Rowling*, edited by Lana A. Whited, U of Missouri P, 2023, pp. 185–200.

Ostry, Elaine. "Accepting Mudbloods: The Ambivalent Social Vision of J. K. Rowling's Fairy Tales." *Reading Harry Potter: Critical Essays*, edited by Giselle Liza Anatol, Praeger, 2003, pp. 89–101.

Park, Julia. "Class and Socioeconomic Identity in Harry Potter's England." *Reading Harry Potter: Critical Essays*, edited by Giselle Liza Anatol, Prager, 2003, pp. 179–89.

Pollvogt, Susannah W. "Unconstitutional Animus." *Fordham Law Review*, vol. 81, no. 2, 2013, pp. 887–937.

Pond, Julia. "A Story of the Exceptional: Fate and Free Will in the Harry Potter Series." *Children's Literature*, vol. 38, 2010, pp. 181–206. *Project Muse*, muse.jhu.edu/article/380767.

Pugh, Tison, and David L. Wallace. "Heteronormative Heroism and Queering the School Story in J. K. Rowling's *Harry Potter* Series." *Children's Literature Association Quarterly*, vol. 31, no. 3, fall 2006, pp. 260–81. *Project Muse*, doi.org/10.1353/chq.2006.0053.

Pugh, Tison, and David L. Wallace. "A Postscript to 'Heteronormative Heroism and Queering the School Story in J. K. Rowling's *Harry Potter* Series.'" *Children's Literature Association Quarterly*, vol. 33, no. 2, summer 2008, pp. 188–92. *Project Muse*, doi.org /10.1353/chq.0.0009.

Rao, Sridevi, and Preethi Gorecki. "Is Dobby a Free Elf?" *Harry Potter and the Other: Race, Justice, and Difference in the Wizarding World*, edited by Sarah Park Dahlen and Ebony Elizabeth Thomas, UP of Mississippi, 2022, pp. 276–86.

Ravn, Signe, and Steven Roberts. "Young Masculinities: Masculinities in Youth Studies." *Routledge International Handbook of Masculinity Studies*, edited by Lucas Gottzén et al., Routledge, 2020, pp. 183–91.

"Responding to Transgender Victims of Sexual Assault." *Office for Victims of Crime*, June 2014, ovc.ojp.gov/sites/g/files/xyckuh226/files/pubs/forge/sexual_numbers.html.

Robinson, Stefan, et al. "Privileging the Bromance: A Critical Appraisal of Romantic and
     Bromantic Relationships." *Men and Masculinities*, vol. 22, no. 5, 2019, pp. 850–71.
Romano, Aja. "Harry Potter and the Author Who Failed Us." *Vox*, 11 Jun. 2020, vox.com
     /culture/21285396/jk-rowling-transphobic-backlash-harry-potter.
Romano, Aja. "Is J.K. Rowling Transphobic? Let Her Speak for Herself." *Vox*, 16 Mar. 2023, vox.
     com/culture/23622610/jk-rowling-transphobic-statements-timeline-history-controversy.
Rosenberg, Alyssa. "There Has Never Been a Better Time to Read J. K. Rowling's Books."
     Washington Post, 24 Sept. 2020, washingtonpost.com/opinions/2020/09/24
     /jk-rowling-controversy-transgender-harry-potter-author-statements-women/.
Rowling, J. K. *Fantastic Beasts and Where to Find Them*. Arthur A. Levine Books, 2017.
Rowling, J. K. *Harry Potter and the Chamber of Secrets*. Scholastic, 1998.
Rowling, J. K. *Harry Potter and the Deathly Hallows*. Arthur A. Levine Books, 2007.
Rowling, J. K. *Harry Potter and the Goblet of Fire*. Arthur A. Levine Books, 2000.
Rowling, J. K. *Harry Potter and the Half-Blood Prince*. Arthur A. Levine Books, 2005.
Rowling, J. K. *Harry Potter and the Order of the Phoenix*. Arthur A. Levine Books, 2003.
Rowling, J. K. *Harry Potter and the Prisoner of Azkaban*. Scholastic, 1999.
Rowling, J. K. *Harry Potter and the Sorcerer's Stone*. Scholastic, 1997.
Rowling, J. K. [@jk_rowling]. "The idea that women like me, who've been empathetic to
     trans people for decades, feeling kinship because they're vulnerable in the same way as
     women—ie, to male violence—'hate' trans people because they think sex is real and has
     lived consequences—is a nonsense." *Twitter*, 6 Jun. 2020, twitter.com/jk_rowling
     /status/1269406094595588096.
Rowling, J. K. [@jk_rowling]. "If sex isn't real, there's no same-sex attraction. If sex isn't real,
     the lived reality of women globally is erased. I know and love trans people, but erasing
     the concept of sex removes the ability of many to meaningfully discuss their lives. It
     isn't hate to speak the truth." *Twitter*, 6 Jun. 2020, twitter.com/jk_rowling/status/1269389
     298664701952?lang=en.
Rowling, J. K. "J. K. Rowling Writes about Her Reasons for Speaking out on Sex and Gender
     Issues." *JKRowling*, 10 Jun. 2020, jkrowling.com/opinions/j-k-rowling-writes-about-her
     -reasons-for-speaking-out-on-sex-and-gender-issues/.
Saidel, Eric. "Sirius Black: Man or Dog?" *The Ultimate Harry Potter and Philosophy:
     Hogwarts for Muggles*, edited by Gregory Bassham, John Wiley and Sons, 2010, pp. 22–34.
Sandberg, Jared. "The Art of Showing Pure Incompetence at an Unwanted Task." *Wall Street
     Journal*, 17 Apr. 2007, wsj.com/articles/SB117675628452071687.
Saraco, Maureen. "Squibs, Disability and Having a Place at Hogwarts School of Witchcraft
     and Wizardry." *Cultural Politics in Harry Potter: Life, Death, and the Politics of Fear*,
     edited by Rubén Jarazo-Álvarez and Pilar Alderete-Diez, Routledge, 2020, pp. 18–31.
"Scholastic Marks 25 Year Anniversary of the Publication of J. K. Rowling's *Harry Potter
     and the Sorcerer's Stone*." *Scholastic*, 6 Feb. 2023, mediaroom.scholastic.com/press-release
     /scholastic-marks-25-year-anniversary-publication-jk-rowling-s-harry-potter-and
     -sorcere.
Schuck, Raymond I. "'The Anti-Racist-White-Hero Premise': Whiteness and the *Harry
     Potter* Series." *Wizards vs. Muggles: Essays on Identity and the Harry Potter Universe*,
     edited by Christopher E. Bell, McFarland, 2016, pp. 9–26.
Scully, Jessica Mitzner. "(Dis)Regarding Magical Creatures in the Wizard-Centric World of
     Harry Potter." *Broadening Critical Boundaries in Children's and Young Adult Literature
     and Culture*, edited by Amie A. Doughty, Cambridge Scholars, 2018, pp. 98–118.

Sheltrown, Nicholas. "Harry Potter's World as a Morality Tale of Technology and Media." *Critical Perspectives on Harry Potter*, edited by Elizabeth E. Heilman, Routledge, 2009, pp. 47–64.

Siad, Arnaud, et al. "JK Rowling Hits Back at Putin after He Likened Russia to Her in Rant against Cancel Culture." *CNN*, 25 Mar. 2022, cnn.com/2022/03/25/world/jk-rowling-putin-intl-scli-gbr/index.html.

Stephens, Rebecca L. "The Lightning Bolt Scar as a Lightning Rod: J. K. Rowling's Harry Potter Series and the Rhetoric of the Extreme Right." *Reading Harry Potter Again: New Critical Essays*, edited by Giselle Liza Anatol, Praeger, 2009, pp. 13–30.

Stetka, Bret. "Why Everyone Should Read Harry Potter." *Scientific American*, 9 Sept. 2014, scientificamerican.com/article/why-everyone-should-read-harry-potter/.

Stevens, Ashlie D. "'Harry Potter' and the Problematic Creator—What's Left for a Fandom Raised on False Tolerance?" *Salon*, 27 Jan. 2021, salon.com/2021/01/27/harry-potter-tv-series-jk-rowling-problematic-fandom/.

Stitch. "On Harry Potter, JK Rowling's Transmisogyny, and What We Owe Each Other." *Teen Vogue*, 7 Jan. 2022, teenvogue.com/story/harry-potter-jk-rowling-transmisogyny-what-we-owe-each-other.

Stotzer, Rebecca L. "Data Sources Hindering Our Understanding of Transgender Murders." *American Journal of Public Health*, vol. 107, no. 9, Sept. 2017, pp. 1362–63, doi.org/10.2105/AJPH.2017.303973.

Sugrue, Karen. "Albus Dumbledore and the Curse of Toxic Masculinity." *Toxic Masculinity: Mapping the Monstrous in Our Heroes*, edited by Esther De Dauw and Daniel J. Connell, UP of Mississippi, 2020, pp. 142–56.

Sundmark, Bjorn. "Of Memes and Muggles: Harry Potter, Facebook and the 2016 Presidential Campaign." *Harry Potter and Convergence Culture*, edited by Amanda Firestone and Leisa A. Clarke, McFarland, 2018, pp. 163–74.

Sutton-Ramspeck, Beth. *Harry Potter and Resistance*. Routledge, 2022.

Tamai, Lily Anne Welty, and Paul Spickard. "Half-Blood: Mixed-Race Tropes Old and New in Harry Potter's World." *Harry Potter and the Other: Race, Justice, and Difference in the Wizarding World*, edited by Sarah Park Dahlen and Ebony Elizabeth Thomas, UP of Mississippi, 2022, pp. 144–63.

Teare, Elizabeth. "Harry Potter and the Technology of Magic." *The Ivory Tower and Harry Potter: Perspectives on a Literary Phenomenon*, edited by Lana A. Whited, U of Missouri P, 2002, pp. 329–42.

Thompson, William V. "From Teenage Witch to Social Activist: Hermione Granger as Female Locus." *Hermione Granger Saves the World: Essays on the Feminist Heroine of Hogwarts*, edited by Christopher E. Bell, McFarland, 2012, pp. 181–97.

Thorne, Jack, et al. *Harry Potter and the Cursed Child, Parts One and Two*. Arthur A. Levine Books, 2016.

Trites, Roberta Seelinger. "The Harry Potter Novels as a Test Case for Adolescent Literature." *Style*, vol. 35, no. 3, fall 2001, pp. 472–85. *JSTOR*, jstor.org/stable/10.5325/style.35.3.472.

Uspenskiy, Andrey. "'Wumben, Wimpund, Woomud': An Exploration of Social Censure in the Internet Age." *Morningside Review*, vol. 18, 2022, journals.library.columbia.edu/index.php/TMR/article/view/8292.

Vezzali, Loris, et al. "The Greatest Magic of Harry Potter: Reducing Prejudice." *Journal of Applied Social Psychology*, vol. 45, no. 2, Feb. 2015, pp. 105–21, doi.org/10.1111/jasp.12279.

Vogels, Christina. "'It's Called Being *Her* Dog': Young Men Talk about Being Boyfriends, Homosociality and the Expelling of Femininity in Aotearoa/New Zealand." *Young*, vol. 28, no. 3, 2020, pp. 225–41. *Sage*, doi.org/10.1177/1103308819858806.

Vujin, Bojana S., and Viktorija E. Krombholc. "High-Voiced Dark Lords and Boggarts in Drag: Feminine-Coded Villainy in the *Harry Potter* Series." *Collection of Papers of the Faculty of Philosophy*, vol. 49, no. 3, 2019, pp. 23–38.

Wannamaker, Annette. "Men in Cloaks and High-Heeled Boots, Men Wielding Pink Umbrellas: Witchy Masculinities in the *Harry Potter* novels." *Looking Glass*, vol. 20, no. 1, 2017, pp. 19–33.

Weiss, Meri. "The Role of Maternal Females in Harry Potter's Journey." *Legilimens! Perspectives in Harry Potter Studies*, edited by Christopher Bell, Cambridge Scholars, 2013, pp. 19–31.

Wente, Sarah. "The Making of a New World: Nazi Ideology and Its Influence on Harry Potter." *A Wizard of Their Age: Critical Essays from the Harry Potter Generation*, edited by Cecilia Konchar Farr, State U of New York P, 2015, pp. 89–112.

Wheaton, Sarah. "The Metamorphosis of J.K. Rowling." *Politico*, 3 Jul. 2022, politico.com /news/2022/07/03/the-metamorphosis-of-j-k-rowling-00043835.

Whited, Lana A. "Introduction." *The Ivory Tower, Harry Potter, and Beyond: More Essays on the Works of J.K. Rowling*, edited by Whited, U of Missouri P, 2023, pp. 3–18.

Wilson, Charles D. "The Failed Wizard Justice System: Race and Access to Justice in Harry Potter." *Harry Potter and the Other: Race, Justice, and Difference in the Wizarding World*, edited by Sarah Park Dalen and Ebony Elizabeth Thomas, UP of Mississippi, 2022, pp. 287–303.

"World Exclusive Interview with J.K. Rowling." *South West News Service*, 8 Jul. 2000, accio -quote.org/articles/2000/0700-swns-alfie.htm.

Yu, Mallory. "Harry Potter's Magic Fades When His Creator Tweets." *NPR*, 10 Jun. 2020, npr.org /2020/06/10/873472683/harry-potters-magic-fades-when-his-creator-tweets.

INDEX

ABOUT THE AUTHOR

Keridiana Chez is an associate professor of English at Borough of Manhattan Community College, part of City University of New York. She is the author of *Victorian Dogs, Victorian Men: Affect and Animals in Nineteenth-Century Literature and Culture* (2017) and various essays on human-animal studies and *Harry Potter*, published in edited collections and journals such as *Victorian Review* and the *Journal of American Culture*.

www.ingramcontent.com/pod-product-compliance
Lightning Source LLC
Chambersburg PA
CBHW030822270326
41928CB00007B/859

9 781496 857323